JAMES M. KAUFFMAN
AND TIMOTHY J. LANDRUM

Children and Youth with Emotional and Behavioral Disorders

A History of Their Education

An International Publisher
8700 Shoal Creek Boulevard
Austin, Texas 78757-6897
800/897-3202   Fax 800/397-7633
www.proedinc.com

© 2006 by PRO-ED, Inc.
8700 Shoal Creek Boulevard
Austin, Texas 78757-6897
800/897-3202   Fax 800/397-7633
www.proedinc.com

Library of Congress Cataloging-in-Publication Data

Kauffman, James M.
   Children and youth with emotional and behavioral disorders : a history of their
education/James M. Kauffman and Timothy J. Landrum.
      p. cm.
   Includes bibliographical references and index.
   ISBN 1-4164-0054-0 (alk. paper)
   1. Mentally ill children—Education—History.   2. Problem children—Education—
History.   3. Special education—History.   I. Landrum, Timothy J.   II. Title.

LC4165.K38   2006
371.94—dc22

2004060083

Art Director: Jason Crosier
Designer: Nancy McKinney-Point
This book is designed in Goudy.

Printed in the United States of America

1 2 3 4 5 6 7 8 9 10   09 08 07 06 05

Children and Youth
with Emotional and Behavioral Disorders

Contents

Preface

We have tried in this volume to describe some of the events that have shaped special education for students with emotional or behavioral disorders into what special education has become. However, we have not been satisfied merely to recount events and recall individuals. We also have tried to draw reasonable connections from past to present and to highlight how succeeding generations of special educators and those in related disciplines used, or failed to use, the insights of those who struggled earlier with the same or similar problems.

We are not under the illusion that knowing what is in this book will allow any of us to escape making errors or avoid all the errors of the past. True, we often seem not to learn from history, but we cannot learn from what we do not know, and many in our profession know little of our history. We believe the errors of the past, now clearer to us than when they were in the making, might in some cases be avoidable. We also believe that we can see the gradual accumulation of evidence supporting effective practices.

History does, actually, consist of a sequence of events. Consequently, organizing the discussion of events in chronological order is necessary. However, our division of chapters and headings for discussion into chronological periods is arbitrary. Any chronology is an arbitrary division of time into blocks (Gould, 1997b). We divided our discussion into periods that seemed manageable to us, given the length of this book, but we recognize that they are both arbitrary and overlapping.

Knowledge of the sequence of events is necessary, but it is insufficient for making sense of what happened. Making sense of things requires knowing the zeitgeist, the general public attitudes toward the problems of the times, and the political movements reflecting or amplifying those attitudes. Ours is a short history. We do not discuss many of the social and political movements that have affected special education and the management of social deviance; for that depth of understanding, one has to read many histories. Neither is ours a comprehensive history. A detailed history would require a massive volume, and a comprehensive history would require multiple large volumes. We make no claim to have included all of the important individuals or events that may have affected the direction of the field. We encourage those who know of other important events in the history of our field to do two things: First, write about them; second, let us know about them. Our goal for this volume was to capture historical highlights and make sense of them.

This book is best considered as only a starting point for understanding the origins and development of the field. Our view is that beginning to understand our origins is an important first step. "We must realize that only by trying to determine where we have been and where we are going can we be certain that the process of getting there will continue to be rewarding" (Kauffman, 1974b, p. iii). Our journey in this field of special education has been very rewarding, not so much in monetary terms as in the consequence of finding things out. Richard Feynman, one of our era's great geniuses, wrote an entire book called *The Pleasure of Finding Things Out* (Feynman, 1999).

In preparing this book, we found out many things we did not know about the history of our field. We all need to find out more things, not merely about our history but also about what works to achieve particular goals and what does not work in educating youngsters with emotional or behavioral disorders. The overarching goal of our field has been and must remain this: Make the lives of our students and their families better.

We owe thanks to many for seeing us through the preparation of this manuscript. We thank Don Hammill and Lee Wiederholt for their confidence in our work. Our editors at PRO-ED, particularly Chris Anne Worsham and Becky Shore, were extraordinarily helpful. Colleagues Maggie Coleman and Ed Sabornie reviewed the manuscript and gave us many helpful comments.

1 Why a History and What Kind?

K NOWING the history of a field of study can help students in that field make better sense of current events. Without knowledge of their field's history, students may misjudge the meaning of what they read and hear. They are likely to give inaccurate or incomplete answers to important questions, be unable to discriminate important from unimportant questions, or be misled easily by rhetoric about ideas that have been given a fair test and been discredited by reliable data. Or they may be unable to add reasonable qualifiers to their answers, assuming that their answers should be unqualified.

The education of students with emotional or behavioral disorders is a case in point. Consider some basic questions that might be posed in the early 21st century:

- How does special education harm or help students with emotional or behavioral disorders?
- What do we know about the most effective means of helping students with emotional or behavioral disorders?
- For a student with emotional or behavioral disorders, how positive or negative is the event of being identified as needing special education?
- What are the alternatives to special education for students with emotional or behavioral disorders?
- Could the answers to these questions depend on many things and be different for different students?

We will be more specific. What should be said in response to the following, which presumably includes special education for children and youth with emotional and behavioral disorders? How does the history of special education suggest we should answer?

What is known about the education of students labeled as handicapped? First, separate special education does not work. It does not do so by any measure of assessment—learning, development of self-esteem and social skills or preparation as student, worker, or citizen. Its failure is costly in several currencies—in dollars, in public confidence and, most importantly, in students' lives. (Gartner & Lipsky, 1989, p. 26)

We might assume that special education will work if it is not separate. But, even if we did, what would we say about identifying students for special education? How accurate is the following statement? Does it apply specifically to students with emotional or behavioral disorders? What does the history of the field suggest? Has special education ever worked—or do we have any reason to believe that it could—without sorting those who need it from those who don't (see Kauffman & Hallahan, 2005b)?

> *Special education plays a sorting role, both for those consigned to it and for those students who remain in general education. It limits expectations of the former, and gnarls the attitudes of the latter.... Thus, the system of special education, and the attitudes towards disability that undergird it, have harmful consequences for both those labeled "disabled" and those not. Among those labeled, their capacity is denied and, thus, expectations of them are limited. Those not labeled are encouraged to believe that people with disabilities are limited and, thus, they are encouraged to offer sympathy toward, but not to value the participation of, persons with disabilities. Neither view provides a basis for a society of inclusion and equity.* (Lipsky & Gartner, 1996, pp. 767–768)

We could assume that special education is a failed or evil practice, that it is separate and therefore unequal. But then how should we evaluate the answers to questions about the viability and value of special education in the early 21st century? How does history suggest the story of special education should be written? Would the story be much like an obituary, an accident report, the report of a religious conversion, a reincarnation, or none of these (Kauffman, 1999–2000)? To what extent or in what ways is the following accurate or inaccurate, and what does it have to do with the history of special education?

> *On December 9, 1993, special education was mugged in a dark alley. The thugs were Joe Shapiro and his gang at* U.S. News and World Report *(cf. Shapiro et al., 1993). Their brass knuckles and tire irons were the half-truths and full-blown distortions they patched together (with the finesse of*

a Mike Tyson) into a cover story entitled "Separate and Unequal: How Special Education Programs Are Cheating Our Children and Costing Tax-payers Billions Each Year." (Fuchs & Fuchs, 1995, p. 363)

Alternatively, we might assume that special education improves the prospects for students with emotional or behavioral disorders. How should the following conclusion be evaluated? The authors reach their conclusion after making arguments for maintaining a full continuum of placement options for students with emotional and behavioral disorders, but is it justified by history, evidence, and logic?

Students with EBD face an increasingly bleak future without treatment that is appropriately specialized and intensive. At the same time that special education programs come under increasing attack and are being dismantled in favor of general education classes, 90% of the general public suggests that "troublemakers" should be removed from school.... Thus, the hostile intentions perceived by students with behavior problems may truly be paranoid, but they are not groundless. Only a society that is indifferent to the plight of its children could eliminate the supports that these children need to develop into the kind of people that society desires and then punish them for failing to do so because they cannot flourish in the same social context as typically developing children. A caring society will provide the alternative environments that are required to be supportive of the educational needs of all of its children. (Brigham & Kauffman, 1998, p. 32)

We might assume that special education is a legitimate profession, that its purpose is to give children and youth with emotional or behavioral disorders a fairer chance in school, and that it has often been successful. But is the following a generally accurate portrayal of special education in the early 21st century? What historical events and trends might lead someone to make such a statement?

I believe our field stands as a lighthouse beacon of hope, caring and unconditional support for these at-risk children and youth to whom life has dealt such a cruel hand. I have been a researcher in the area of school-related behavior disorders for over three decades. During that time, I have been proud to call myself a member of the field [of emotional and behavioral disorders] which brings together dedicated professionals from diverse backgrounds who work together so well on behalf of at-risk children. Our field models and demonstrates positive values and best practices that can make a real difference in the lives of children and youth with emotional and behavioral disorders and those of their families. (Walker, 2003)

Today's circumstances and views are grounded in the past. It is therefore critically important that we examine what has transpired in the past. No one today can give good answers to the preceding questions without understanding what has happened in past decades and centuries. Trying to understand as objectively as possible what has happened in the past will help us ask better questions and construct better answers, not only to current issues but also to those the future will bring.

No history is entirely objective or unbiased. All writers of history decide what events to include and what to exclude, how to present events and what to say about them. But the alternative to writing a biased history is to write none at all. We encourage our readers to think about the events we present and the way we present them, to check the veracity of our accounts whenever possible, and to question our interpretations of history. Questioning ourselves, as well as questioning others, and trying to formulate defensible answers help us make better sense of the world and, ultimately, help the children and youth we special educators are dedicated to serve.

....

The Importance of Historical Perspective

As we have suggested, the connectedness of current issues to past problems is an important concept. We cannot understand today's difficulties very well if we assume they emerge from present circumstances alone. Although knowledge of history is no guarantee that we will not repeat our mistakes, ignorance of history virtually ensures that we will make no progress (Cole, 2005; Kauffman, 1976, 1981, 1993, 1999e, 2005a; Kauffman, Brigham, & Mock, 2004; Kauffman & Smucker, 1995).

Consideration of the historical background of current issues and contemporary practices will serve us well (Smith, 1998). In fact, the late special educator Burton Blatt wrote, "History can be a strength of society or its anchor. We can learn from it or not.... In this field we call special education, history has not served us well. We have not learned from it" (Blatt, 1975, p. 404). In the 1960s, Blatt published a historically significant, scathing exposé of conditions in institutions, *Christmas in Purgatory* (Blatt & Kaplan, 1966; see also http://www .disabilitymuseum.org/lib/docs/1782card.htm). He did not live to see the 21st century exposé of the squalid conditions and abuse in community facilities to which many residents of institutions were moved (Fallis, 2004a, 2004b, 2004c, 2004d). Indeed, Blatt was right—we did not learn from history that changing people's placement does not permanently alter the way they are treated. But we *could have* learned that lesson from our history. Blatt also noted, "History is the basic science. From history flows more than knowledge, more than prescription, more than how it was—how we might try to make it become" (1975, p. 402).

Another sage writing about the history of special education noted, "Yes, almost every intervention approach has its successes.... And so we repeat and repeat and again repeat the outworn, the discredited, the valueless" (Mann, 1979, pp. 541–542). Indeed, much of what passes for "progressive" in the early 21st century has a long history of failure (Kauffman, 2002). In some ways, our field seems perversely determined to embrace failed ideas and reject demonstrated success, especially if the generally successful is not perfect.

Human beings have a long history of recycling ideas. Perhaps the saying "There is nothing new under the sun," written several thousand years ago, is an even more astute observation today. Dig around in the past, and you will find the roots of nearly every idea that anyone puts forward today. This is a concept to which we return repeatedly in this book, especially in Chapters 5 and 6.

Institutional memories as well as personal memories are short and often inaccurate. But reliable information about the past depends on knowing facts, not on personal memories. Nobel laureate Gabriel Garcia Marquez described the difference between personal memory and truth in his memoir, *Living to Tell the Tale* (2003): "The memory is clear, but there is no possibility that it is true" (p. 63). Marquez also distinguishes between factual truth and the truth of one's personal experience, which may not correspond to fact (see especially pp. 261–271). To the extent possible, we have tried to convey historical facts, with interpretation and personal views confined primarily to Chapter 6.

The Importance of Historical Sources

Histories may be biased in many ways, but one thing that is certain to make any history inaccurate is reliance on other than primary sources. We have not been able to rely exclusively on first-hand or primary sources, although we have done our best to search for books, journal articles, and other documents in their original or in facsimile editions rather than rely heavily on compilations and indexes.

As an example of the kind of misstatement of fact that can occur when one relies on secondary rather than primary sources, consider the statement of Rubenstein, who wrote, "There is no indication of a single article dealing specifically with insanity in childhood in any of the first forty-five volumes of the *American Journal of Insanity*" (Rubenstein, 1948, p. 315). However, Rubenstein had based his statement on an *index* of the first 45 volumes of the *American Journal of Insanity* compiled by Wise in 1889, not on a perusal of the journal itself. Had Rubenstein examined the first 45 volumes, he would have found numerous articles dealing with children. Volume 1 includes descriptions of young lunatics in asylums and case descriptions of insanity in children said to be induced through imitation. Volume 2 includes an article by Brigham (1845a) describing selected cases of insanity in children and a description by Ray (1846) of special education for "idiots" and residents of hospitals for the insane, including children and youth. Volume 3 contains an article on the effects of music on a neurotic 17-year-old boy and several other "interesting cases" involving children. (See Kauffman, 1976, for further examples.)

Reliance on indexes can be extraordinarily misleading. Many indexes are compiled by freelancers who are not familiar with the field or the work of authors who are prominent in the field. Even if the index is compiled by the author of a book or the editor of a journal, there is no assurance that it will represent every idea of importance mentioned. For example, were we to consult the index to Kanner's (1964) *History of the Care and Treatment of the Mentally Retarded*, we would find no reference to affect, autism, disordered behavior, emotional disturbance, maladaptive behavior, social adaptation, psychosis, psychotic, or any other entry referring to the problem of disordered behavior of people with mental retardation, although such behavior problems are well known and were even recognized by Kanner himself (cf. Kanner, 1960).

Other misconceptions have been fostered by careless reading. For example, in a single paragraph devoted to "the great Esquirol," Kanner (1962) gives the impression that Esquirol (1845) does not give attention to children, except in a passing, and mistaken, reference to "two little homicidal maniacs." However, perusal of Esquirol's work reveals a discussion of the relationship of age to madness and the particular forms of insanity most common in childhood, behavior problems related to dentition, epilepsy in childhood, suicide in childhood, incendiarism (fire setting; see also Esquirol, 1849) in childhood, and homicidal monomania in children, as well as childhood idiocy. Moreover, Esquirol's description of the "three little homicidal maniacs" is far more detailed than Kanner suggests and differs in several ways from his account. Esquirol's discussion is embedded in the context of a more general exposition on homicidal monomania and goes beyond mere description. In summing up his observations about these three children, Esquirol (1845) concluded,

> *These three cases are pregnant with meaning. Was it not the want of a due degree of moral and intellectual development, and the vicious education of these three little girls, that deprived them of the discernment necessary to appreciate the horrid nature of the acts which they committed? Did not the habit of onanism [masturbation], contracted at the age of four years, impair their developments in the case of the first? Did not the inconsiderate conversation of the grandparents make a profound and fatal impression upon the mind and heart of the subject of the second case? As for the third, nothing corrected the habits of wickedness, contracted in infancy.* (p. 372)

We may well disagree with Esquirol's guesses about the causes of these children's behavior. However, his statement is hardly consonant with Kanner's suggestion that in the first half of the 19th century there was *no* comprehension of children's behavior disorders that manifested themselves in disorganized feeling, thinking, and acting and that the brief sketches of behavior disorders by Esquirol and others carried the implication of *inherent* evil. Esquirol and other physicians of his era often described how environmental events or experiences contributed to problem behavior, which is a very contemporary and increasingly

7

well substantiated idea (Kauffman, 2005a; Walker, Ramsey, & Gresham, 2004).

History of Special Education for Emotional or Behavioral Disorders

No doubt teachers have always faced the problem of disorderly, disruptive behavior. No doubt, either, that students with emotional and behavioral disorders have presented problems in many, if not all, cultures of the world (Hallenbeck & Kauffman, 1994; Winzer, 2005).

Throughout recorded history, one can find examples of children's behavior that angered and disappointed their parents or other adults and violated established codes of conduct (Braaten, 1985; Cavan & Ferdinand, 1975; Kazdin, 1978; Winzer, 1993, 2005). Furthermore, throughout history, people in every culture have sought to conceptualize unusual or disturbing human behavior in terms of causal factors and the implications of those factors for eliminating, controlling, and preventing deviant acts. Although a myriad of causes and remedies have been suggested over the centuries, several conceptual themes have remained remarkably consistent for thousands of years; contemporary versions are merely elaborations and extensions of their ancient counterparts (Kauffman, 1974a, 1974c). For purposes of explanation and control of behavior, humans have been conceptualized as spiritual beings, biological organisms, rational and feeling individuals, and products of their environments.

However, special education as we know it has not always existed. Special education as a means of addressing the problems of children with disabilities did not begin with the recognition of emotional and behavioral disorders. In fact, special education for the youngsters who are the focus of this volume emerged only gradually over many decades, primarily in the 20th century. The historical roots of special education for children with emotional and behavioral disorders are not easy to identify, for although such children have been recognized for thousands of years, it is only in relatively recent times that systematic special education for them has been devised. As Lewis (1974) stated,

When charting the growth of this field, one must make an arbitrary decision concerning a starting point. No matter where one begins, examples of earlier programs or treatments probably can be identified. Tracing the history of the field presents great difficulty because these children have been subsumed under so many different labels and because labeling itself frequently has been determined by the sociological and scientific conditions of the moment. Thus, the beginning of the field of education for the disturbed child is difficult to find; it is lost not only in the confusions of sociological history but also in the myriad of disciplines that crisscross its development. (p. 5)

To the extent possible, we focus on the history of *education* for children with emotional and behavioral disorders (also referred to by many other labels, including *disturbed* and *maladjusted*) and on other interventions directly relevant to educational concerns. An exclusively educational focus is not possible, however, for the conceptual foundations of special education are found mostly in the disciplines of psychology and psychiatry. The historical roots of special education are thus intertwined with the histories of other fields of study and practice, though education has come to play an increasingly prominent role in the treatment of children's emotional and behavioral disorders over the years. As our brief history unfolds in the following chapters, therefore, it becomes increasingly oriented toward special education.

Life seems increasingly complicated by the expansion of knowledge, the development of technologies, and political change. We are tempted to believe that in an earlier era, when life was simpler, the issues involving behavioral deviance and emotional disorders were less difficult. Perhaps life was simpler long ago in some respects, but much of the historical literature suggests that questions about how to identify social deviance and what to do about it have always been perplexing.

Who should have the power to identify children and youth who need special education because of their emotional or behavioral disorders? Indeed, who should be given the authority to declare that a child has such a disorder or mental illness? Once identified, how should these children be taught? And where should they be taught? *Who, how,* and *where* are perpetual questions in the field of learning disabilities, as Bateman (1994) has pointed out. We see them as perpetual questions in the field of emotional and behavioral disorders, as well. And to those questions we would add the question of *what* students should be taught. *Who, how, where,* and *what* are questions that involve the core concepts of contemporary special education, and they will not go away (Kauffman & Hallahan, 2005b). But supposing that these questions are new is to misunderstand what previous generations had to confront and how special education has evolved.

Unfortunately, as professionals in a field, we appear highly likely to repeat our mistakes, partly because we do not know what has been tried and failed or tried with success. Maybe it is unreasonable to expect that we will learn much from history, as failure to learn from the past, especially the distant past, is a common characteristic of human beings. But there are things we *could* learn from our history. For example, we should know by now that unrestrained advocacy is self-defeating. Our history includes extreme enthusiasm for institutions and for special classes. We could observe that overenthusiasm for inclusion is likely to suffer the same fate as overenthusiasm for what many people now see as exclusionary practices. In fact, we might expect that unrestrained advocacy for full inclusion has already laid the foundation for the unrestrained advocacy of full separation of exceptional children from the educational mainstream.

There is still something of the adolescent in our views of the world and our disdain as a profession for our history. That adolescent character was observed in the last century (Kauffman, 1974b, 1984), but it persists. We are not really a very old or very mature profession as professions go. Perhaps that, in some ways, is to our advantage, as it frees us from some of the stodginess that can accompany age. But it is not without its problems. We find ourselves pulled in opposite directions, not knowing whether we should separate ourselves from the mainstream of education and assert our difference and independence or embrace and merge with the disciplines of our origins (general education, for example). There is an awkwardness about us, a self-consciousness and lack of self-assurance. We have a lot of self-doubts. In some ways, that is good, for it keeps us open to change; in other ways, it demonstrates our immaturity and tentativeness as a profession.

Special educators still wonder about what is expected of them by the public (see Walker, Forness, et al., 1998). As special educators, we are uncertain about what we should expect of ourselves—whether, for example, we should seek merely significant improvement in our students or be expected to make them "normal" or indistinguishable from typical students, and whether we need additional resources or need simply to make better use of those already given to us. Some question whether we should try to bring about changes in our students at all, suggesting that we should seek changes in ourselves and in our society instead. Moreover, the attention span of those who provide our financial resources is short, meaning that good experimental data and longitudinal studies are virtually nonexistent. As Cruickshank observed in the early 1970s,

> *Not one of the persons included in this book [important figures in the development of special education for children with emotional and behavioral disorders] has been able to apply his theory to a selected group of children and, with adequate funding, to follow those children through childhood and adolescence, to observe their young adult adjustment, and to factor out those related theoretical issues which produced positive growth in children. There is an appalling dearth of longitudinal studies in all aspects of growth and development of exceptional children.* (Cruickshank, 1974, p. x)

More longitudinal data may be available in the early 21st century than was available in 1975, but the neglect of long-term outcomes is still a matter of considerable disappointment, and planning for the study of long-term consequences of social policy is typically ignored. For example, we do not know of any studies designed from the time of its inception to study the long-term effects on any group of the No Child Left Behind Act, passed by the United States Congress and signed by President George W. Bush in 2002. Likewise, assessment of the long-term effects of the Individuals with Disabilities Education Act (signed into law in 1975 by President Gerald Ford) has been haphazard, at best.

Perhaps it is true that the only thing we learn from history is that we don't really learn from it. In 1984, one of special education's 20th-century pioneers commented about the history of our field,

> *The history of special education has indicated that we tend to move enthusiastically in one direction, then become disillusioned with that program, and then become enthusiastic in another direction. We first thought that residen-*

*tial schools would solve the problems of the care and education of the handi-
capped. After fifty years of building institutions, we found this procedure
was not the answer. We then became enthusiastic about day schools and
self-contained special classes in public schools. After fifty or more years, we
decided that these classes were not the answer. We then became enthusiastic
over mainstreaming. Today, some feel that mainstreaming is not the answer,
especially for the mentally retarded. Many are raising questions about our
future in special education.* (Kirk, 1984, p. 53)

As Kirk notes, we have a history of lurching from one enthusiasm
to another. Beginning in the late 20th century, there was great enthusiasm for what was called *mainstreaming* and has now come to be known
as *inclusion*. Probably, *inclusion* will yield to a new term (perhaps having
to do with community) or an ostensibly new program (perhaps special
schools or classes). Nevertheless, we believe that our field does not
have to be caught in a vicious and perpetual cycle of enthusiasm, disappointment, forgetting, and rediscovery.

A firm grip on our history might make us less apologetic about
our existence as a distinct part of education. Gerber (1996) has pointed
out that special education has, historically, been the *added* structure requiring and enabling public education to accommodate students with
disabilities, to become truly *universal* public education. If special education is abandoned, as Kirk's comments seem to suggest, it will certainly
be reinvented (Kauffman, 1999–2000). This is true simply because the
variability found in the general population, noted long ago by Horn
(1924), will not disappear, and something other than general education is required to address this variability, as noted by Horn, Singer
(1988), and many others (e.g., Kauffman & Hallahan, 2005b).

Nearly everyone would like to see all students in our schools, including those with disabilities, learn more than they do now. However, the achievement of that outcome and the group comparisons
that make the most sense are controversial issues of the 21st century
(Kauffman, 2004b, 2005c; Kauffman & Wiley, 2004).

The field of special education for children with emotional and
behavioral disorders has been largely characterized by the gradual
accumulation of scientific evidence about what is helpful and what
is not (Kauffman, 1999d). However, some have suggested that non-
scientific methods should guide the field (e.g., Gallagher, 1998, 2004),

and the basic ideas that should guide special education remain controversial.

We trust that the remainder of this book will inform readers of our history and prompt thinking about what the future of our field might hold—and what we hope it will hold. We do not claim to know where the field is headed, but there may be clues in our past.

2 Before the Twentieth Century

A S noted earlier, we have substantial reason to believe that what are today referred to as emotional and behavioral disorders have always existed, although they may have been known by other names. For example, the biblical story of the Prodigal Son could be taken as a story of adolescent delinquency, if not disordered behavior. In fact, most ancient literature includes descriptions of behavior that from our current perspective might be considered deranged, disordered, or reflecting one sort or another of what we now call mental illness. Perhaps the Old Testament's King David suffered from depression or bipolar disorder. Regardless of how we label or describe it, we know that both the disordered behavior of youngsters and the treatment of it have historical roots that go back centuries, if not millennia (cf. Kazdin, 1978; Reisman, 1976).

The identification of the disorders we say today are emotional or behavioral cannot be understood except as a part of special education for children with a variety of other disabilities (Kauffman, 1976, 1979, 1981; Kauffman, Brigham, & Mock, 2004). We know that children with any identifying disability were not generally well treated by most societies prior to the 19th century. Before the rise of psychiatry and the recognition of "insanity" as a treatable condition rather than a sign of sin, disfavor by a deity, or demon possession, deviant behavior was most often punished harshly or treated by a variety of cruel and unproven methods. As we shall see later in this history, some seem to have forgotten the contempt with which deviant individuals were treated in the prescientific era.

Before the Nineteenth Century

We often do not think of psychiatry as having its roots in medical practice before 1800. However, William Battie published his A Treatise on Madness in 1758. As Brussel (1969) notes, Battie was the first teacher of psychiatry in England, perhaps the first in the world. And some of his insights, although gained by his observation and experience about a quarter of a millennium ago, seem quite consistent with current thinking:

> *Besides being a psychiatric first, A Treatise on Madness contains some revolutionary (for that time) ideas, many of which are valid by today's criteria. At least Battie sponsored "change"; to throw off the yoke of antiquated and unproven isms and give thought to new concepts even if they turn out to be wrong when given a clinical try-out. Today we call this research. When one reads this book and appreciates how "modern" Battie's medical reasoning is, it is understandable that he would be a minority of one among his contemporary colleagues who, a dozen years after Battie's death, advocated drastic purging, blistering of the skull, bleeding, induction of vomiting, and other similar measures for George III in his first attack of insanity in 1788. Certainly he treated his patients, both at St. Luke's and at his own private hospital, more humanely than did Monro [in another English mental hospital] at Bethlehem.*
>
> *Among his tenets, many of them "firsts," are his (correct) antipathy for violent purging as treatment of the insane. He separates each psychiatric symptom and maintains that a definition must say what madness is and is not. (Ask any contemporary psychiatrist to define "psychosis" and watch his embarrassment!)* (Brussel, 1969, pp. v–vi)

In Battie's own words, careful observation and testing of ideas are more important than philosophy or ideology, a principle of enormous importance to special education in the current century (see Kauffman, 2002; Kauffman, Brigham, & Mock, 2004). He also notes that definition is critically important, recalling for us the present-day importance of defining not only what special education is but what it is not (see Kauffman & Hallahan, 2005b):

> *In order therefore to avoid this mischievous confusion of sentiment as well as language, and that we may fix a clear and determinate meaning to the Word Madness; we must for some time at least quit the schools of Philosophy, and content ourselves with a vulgar apprehension of things; we must reject not only every supposed cause of Madness, but also every symptom which does not necessarily belong to it, and retain no one phenomenon but what is essential, that is without which the word Madness becomes nugatory*

and conveys no idea whatever: or, in other words, no definition of Madness can be safe which does not, with regard at least to some particular symptoms, determine what it is not, as well as what it is. (Battie, 1758, p. 4)

Still, prior to the 19th century, children and youth with nearly any significant disability typically were, at best, only protected from abuse. We know of few systematic attempts to teach them. Emotional or behavioral disorders were believed to be evidence of Satan's power, and children and adolescents were often punished under the law as adults (Bremner, 1970; Despert, 1965). Abuse, neglect, cruel medical treatments (e.g., bleeding and purging), and harsh punishment were common and often accepted. Not until the period following the American and French revolutions in the closing years of the 18th century did kind and effective treatment of the "insane" and "idiots" (terms then used to designate people with mental illness and mental retardation) begin to appear. In that era of political and social revolution, emphasis on individual freedom, human dignity, philanthropy, and public education set the stage for humane treatment and education of people with disabilities.

Immediately after the French Revolution, Phillipe Pinel, a distinguished French physician and one of the earliest psychiatrists, unchained several people who were chronically mentally ill and had been brutally confined for years in the Bicêtre Hospital in Paris. When treated with kindness, respect, and the expectation that they would behave appropriately, these formerly deranged, regressed patients showed dramatic improvement. Pinel's revolutionary and humane methods became widely known and were used in Europe and the United States during the first half of the 19th century. His approach, later elaborated by his students and admirers, became known as *moral treatment*.

One of Pinel's students was Jean Marc Gaspard Itard, another French physician. In the late 1700s and early 1800s, Itard attempted to teach "the wild boy of Aveyron" (Itard, 1962). The boy, Victor, was found in the forest, where he had apparently been abandoned at an early age. Pinel believed that Victor had severe mental retardation ("idiocy," in the language of the day), but it is clear from Itard's description that Victor also exhibited many of the behaviors characteristic of severe mental illness. Itard was convinced that Victor could be taught practical skills, including speech. Although Victor never uttered more than a few words, Itard was remarkably successful in teaching him many skills. Itard's work with Victor provided the basis for the teaching methods of Edward Seguin and 19th-century educators of "idiots." Itard's book, *The Wild Boy of Aveyron*, remains a fascinating and moving classic in the education of students with disabilities. Seguin's book, *Idiocy and Its Treatment by the Physiological Method* (1866), has become another classic in the history of special education. In fact, some later writers have drawn direct connections from the work of Itard and Seguin to popular approaches in special education of the 20th century (e.g., Ball, 1971).

Contemporary educational methods for students with a variety of disabilities are grounded in many of the principles expounded by Itard two centuries ago and by Seguin in the middle of the 19th century, although the story of the Wild Boy is often misinterpreted or misrepresented (see Lane, 1976; Shattuck, 1994). Moreover, Itard's work remains a reference point today for intervention with children who are found to have been closeted away and abused by their parents (cf. Raymer, 1992). In fact, Hallahan and Kauffman (2006) suggest that Itard and his students first articulated what are now basic special education principles:

- *individualized instruction,* meaning that the student's characteristics rather than prescribed curriculum content provide the basis for teaching
- *sequenced educational tasks,* beginning with those the student can perform successfully and gradually becoming more complex
- *stimulation and awakening of the student's senses,* with the aim of making the child more aware of and responsive to educational tasks
- *purposeful arrangement of the student's environment,* allowing the structure of events to lead naturally to learning
- *immediate reinforcement* for correct responses so that the student learns efficiently
- *emphasis on functional skills* that allow the student to become as self-sufficient and self-actualized as possible
- *the assumption that every student can learn something worthwhile* or improve to some degree

Besides the work of Pinel and Itard in Europe, developments in the United States in the late 1700s were a prelude to education for children and youth with emotional or behavioral disorders. Most important was the influential writing of Dr. Benjamin Rush of Philadelphia, often considered the father of American psychiatry. After the American Revolution, Dr. Rush became a strong proponent of public education and public support for schools for poor children. His writings argued vehemently and eloquently against corporal punishment and cruel discipline and for kind and prudent methods of behavior control. His words, first published in 1790 in *The Universal Asylum and Columbian Magazine*, have the ring of present-day child advocacy and appeal for more caring relationships with children:

> I conceive corporal punishments, inflicted in an arbitrary manner, to be contrary to the spirit of liberty, and that they should not be tolerated in a free government. Why should not children be protected from violence and injuries, as well as white and black servants? Had I influence enough in our legislature to obtain only a single law, it should be to make the punishment for striking a schoolboy, the same as for assaulting and beating an adult member of society....
>
> The world was created in love. It is sustained by love. Nations and families that are happy, are made so only by love. Let us extend this divine principle, to those little communities which we call schools. Children are capable of loving in a high degree. They may therefore be governed by love. (Bremner, 1970, pp. 222–223)

Rush did not advocate the abandonment of discipline. He suggested mild forms of punishment in school: admonishing the child privately, confining the child after school hours, and requiring the child to hold a small sign of disgrace in the presence of the other children. If the child did not respond to those methods, Rush recommended dismissing the child from school and turning the business of discipline over to the parents. His emphasis on education and love-oriented methods of control had a profound influence on the early years of American psychiatry and the moral therapy employed in many American "lunatic asylums" during the first half of the 19th century.

19

....

The Nineteenth Century

Most 20th-century descriptions of 19th-century treatment of young-sters with emotional or behavioral disorders have been brief and nega-tive (Despert, 1965; Kanner, 1957, 1962; Lewis, 1974; Rubenstein, 1948). Only relatively recently has the history of public education for such children and youth been traced (Berkowitz & Rothman, 1967a; Hoffman, 1974a, 1975). The literature of the 19th century is meager by current standards; children in this literature are often looked upon and treated psychologically as miniature adults; and bizarre ideas (such as the notions that insanity could be caused by masturbating, by study-ing too hard, or by watching someone have an epileptic seizure) are persistent. Most histories of childhood emotional and behavioral dis-orders consistently contain certain inaccuracies and distortions that lead to underestimating the value of the 19th-century literature in ap-proaching present-day problems (Kauffman, 1976).

However, dismissing the 19th century as an era in which no one recognized, much less cared about, children with emotional and be-havioral disorders is not entirely justified. As Berkowitz and Rothman (1967a) noted,

> *The original war on poverty [President Lyndon B. Johnson declared the 20th century's war on poverty in the 1960s] may well have started in 1805, when New York City established a school for its "pauper" children—forty in number. Not only was this the beginning of New York City's school system, it was also the beginning of New York City's concern for special children— the special children, in this case, being the "pauper" children. This interest and concern in both public education and in special children expanded as the city grew so that in 1898 the New York City Board of Education was responsible for the educational program of fifty-eight "corporate" schools. These schools were situated in residential institutions for dependent, des-titute, neglected and physically handicapped children. In the light of our present knowledge, it is certainly reasonable to assume that many of these children had serious emotional problems.* (p. 5)

The 19th-century literature on "insanity" and "idiocy," in which we find most of the literature on youngsters' emotional and behavioral disorders, leads us to conclude that nearly every current important issue has been an issue for over two centuries. Whether these issues persist because of the intractability of the sociopsychological problems they represent or because of the ineptness with which potential solutions have been implemented is moot.

It is important to note that in the early 19th century, physicians gradually became the individuals most responsible for disabilities involving what was then called madness or lunacy (now called mental illness) (Scull, 1975). The physicians involved in "madness" gradually became what we know today as psychiatrists, whose systems of classification and treatment dominate contemporary views of emotional and behavioral disorders (see Kauffman, 2005a; Phillips, Draguns, & Bartlett, 1975; Prugh, Engel, & Morse, 1975; Rutherford, Quinn, & Mathur, 2004). However, as we have noted, the earliest instances in which madness or mental illness was an object of study and extensive writing date from the 18th century (e.g., Battie, 1758).

Scull attempted to explain "just how that segment of the medical profession which we now call psychiatry captured control over insanity; or, to put it another way, how those known in the early nineteenth century as mad-doctors first acquired a monopolistic power to define and treat lunatics" (1975, p. 218). Scull's observations and others' like his became the basis for later attacks on modern ideas of treatment. For example, Skrtic and Sailor (1996) commented,

> The notion of disciplinary power raises serious moral and political questions for the social professions—questions concerning the nature and effects of the practices and discourses of investigation, surveillance, medicalization, objectification, treatment, confinement, and exclusion that these professions have developed and refined over the course of this [20th] century. (p. 275)

Regardless of how one views the moral, philosophical, and political questions involved, Skrtic and Sailor seem to have attributed at least the initial development of the objective medical study of mental illness to the wrong century. True, refinement of the study of mental illness has been continuous since its inception, but such study began in the 18th century and was extensively developed in the 19th century. Two decades before Skrtic's and Sailor's comments, Scull (1975) had stated in his review of early 19th-century psychiatry,

Just as in the case of bodily illness, where a profession is granted the authority to label one person's discomfort an illness and another's not, so too with mental distress, the psychiatrists possess the ultimate power to assign one person to the status of being mentally ill, and to refuse the designation to another. And it is contact with society's official experts in this area, rather than manifestations of specific behavioral or mental disturbance, which most firmly and legitimately affixes the label in the eyes of the layman. (pp. 220–221)

Certainly, an important issue is who should have the power to determine that someone has a "mental illness" or an emotional or behavioral disorder. One point of view is that no one should have such power, but that view is hardly consistent with our ideas of social justice, for then such disorders would be addressed only in a haphazard way, if at all. Another point of view is that political entities, such as government or party officials, should have such power, but historian Robert Conquest's reflections on the abuses of political power in the 20th century suggest that giving such power to political entities would not be wise, as such entities might abuse their power for political gain (Conquest, 2000). It is hard to know just who in any humane society should be so entrusted, but it is likely that someone will have—and should have—such power.

Scull (1975) might be overstating the "monopolistic power" of psychiatrists to define mental illness, although psychiatry is the obvious discipline to which people now defer in such judgments. We might note two things about the comments of writers such as Skrtic and Sailor (1996) and Scull. First, evidence increasingly points to a physiological component in what we now call emotional and behavioral disorders of both children and adults. Evidence also increasingly implicates complex physiological processes *in interaction with environmental events* (see Goldapple et al., 2004; Pinker, 2002). If physicians are not justifiably the leaders in identifying and treating such disorders, then we wonder who should be. Still, medicine is not and should not be the only discipline involved. Second, the issues raised by Scull and Skrtic and Sailor are likely perpetual. They are neither new nor entirely resolvable in a way that is satisfactory to all.

Mental Retardation and Emotional or Behavioral Disorders

One reason the 19th century is often dismissed as an unimportant era in the field of emotional or behavioral disorders is that the relationship between it and that of mental retardation is overlooked. It is clear to many writers that individuals with mental retardation and those with emotional disturbance are not as different in their characteristics as was assumed several decades ago, regardless of whether one considers mild and moderate retardation or disturbance or those with severe and profound disabilities (Balthazar & Stevens, 1975; Barrett, 1986; Crissy, 1975; DeMyer et al., 1974; Kanner, 1960; Menolascino, 1972, 1990). Nineteenth-century writers recognized the great similarity between mental retardation and mental illness. Not until 1886 was there a legal separation between "insanity" and "feeblemindedness" in England (Hayman, 1939).

Some 19th-century descriptions of "idiocy" and its varieties present a picture of youngsters who today might well be said to have schizophrenia or autism. Itard's (1962) description of Victor, written at the end of the 18th century, is important as a study of emotional or behavioral disorders as well as a treatise on mental retardation. Esquirol (1845), a French physician, describes in considerable detail the physical and behavioral features of an 11-year-old "imbecile" admitted to the Salpetriere Hospital:

> R. *usually sits with her knees crossed, her hands beneath her apron, and is almost constantly raising or depressing her shoulders. Her physical health is good, and she has a good appetite. She is a gourmand, worrying herself much about what she shall have to eat at her meals; and if she sees one of her companions eating, cries and calls for something for herself. Whilst with her parents, she is accustomed to escape and run to the shop of a pastrycook who lived near, and devour the first pie that she saw. She was also in the habit of entering a grocer's shop, seizing upon the bottles of liquor, and if they attempted to prevent her from drinking, dashed them upon the ground.... She is cunning and conceited. On wetting the bed, as she sometimes does, she defends herself, and accuses the servant girl of it. She detests her roommate, who is mute, and poorly clad. She has been caught thrusting needles into the blistered surface, which had been made upon the person of her wretched companion.* (p. 450)

The description of Charles Emile, a 15-year-old "idiot" at the Bicêtre, also contains reference to severely disordered behavior. Brigham (1845b) summarized the observations of Voisin, a physician at the Bicêtre, who said of Charles:

> *He was wholly an animal. He was without attachment; overturned everything in his way, but without courage or intent; possessed no tact, intelligence, power of dissimulation, or sense of propriety; and was awkward to excess. His* **moral sentiments** *are described as* **null**, *except the love of approbation, and a noisy instinctive gaiety, independent of the external world.... Devouring everything, however disgusting, brutally sensual, passionate—breaking, tearing, and burning whatever he could lay his hand upon; and if prevented from doing so, pinching, biting, scratching, and tearing himself, until he was covered with blood. He had the particularity of being so attracted by the eyes of his brothers, sisters, and playfellows, as to make the most persevering efforts to push them out with his fingers.... When any attempt was made to associate him with the other patients, he would start away with a sharp cry, and then come back to them hastily.* (p. 336)

Today, some of the children and youth then served in institutions for the deaf and the blind, and for mental retardation, would likely be said to have autism or other severe developmental disorders. The eminent American educator of students with disabilities Samuel Gridley Howe understood the difficulty in distinguishing students with mental retardation from those with emotional or behavioral disorders. He used the term *simulative idiocy* (Howe, 1852) to describe the problem that today would be termed *pseudoretardation*—the *appearance* of mental retardation presented by a nonretarded person.

The great reformer Dorothea Dix reported in 1844 the shock of finding a little girl in an asylum:

> *[I saw] a little girl, about nine or ten years of age, who suffered the four-fold calamity of being blind, deaf, dumb, and insane. I can conceive of no condition so pitiable as that of this unfortunate little creature, the chief movements of whose broken mind, were exhibited in restlessness, and violent efforts to escape, and unnatural screams of terror.* (Bremner, 1970, p. 777)

There is little doubt that institutions for the deaf and blind and those with mental retardation served children who would fall into the contemporary categories of autistic or emotionally disturbed. In short, the close relationship between mental retardation and emotional or behavioral disorders in children (and in adults as well) was known in the 19th century, and the observations of many 19th-century writers are surprisingly consonant with contemporary emphases on the similarities and overlapping characteristics, etiologies, and interventions for these groups.

As far as treatment is concerned, the historical reviews of Hoffman (1974a, 1974b, 1975) make it clear that the public schools of the late 19th century made provisions for inept and unruly students who today would be said to have emotional disturbance, learning disabilities, or mental retardation. "Incorrigible," "defective," and non–English-speaking children were typically lumped together in special "ungraded" classes—much like many noncategorical classes of the present era—with little or no regard for their specific educational needs. Thus, early public education for children with emotional or behavioral disorders must be viewed in the context of attempts to deal with the problem of mental retardation, as well.

Theories of Etiology

By the end of the 18th century, the belief that emotional and behavioral disorders were caused by demon possession and should be treated by religious means was no longer in vogue among the experts. Nineteenth-century writers, however, were undeniably preoccupied with a relationship between masturbation and insanity, particularly insanity in children and youth. The prevailing belief was that masturbation caused (or at least aggravated) insanity (Hare, 1962; Rie, 1971). The idea that masturbation was an intolerably horrible, debasing practice had not been laid to rest by the end of the 19th century. Castration and ovariotomy were still being used in the 1890s and early 1900s in attempts to stop masturbation and sexual interests in "idiotic," "imbecile," "feebleminded," and epileptic children and youth, many of whom exhibited disturbing behavior (see Bremner, 1971, pp. 855–857).

Nevertheless, some writers questioned the causal relationship between masturbation and insanity long before the beginning of the 20th century. Although Stribling (1842) referred to masturbation as a "detestable vice" and a "degrading habit," he clearly understood that it was mistaken as a cause of insanity:

> There is no subject connected with insanity of more interest than the causes from which it proceeds; and there is none certainly in regard to which the enquirer has more difficulty to ascertain the truth. The ignorance of some, and the aversion of others to disclosing the circumstances (which are often of a delicate character) connected with the origin of the patient's malady, are obstacles frequently to be encountered in such investigations—whilst even with the intelligent and communicative, it too often occurs that cause and effect are so confounded, as that the one is improperly made to take the place of the other....
>
> Masturbation ... as a cause of insanity, we are induced to think is often much exaggerated. Intellect is the great regulator of the human passions and propensities; and as we possess the latter in common with and to as great a degree as other animals, it is only by the former that we are distinguished from and elevated above them. When therefore the mind is thrown into chaos, and man is no longer a rational creature, his animal nature acquires the ascendancy and directs his actions. In this state, too, he is almost invariably cut off from intercourse with his kind, and hence this detestable vice in too many instances becomes his daily habit. When, therefore, in this condition it is first observed, the beholder, forgetting the circumstances which preceded, at once imagines that as no other cause for the mental disorder had ever been assigned, he has made the important discovery; and thus, what in most cases was merely the result of reason dethroned, is chronicled as the monster which expelled her from her empire. (pp. 22–23)

Actually, in many respects, including the difficulty of pinpointing causes and the delicacy of inquiring into personal history, Stribling's observations seem quite contemporary. He saw the error of the assumption *post hoc, ergo propter hoc* (after the fact, therefore because of it). Whereas Stribling questioned the cause–effect relationship between masturbation and insanity, Jarvis (1852) noted that masturbation could not be evaluated as a factor in any increase in insanity simply because "we have no means of knowing whether masturbation increases or diminishes" (p. 354).

Some psychiatrists of the early 19th century identified etiological factors in youngsters' emotional and behavioral disorders that are today given serious consideration. For example, Parkinson in 1807 and West in 1848 (in Hunter & Macalpine, 1963) pointed to the interaction of temperament and child rearing, overprotection, over-indulgence, and inconsistency of discipline as factors in the development of troublesome behavior. Parkinson's perspectives are consistent with the 20th-century findings of Thomas, Chess, and Birch (1968) and Keogh (2003) on temperament and child rearing. In Parkinson's words, written in 1807,

> *That children are born with various dispositions is undoubtedly true; but it is also true, that by due management, these may be so changed and meliorated by the attention of a parent, that not only little blemishes may be smoothed away, but even those circumstances which more offensively distinguish the child, may, by proper management become the characteristic ornaments of the man.... On the treatment of the child receives from his parents during the infantine stage of his life, will, perhaps, depend much of the misery or happiness he may experience, not only in his passage through this, but through the other stages of his existence.* (Hunter & Macalpine, 1963, p. 616)

Note also the contemporary flavor of Parkinson's observations on child rearing in the following excerpt from his 1807 treatise:

> *If, on the one hand, every little sally of passion and impatience is immediately controuled; if those things which are admissible are regularly permitted, and those which are improper are as regularly withheld, the wily little creature will soon learn to distinguish that which is allowed of, from that which is prohibited. He will, indeed, urge his claim, for that to which he has been taught he has a right, with manly boldness; but will not harass himself and his attendants, with ceaseless whinings or ravings, to obtain that which uniform prohibition has placed beyond his experience. But a melancholy reverse appears, if, on the other hand, no consistency is observed in his management; if, at one time, the slightest indulgence is refused, and at another the most extravagant, and even injurious cravings, are satisfied, just as the caprice of the parent may induce him to gratify his ill humour, by thwarting another; or to amuse his moments of ennui, by playing with his child as a monkey, and exciting it to those acts of mischief and audacity for which, in the next moment, it may suffer a severe correction. Continually undergoing either disappointment or punishment; or engaged in extorting gratifications, which*

27

he often triumphs at having gained by an artful display of passion; his time passes on, until at last the poor child frequently manifests ill nature sufficient to render him odious to all around him, and acquires pride and meanness sufficient to render him the little hated tyrant of his playfellows and inferiors. (Hunter & Macalpine, 1963, pp. 616–617)

These comments of Parkinson, written about two centuries ago, are extraordinarily consistent with contemporary research on inconsistency in child rearing and teaching. With few changes in the language, they could have been written as summaries of research reviewed by Haring and Phillips (1962), Patterson (1982), or Walker, Ramsey, and Gresham (2004).

Nevertheless, many of the presumed causes of mental illness listed by 19th-century writers seem laughable from a contemporary perspective: "idleness and ennui," "pecuniary embarrassment," "sedentary and studious habits," "inhaling tobacco fumes," "gold fever," "indulgence of temper" (Stribling, 1842); "suppression of hemorrhoids," "kick on the stomach," "bathing in cold water," "sleeping in a barn filled with new hay," "study of metaphysics," "reading vile books," "license question," "preaching sixteen days and nights," "celibacy," "sudden joy," "ecstatic admiration of works of art," "mortified pride," "Mormonism," "duel," "struggle between the religious principle and power of passion" (Jarvis, 1852); "feebleness of intellect," "uterine derangement," "suppression of menses," "suppressed masturbation," "cerebral softening," "bad whiskey," "women," "worms," "politics," "Salvation Army," "novel reading," "seduction," and "laziness" (among those listed as reasons for admission to the West Virginia Hospital for the Insane at Weston, 1864–1889).

Although biological causes of mental retardation and emotional and behavioral disorders were recognized during the first half of the 19th century, the emphasis was on environmental factors, especially early discipline and training. It is not surprising that interventions in that period centered on environmental controls—providing the proper sensory stimulation, discipline, and instruction.

As Hoffman (1974a, 1974b, 1975) noted, the influence of Darwinist thought in the late 19th century was profound. British philosopher Herbert Spencer and the American spokesperson for social Darwinism in the United States, William Graham Sumner, saw the seeds of social decay and destruction in the unchecked propagation of the lower classes and defective individuals, as did Dr. Walter E. Fernald, distinguished medical superintendent of the Massachusetts School for the Feebleminded (Barrows, 1893). The ideas of social evolution, survival of the fittest, and eugenics led inevitably to the writing and influence of Henry H. Goddard, an early 20th-century progenitor of special education (Balthazar & Stevens, 1975; Smith, 1962). The favored position in the late 19th and early 20th centuries was that undesirable behavioral traits represented inherited flaws and that intervention should be limited to selective breeding. Contemporary sciences acknowledge the importance of genetic influences on behavior without seeing it as the only critical influence or recommending eugenics (selective breeding) as a social policy (e.g., Pinker, 2002; Weiner, 1999; Wilson, 1998).

Intervention

Many children and youth, including those with emotional or behavioral disorders and limited intellect, were undoubtedly neglected and abused in the 19th century. Bremner (1970, 1971), Hoffman (1974a, 1975), and Rothman (1971) amply document the cruel discipline, forced labor, and other inhumanities suffered by children and youth in the 1800s (see also Forehand & McKinney, 1993). Although many 19th-century attempts at education and treatment were primitive compared to the best that can now be offered, some youngsters with emotional or behavioral disorders in the 19th century received considerably better care than many similar children receive today. If we were to concentrate on the neglect and abuse in institutions, schools, detention centers, streets, and homes in the early 21st century, we might justifiably conclude that the plight of such children and youth has not improved much in all the intervening years.

Dorothea Dix, the great advocate of institutions for the insane, was herself apparently of questionable emotional stability, and her advocacy for institutions was undoubtedly based in part on her own experience of privilege (see Dumont, 1995; Gollaher, 1995). Her advocacy of institutional care for people who were said to be mad or insane apparently improved their lives, as institutions of her era were almost always better than the jails, almshouses, and streets on which these people were found. However, before the beginning of the 20th century, the institutions for which Dix advocated had become overcrowded and ineffective. Her zealous advocacy for institutionalization led, perhaps inexorably, to the deinstitutionalization movement beginning in the 1960s. In fact, we seem to have come full circle since the days of Dix, as most adults with serious mental illness are now found outside of mental hospitals. And these mentally ill people are not receiving effective treatment or living successfully in their communities—they are on the streets and in jails (see Davenport, 2004; Lamb & Weinberger, 2001; Patton, Mondale, & Monmaney, 1988). Moreover, the neglect of children's mental health in the 20th and 21st centuries is nothing less than scandalous (Knitzer, 1982; U.S. Department of Health and Human Services, 2001), and fewer than 1% of schoolchildren in the United States were receiving special education for emotional or behavioral disorders in the opening years of this 21st century (Kauffman, 2005b). Many children remain in poverty (Knitzer & Aber, 1995).

Contrasting the best contemporary thinking and treatment to the worst of the 19th century creates a dark and distorted vision of that century, with its references to imprisonment, cruelty, punishment, neglect, ignorance, bizarre ideas (masturbatory insanity), and absence of effective education and treatment for youngsters with emotional or behavioral disorders (Despert, 1965; Kanner, 1962; Rie, 1971; Rubenstein, 1948). As it happens, many 19th-century leaders in the treatment of children with emotional or behavioral disorders were more enlightened than their critics have assumed. Unfortunately, some of their brightest successes, such as moral treatment, have usually been ignored.

Seldom has moral treatment been mentioned in connection with children and youths. "*Moral treatment*, in modern technical jargon, is what we mean by resocialization by means of a growing list of therapies with prefaces such as recreational, occupational, industrial, music—with physical education thrown in for good measure" (Bockoven, 1956, p. 303). Bockoven's detailed review of moral therapy provides the richest description of that intervention since the 19th century (Bockoven, 1956, 1972). He points out that these therapies—recreational, occupational, industrial, musical, for example—do not add up to moral treatment, which implies an integrated total treatment program (see Brigham, 1847, for a succinct 19th-century description of moral treatment). The term *moral treatment* did not, as some have surmised, connote religious training or training in ethics. Originally, as translated from Pinel's work, *moral treatment* meant *psychological as opposed to medical* treatment of insanity, and it included every therapeutic endeavor other than medication or surgery. (For further discussion of moral treatment, see Bockoven, 1972; Caplan, 1969; Carlson and Dain, 1960; Grob, 1973; Menninger, 1963; Rees, 1957; and Ullmann and Krasner, 1969.)

Rie (1971) discusses the moral treatment of the 1800s but largely discounts its relevance for child psychopathology because youngsters were not admitted to institutions in great numbers. Yet children and youth did find their way into institutions and were treated by moral therapists during the first half of the 19th century (*Annual Reports of the Court of Directors of the Western Lunatic Asylum, 1836–1850, 1870;* Esquirol, 1845; Hunter & Macalpine, 1974; Mayo, 1839). For example, Francis Stribling, a prominent moral therapist of the early 1800s, reports that of 122 patients in the Western Lunatic Asylum in Staunton, Virginia, during 1841, 9 were under the age of 20 and 2 were under the age of 15 (Stribling, 1842). Thus, we need to include moral treatment in the types of care offered to children and youths in that era.

Moral therapists emphasized constructive activity, kindness, minimum restraint, structure, routine, and consistency in treatment. Furthermore, obedience to authority and conformity to rules were primary features of child-care institutions and child-rearing dogma in mid-19th-century America (Rothman, 1971). Rothman indicates that the emphasis on obedience and conformity was sometimes carried to ridiculous or even harmful extremes, that some youngsters languished in jails or poorhouses, and that the concepts of structure, consistency, and reeducation were sometimes distorted to include cruel and excessive punishment. Still, it is evident from the writing of moral therapists that humane, nonpunitive care was the goal. Mayo (1839) provides an example of the type of treatment given to children and youth with emotional or behavioral disorders by moral therapists in his description of the case of a youth he calls N. B. Although written in the language of the day and consistent with social conventions of the era, the richness of the description of N. B., Mayo's rationale for particular decisions, and the treatment itself in many respects reflect the thinking of late-20th- and early-21st-century special educators (e.g., in the generally sympathetic description of the youth, the detailed depiction of conduct disorder, the obvious sympathy for the distraught youth, the attempt to treat N. B. in the community or in the least restrictive setting, the observation that regular educational procedures were ineffective, the emphasis on consistency and structure, and the generally supportive, nonviolent approach):

N. B., aged 16, was described to me by his father, who came to consult me, in regard to his management, as a boy of singularly unruly and intractable character; selfish, wayward, violent without ground or motive, and liable under the paroxysm of his moodiness to do personal mischief to others; not, however, of a physically bold character. He is of a fair understanding, and exhibits considerable acuteness in sophisticated apologies for his wayward conduct. He has made little progress in any kind of study. His fancy is vivid, supplying him profusely with sarcastic imagery. He has been subjected at different times, and equally without effect, to a firmly mild and to a rigid discipline. In the course of these measures, solitary confinement has been tried; but to this he was impassive. It produced no effect.

He was last in a very good [school] in a town in ——, where he drew a knife upon one of the officers of the establishment, while admonishing him; and produced a deep feeling of aversion in the minds of his companions, by the undisguised pleasure which he showed at some bloodshed which took place in this town during the disturbance of 18——.

He has not appeared to be sensually disposed, and he is careful of property. His bodily health is good, and he has never had any cerebral affection. This boy was further described to me as progressively becoming worse in his conduct, and more savagely violent to his relatives. Still I easily discovered that he was unfavourably situated; for his relations appeared to be at once irritable and affectionate; and the total failure of various plans of education was throwing him entirely upon their hands.

As an instance of the miserable pleasure which he took in exciting disgust and pain, I was told, that when 13 years old, he stripped himself naked and exposed himself to his sisters.

When I saw him (December 8th, 18——), he received me courteously but suspiciously, his demeanor was soft, but there was a bad expression about his mouth; I believe his eyes gave him the appearance of softness; they were large and dark; his skin was smooth; he was small for his age, not having grown for some years. On my addressing him in regard to his peculiarities, he equivocated and became irritable; and he asserted that he was under impulses which he could not resist. He spoke unkindly of his father, and tried to snatch out of my hand a very wicked letter written by himself to one of his relatives, which I produced as an evidence of his misconduct. This peculiarity seemed to pervade his views of his own conduct,—that he contemplated past offenses, not only as what could not be recalled, but also, as what ought not to be remembered to his disadvantage.

Having satisfied my mind by careful observation, that the accounts given by his relatives were substantially correct, and that the ordinary principles of education, however skillfully applied, would here lead to no salutary result, I suggested the following line of treatment, as calculated to give him his best chance of moral improvement. Let him reside in the neighborhood or, if possible, in the family of some person competent to undertake this charge, under the attendance of two trustworthy men, who should be subject to the authority of the superior above alluded to; one of these persons should be in constant attendance upon him; but if coercion should be required in order to induce him to comply with reasonable requests, both should be employed so as not to make such violence necessary as should produce the slightest bodily pain. The object of this plan would be to accustom him to obedience, and by keeping him in a constant state of the exercise of this quality, for such a length of time as might form a habit, to adapt him to live in society afterwards, on terms of acquiescence in its rules.

Now the principle of management suggested here, is that ordinarily applied to insane patients alone; but this young man could not be considered insane in any accredited use of the term. He was totally free from false perception, or inconsequential thoughts; he was neat in his person, agreeable in his address, and of an intellect above rather than below par. Yet, education in its appeal to the moral principle had been tried on him in many various forms with total unsuccess: youth was advancing into manhood; and his chances of attaining a state, in which he might be a safe member of society, were becoming slender according to any of the usual methods of moral education.

The case seemed to warrant the application of the principle recommended; and after much thought, I determined to try it in the only way in which it was practicable to me, namely; in the walls of an establishment, a few miles from the place in which I resided, the proprietor of which was well known to me for excellent judgment and an amiable character.

I took him to this establishment, accompanied by his father and another relative, showed him at once into his apartment; and briefly told him why he was placed there; and how inflexible he would find his restraint there, until he should have gained habits of self-control. At the same time I pointed out

33

to him the beautiful and wide grounds of the establishment, and the many comforts and enjoyments which he might command by strict obedience. This I stated to him in the presence of his two relatives, whom I then at once removed from the room. When I saw him about an hour afterwards, the nearest approach to surprise and annoyance which he made, was the expression, "that he never was in such a lurch before." He wished to see his father again before he left the house, not however, apparently from motives of feeling, but in order to address some persuasives to him against the scheme. I refused this interview.

For about a fortnight he behaved extremely well. He then lost his self-command, kicked his attendant, and struck him with a bottle of medicine. On this, I went over to see him; he vindicated himself with his usual ingenuity; but looked grave and somewhat frightened,—when I told him that if he repeated this offence, he would be placed in a strait waistcoat, not indeed as a punishment, but as a means of supplying his deficiency of self-control. He expresses no kindly feeling towards his relatives; but confesses the fitness of his treatment and confinement. It appears to me, that he is tranquilized by his utter inability to resist.

January 16th, 18——. Visiting N. B. today, I told him, that he might write letters to his father or uncle, but that he would at present receive none from them. To have refused him permission to write letters would have been tyrannical; besides, they would afford insight into his character; to have allowed him to receive letters, would have been an interference with that principle of entire separation from his family, which I wished to maintain, until he should have learned the value of those ties to which he has been indifferent. He made complaints in very unimportant matters against his servant, to which I paid attention, but gave no credence. Great unfairness in these remarks. I have endeavoured to make him understand, that in dealing with Mr. N——, the proprietor of the establishment, and myself he can neither enjoy the pleasure of making us angry, nor hope for advantage from sophistry. But that strict justice will be done him, upon the terms originally stated to him.

In a letter to his father about this time, I observe—"the plan evidently works well. He is practicing self-restraint successfully; not indeed from conviction of its moral fitness, but from having ascertained its necessity. He is aware of the state of entire subjection in which he is placed; and yet his spirits do not flag, neither does his health suffer. It is curious, that he has ceased to use his old argument in conversation with me, that past conduct ought not to *be taken into the account in regard to present proceedings." From the time above alluded to, during his stay at the establishment, which I continued for fourteen months, no further outbreak against authority took place. He ceased to be violent, because the indulgence of violence would imply risk of inconvenience to himself, without the comfort which he had formerly derived from it in exciting the anger of his friends or giving them pain.* (Mayo, 1839, pp. 68–70)

By the middle of the 19th century, educators were providing programs for students with limited intelligence and emotional or behavioral disorders. Schools in asylums for "insane" and "idiotic" students flourished for a time under the leadership of humanistic teachers who developed explicit teaching methods (Brigham, 1845b, 1847, 1848; Howe, 1851, 1852; Ray, 1846). As Bockoven (1956) notes, education was a prominent part of moral treatment. Teaching and learning were considered conducive to mental health—a concept that can hardly be considered bizarre or antiquated.

Most of the education for students with severe emotional or behavioral disorders, aside from the academic instruction offered in asylums for the insane, was provided under the rubric of education for idiots. The teaching techniques employed by leading educators of students with mental retardation were amazingly modern in many respects—based on individual assessment, highly structured, systematic, directive, and multisensory, with emphasis on training in self-help and daily living skills for those with severe disabilities, frequent use of games and songs, and suffusion with positive reinforcement (Brigham, 1848; Itard, 1962; Ray, 1846; Seguin, 1866). Despite the overenthusiasm and excessive claims of success by moral therapists and early educators of students with mental retardation (Howe, Itard, and Seguin), the basic soundness of their work and the changes they were able to produce remain impressive (Balthazar & Stevens, 1975). At mid-19th century, the prevailing attitude was one of hope and belief that every student with disabilities could be helped. As Brigham (1845b) states,

The interesting question is, to what extent can careful and skillful instruction make up for these natural deficiencies [of idiotic children]; and, as already done for the deaf, the dumb, and the blind, reclaim for these unfinished

*creatures the powers and privilege of life. The exertions of future philanthro-
pists will answer this question. Improvement must not be looked for beyond
what is strictly relative to the imperfect individual in each case; but it would
seem to be true of idiots, as of the insane in general, that there is no case
incapable of some amendment; that every case may be improved or cured,
up to a certain point—a principle of great general importance in reference to
treatment. (pp. 334–335)*

We are tempted to see personnel recruitment and training as phe-
nomena of recent times, but moral therapists of the 19th century recognized the importance and the difficulty of getting the right people
to work with the insane. Manuals were developed for training attendants to work with patients (see Caplan, 1969), and the difficulty of
hiring people with adequate qualifications was often noted. In fact,
Ray (1852) said of ideal attendants,

*They must manifest patience under the most trying emergencies, control of
temper under the strongest provocations, and a steady perseverance in the
performance of duty, disagreeable and repulsive as it oftentimes is. They
must be kind and considerate, ever ready to sacrifice their own comfort to the
welfare of their charge, cleanly in all their ways, and unsaving of any pains
necessary to render their charge so also. In all respects, their deportment and
demeanor must be precisely such as refined and cultivated persons have indicated as most appropriate to the management of the insane. In short, they
are expected to possess a combination of virtues which, in ordinary walks of
life, would render their possessor one of the shining ornaments of the [hu-
man] race. (pp. 52–53)*

Compare Ray's (1852) depiction of the ideal attendant with the
1966 depiction by Hobbs of the ideal teacher-counselor:

*But most of all a teacher-counselor is a decent adult; educated, well trained;
able to give and receive affection, to live relaxed, and to be firm; a person with private resources for the nourishment and refreshment of his own
life; not an itinerant worker but a professional through and through; a person with a sense of the significance of time, of the usefulness of today and
the promise of tomorrow; a person of hope, quiet confidence, and joy; one
who has committed himself to children and to the proposition that children*

who are emotionally disturbed can be helped by the process of re-education.
(pp. 1106–1107; also, Hobbs, 1974, p. 157)

Individuals having all the characteristics described by Hobbs have always been a minority of those staffing programs for children and youth with emotional and behavioral disorders. Throughout the history of our field, professionals have been able to articulate what we are looking for in those we want to work with the youngsters we serve. However, finding and keeping them has always been another matter. Even in the mid-19th century, the problem was noted:

> *Now, although there can be no objection to a high standard of excellence, that man can be little better than a fool who supposes it will be often reached by persons whom we employ as attendants. They have been prepared for this delicate and responsible duty by no special course of self-discipline, and, we know well enough, are seldom distinguished by the beauty or abundance of their moral endowments. They are, in fact, plain, every-day men and women, with common infirmities of the race, losing their temper under ordinary irritations, and sometimes guilty of downright abuse of their trust.*
> (Ray, 1852, p. 53)

Not much has changed in the discrepancy between the quality of personnel we would like to have and the quality of personnel we are able to attract to the difficult task we ask them to undertake. Finding, training, and keeping employed the teachers we wish for students with emotional and behavioral disorders—those "highly qualified" to teach the most difficult students—is still an extraordinary and largely unmet challenge. We are, in fact, often forced to choose between having no teacher at all in a classroom and employing a plain, everyday man or woman with common human faults.

In the late 19th century, considerable concern was shown also for children and youths who were delinquent, vagrant, aggressive, disobedient, or disadvantaged (i.e., poor or orphaned) but not considered insane or idiotic (Bremner, 1970, 1971; Eggleston, 1987; Rothman, 1971). Many of these youngsters, who today might be said to have mild or moderate disabilities, found their way into jails and almshouses. There was, however, a strong movement to establish child care institutions (such as orphan asylums, reformatories, houses of refuge) for the purpose of reforming and rehabilitating deviant children and youth. The intent was to protect wayward, disabled, and poor youngsters and to provide for their education and training in a humane, familiar atmosphere. Concern for the futures of those exhibiting acting-out behavior was not entirely misguided. Contemporary longitudinal studies tend to confirm what 19th-century writers suspected: aggressive, acting-out, delinquent behavior in youngsters predicts misfortune for their later adjustment (Robins, 1966, 1974, 1979, 1986; Walker et al., 2004).

Intervention in the public schools became a reality only after the enactment of compulsory attendance laws in the closing decades of the 19th century. One reason for enacting compulsory attendance laws was the large number of non–English-speaking immigrant youngsters who poured into the United States during this period. Immigrant children and youths, authorities felt, should be compelled to be socialized and Americanized by the schools. Once the attendance laws were enacted and enforced, many students obviously interfered with the education of the majority and benefited little from the regular classes themselves. Before these youngsters had been compelled to go to school, they had merely dropped out, causing problems only by roaming the streets and committing delinquent acts.

Partly out of concern for such problems, the public schools established ungraded classes. In 1871, authorities in New Haven, Connecticut, opened an ungraded class for truant, disobedient, and insubordinate children. Soon afterward, other cities followed suit, and classes for the socially maladjusted and "backward" students (those with mild mental retardation; those with severe mental retardation were not included in public schools) grew rapidly (Berkowitz & Rothman, 1967a; Hoffman, 1974a, 1974b, 1975). These special classes, as well as corporate schools and similar institutions, eventually became little more than dumping grounds for all manner of misfits. Whether the students who did not want to be in school or the public school administrators were the misfits was as pertinent a question for that era as it is for the present (Cruickshank, Paul, & Junkala, 1969).

Changes Within the Nineteenth Century
The 19th century, like any other, was not a unitary or homogeneous historical period. Between 1850 and 1900, important changes

took place in attitudes toward severe and profound emotional and behavioral disorders and mental retardation, and rather dramatic differences appeared in the type of care afforded in institutions. Optimism, pragmatism, inventiveness, and humane care, associated with moral treatment and model social programs in the first half of the century, turned to pessimism, theorizing, rigidity, and dehumanizing institutionalization after the Civil War. The failure of private philanthropy and public programs to solve the problems of "idiocy," "insanity," and delinquency and to rectify the situations of the poor led to cynicism and disillusionment. More and larger asylums and houses of refuge were not the answers, although some advocates and many legislatures behaved as if they were. The many complex reasons for the retrogression after 1850 include economic, political, social, and professional factors analyzed by Bockoven (1956, 1972), Caplan (1969), Deutsch (1948), Grob (1973), Kanner (1964), Menninger (1963), Rothman (1971), and Ullmann and Krasner (1969). Then, as now, how people with disabilities were treated depended on economic conditions as well as the popular social and political philosophies.

Consider the buoyant optimism of the first half of the 19th century. It was an era in which public and private residential schools for individuals with disabilities were first established in the United States. The mood among special educators before the Civil War was exemplified by the comments of the Reverend Samuel J. May at the ceremony of the laying of the cornerstone of the first permanent, state-supported school built expressly for individuals with mental retardation in the United States. At this ceremony in Syracuse, New York, on September 8, 1854, Reverend May first reflected on the nature of evil and the way the apparent evils of blindness and deafness were transformed into good effects through special education. Then, he said,

> But there was idiocy—idiocy so appalling in its appearance, so hopeless in its nature; what could be the use of such an evil? It were not enough to point to it as a consequence of the violation of some of the essential laws of generation. If that were all, its end would be punishment. I ventured, therefore, to declare with an emphasis enhanced somewhat, perhaps, by a lurking distrust of the prediction, that the time would come when access would be found to the idiotic brain; the light of intelligence admitted into its dark chambers, and

the whole race be benefited by some new discovery on the nature of the mind. It seemed to some of my hearers, more than to myself, a daring conjecture.

Two or three years afterwards I read a brief announcement that in Paris they had succeeded in educating idiots. I flew to her who would be most likely to sympathize in my joy, shouting, "wife, my prophecy is fulfilled. Idiots have been educated." (Seguin, 1866, pp. 11–12)

In many ways, the extreme optimism of Reverend May and his colleagues was echoed about a century later. Achenbach (1974) noted how optimism and pessimism about educating children with disabilities have risen and fallen like waves (see also Achenbach, 1975). The 19th-century idea that all cases of idiocy and insanity could be *cured*, if only the right method were found, may have been given up by special educators of the 20th century. However, the idea of curability was clearly replaced by the 20th-century faith that, if only the right treatment were provided, every child would profit from education and make progress toward a higher level of functioning (Kauffman & Krouse, 1981). Consider the following statement of Abeson, Burgdorf, Casey, Kunz, and McNeil (1975):

With the establishment of the principles of normalization and least restrictive environment has come the recognition that accurate predictions cannot be made of the ultimate achievement and adjustment of any human being. Given appropriate programs of education, therapy, or treatment, all persons will progress. (pp. 277–278)

The notion that if only the correct educational methods are used, all children will achieve competence in basic skills has persisted into the 21st century. It is found in the No Child Left Behind Act and the report of the President's Commission on Excellence in Special Education, which we discuss further in later chapters (see also Kauffman & Wiley, 2004).

Ironically, most historical comment on children's emotional and behavioral disorders seems to favor the last decades of the 19th century as more auspicious than earlier decades in the development of child psychiatry (Alexander & Selsnick, 1966; Harms, 1967; Kanner, 1973c; Rie, 1971; Walk, 1964). However, MacMillan's (1960) review of the literature suggests that the earlier decades of the 19th century provided a richer body of information than did the later decades. His observations seem to be borne out by examination of some of the literature published during the last decades of the century. Certainly, there is little or nothing to be found in the writings of Hammond (1891), Maudsley (1880), or Savage (1891) that improves on earlier works insofar as treatment is concerned. The valuable and insightful work of the late 19th-century psychiatrists (such as Griesinger) reviewed by Harms (1967) is concerned with the theory and diagnosis of psychological disturbances in children and youth.

After the demise of moral treatment about midcentury, psychiatry became increasingly engrossed in varieties of psychodynamic theory, and therapeutic action on behalf of patients often gave way to interest in diagnosis and classification. Institutions had become vast warehouses for the insane. Educational and reform efforts with problem children and delinquents increased in number and size but not in quality or effectiveness. Hoffman (1974a) notes that "in each case, what began as sincere, humanistic efforts toward change were turned into near caricatures of their original purposes" (p. 71). That remains the case, with the movement toward full inclusion as a case in point (see Fuchs & Fuchs, 1994; Kauffman & Hallahan, 2005b; Mock & Kauffman, 2005). Before 1900 it was clear that institutionalization did not necessarily mean treatment and that special class placement could mar a child's identity. It was also clear that institutions and special classes *could*, given the right teachers and circumstances, dramatically improve children's lives, as is true also today (see Fuchs & Fuchs, 1995; Gliona, Gonzales, & Jacobson, 2005; Kauffman, Bantz, & McCullough, 2002).

By the end of the 19th century, several textbooks had been published about the psychiatric disorders of children and youth. These books dealt primarily with etiology and classification and, as Kanner (1960) notes, tended toward fatalism. Psychiatric disorders were assumed to be the irreversible result of widely varied causes such as masturbation, overwork, hard study, religious preoccupation, heredity, degeneracy, or disease. Also, by century's end, the problems of obstreperous children and juvenile delinquents had not been solved. However, some psychologists were hopeful that education and training could overcome problems, regardless of their origins. New efforts were being made by some individuals. For example, Lightner Witmer established a psychoeducational clinic at the University of Pennsylvania in 1896;

Chicago and Denver established the country's first juvenile courts in 1899.

Witmer's clinic was particularly noteworthy because of its connection to schools and its treatment of children with emotional and behavioral disorders:

> Witmer's clinic treated children, referred from the local school systems, whose problems were regarded as primarily learning difficulties of one kind or another. These included children whose behavior in the classroom was unruly and disruptive, and who today might be considered emotionally disturbed; such youngsters were described as having "moral defects." Each child was first examined by a physician and then received a mental examination (antropometric measures, eye tests, reaction time, etc.). Witmer placed considerable emphasis on the diagnosis. His concern was to determine whether the learning problem could be attributed to an arrest of cerebral development or to inadequate methods of education, and to delineate the "defect" precisely. Once an accurate diagnosis was made, treatment could be attempted. The treatment consisted of specific methods of retraining the child to alleviate his particular form of learning defect.... When we examine Witmer's theory and techniques, we find that at first he offered nothing original. His signal contribution was to suggest that psychologists take a new direction and discover new uses for already available methods. (Reisman, 1976, pp. 42–43)

Witmer apparently had some significant successes. He emphasized prevention and straightforward, practical solutions to problems (e.g., identifying the visual problem of a bad speller, fitting him with glasses, and giving him tutoring). His approach was pedagogical in the tradition of those who had come before—namely, Itard and Seguin (Reisman, 1976). In this sense, his strategy for addressing emotional and behavioral problems was extraordinarily contemporary—he saw the importance of teaching both academic skills and appropriate behavior (see Walker et al., 2004, for comparison).

As we shall see in the next chapter, events and trends during the first decades of the 20th century represented a gradual increase in concern for children and youth with emotional or behavioral disorders. Special education for such children was not invented overnight, and it did not suddenly become a widespread feature of American public education. It has emerged over decades only because of the persistent, dedicated work of many advocates.

....

Prelude to the Twentieth Century

Much of the groundwork for the flowering of special education was laid in the 19th century. Public education had been established, and without attempts to mandate universal education, special education had little meaning for average citizens. People of wealth have always been able to purchase services for their children, whether those children have disabilities or not. But special education was to become an integral part of the public education system, one that served families of the poor as well as those of wealth. It was emerging as part of public education in major population centers before the end of the 19th century. In the early 20th century, special education came into its own as a field of study and as a public enterprise.

3 Early Twentieth Century— 1900 to 1960

MANY people assume that special education is entirely a phenomenon of the 20th century. Chapter 2 should have disabused readers of that notion. True, a national organization of special education teachers was not founded until the early 20th century. True, also, that federal legislation was not enacted until the second half of the 20th century. However, we have noted that special education was practiced in some 19th-century institutions and was begun in the public schools of major population centers before the opening of the 20th century.

The early 20th-century literatures of psychology, psychiatry, and education having to do with children are far richer than many imagine. Our discussion cannot begin to mention all of the literature about children's psychological and behavioral development and treatment of social deviance. We have had to pick some sources and ignore others, and in doing so we may have overlooked some important publications or individuals. Readers may want to do their own search and synthesis of the historical literature of this era.

We have chosen to treat the early 20th century as the period from 1900 to 1960 rather than from 1901 to the exact midcentury, because the 1960s seem to mark a new era in special education. We have broken the first six decades of the century into three blocks of time, but these periods overlap; each set of dates represents the approximation of an era, not a rigid demarcation.

....

1900 to 1930

Several important events in the first years of the 20th century gave direction and impetus to concern for children and youth for many years to come. Ellen Key, the Swedish sociologist, awakened great interest with her prophecy that the 20th century would be "the century of the child" (Key, 1909). However, the events and conditions of the late 1900s left us wondering what happened to that idea, even though 1919 was designated as "the year of the child" and child study and special education had become part of American culture before mid-century (see Carstens, 1932; Kelly, 1931). Redl (1966) suggested a more apt title for such times in his phrase "Love of Kids, Neglect of Children, Hatred of Youth." As Brentro, Brokenleg, and Van Bockern (1998) later put it, "The optimism of Key was supplanted by profound ambivalence and even cynicism" (p. 1). At least we can say that in the 1900s, children became a subject of more intense scrutiny by scientists and the larger society than they had been.

Many special educators of the 21st century do not know that President Herbert Hoover called a White House Conference on Child Health and Protection in 1929—and that it was the *third* such conference, the first being held in 1909 (see White House Conference, 1931). Nor do many people know that many of the same concerns that have dogged special education into the 21st century were expressed in reports of that conference—definition, placement, causation, prevention, overrepresentation of minorities, and personnel preparation, for example (see Baker, Crothers, McCord, & Stullken, 1931). But in spite of the concern of the federal government and many states, the last state to pass a child protection law (Georgia) did so only in 2004. Little wonder that federal initiatives regarding children are often greeted with cynicism by child advocates.

Personal narrative played an important role in developments of the early 20th century, as it perhaps always has and always will. Clifford W. Beers, a bright young man who experienced a nervous breakdown in 1900 and later recovered, wrote of his experiences in a mental hospital. His autobiography, *A Mind That Found Itself* (Beers, 1908), had a profound influence on public opinion. At least, the public became aware of mental illness as a problem of individuals and society. Along with the psychiatrist Adolph Meyer and the philosopher and psychologist William James, Beers founded the National Committee for Mental Hygiene in 1909. The mental hygiene movement resulted in efforts of early detection and prevention, including the establishment of mental hygiene programs in schools and the opening of child guidance clinics (see Berkowitz & Rothman, 1967b). These programs and clinics did not, of course, resolve the problems of deviant children, nor did they serve all the children in need of them.

Developments in the treatment of juvenile delinquency were also important. William Healy founded the Juvenile Psychopathic Institute for the psychological and sociological study of juvenile delinquents in 1909. And around this time, Healy and his wife, Augusta Bronner, along with Grace M. Fernald, Julia Lathrop, and others in Chicago, began a systematic study of repeat (recidivist) juvenile offenders that influenced research and theory for many years (Healy, 1915, 1917, 1931; Healy & Bronner, 1926/1969).

Also during these years, the tool that French psychologist Alfred Binet (along with Theodore Simon) designed to measure children's performance and predict their school success became widely used. It was to become known as a test of general "intelligence." Lewis Terman of Stanford University popularized an American adaptation of the Binet–Simon scale, which became known as the Stanford–Binet test of intelligence (see Reisman, 1976; Strauss & Lehtinen, 1947). Binet was trying to invent an instrument that would be useful to schools, but as Sarason and Doris (1979) commented,

> He never dreamed his test would become a task so routinized, so devoid of specificity for action, so assembly line in character, as to defeat everyone's purposes. Public Law 94-142 [later known as IDEA] may well lock this routinization in concrete, not because that is its purpose but because it does not confront some of the major realities of the culture of schools. (p. 390)

Intelligence testing was to become highly controversial in special education, and it soon became painfully obvious that such testing was often misunderstood and misused. During these early years of the 20th century, Henry Goddard and Walter Fernald forwarded the notion that mental retardation, which could now be identified more objectively with the intelligence test, was inseparably linked to criminality and degeneracy (Doll, 1967; Hoffman, 1974a; Smith, 1962). (Stephen Jay Gould's book *The Mismeasure of Man* [1996] was a critique, not of the measurement of intelligence per se, but of the misinterpretation of testing and inappropriate uses of intelligence tests, a point often missed by critics of intelligence tests.)

In the early 20th century, Sigmund Freud and his contemporaries began writing widely on the topics of infant sexuality and human mental development. This work was to have a profound effect on the way children's behavior was viewed and, eventually, on attempts to educate children and youths with emotional or behavioral disorders (Fine,

1991; see also Berkowitz & Rothman, 1960; Bettelheim, 1950, 1961, 1967, 1970; Bettelheim & Sylvester, 1948; Bradby, 1919; A. Freud, 1954, 1965; Kornberg, 1955; Neill, 1927, 1960).

The opening decade of the 20th century was characterized by important beginnings in the field of mental hygiene (i.e., mental health). Many of the ideas first clearly articulated in that era found their way into later developments in special education. Children and youth became objects of scientific study, not merely control, and public programs were begun to foster children's healthy development. Among the first major books on exceptional children was a volume by Groszmann (1917), in which he included chapters on "psychopathic disorders and psychopathic constitutions," school problems, teacher training, and the like.

Concern for the mental and physical health of children expanded greatly after 1910 (Ollendick & Hersen, 1983). In 1911, Arnold Gesell founded the Clinic for Child Development at Yale, and in 1921 he published a small volume on public school policy in relation to exceptionality (Gesell, 1921). In 1912, Congress created the U.S. Children's Bureau to investigate and report on matters pertaining to the welfare of children and children's lives. The bureau's mandate included children from all classes of society. Moreover, the maltreatment of children and their poor development became matters of concern. Early studies of social deviance were published (e.g., Mateer, 1924). Special education had existed for some time, but in the 1920s, it became a field of organized study.

The first college textbooks for teachers planning to work with handicapped children were published in the 1920s (e.g., Hollingworth, 1923; Horn, 1924; Wallin, 1924), and narratives of teachers who saw problem children in school were published (e.g., Sayles & Nudd, 1929). We are tempted to see ourselves as enlightened, but many of the ideas we think of as contemporary are actually nearly a century old. For example, Leta Hollingworth stated in 1923, "The most important single cause of truancy is … that the curriculum does not provide for individual differences" (p. 200). She went on to comment on the cost of the individualization we associate with special education and to note the stultifying effects of requiring the same education for everyone:

The increased cost results from the fact that when education is individual-
ized, the number of pupils occupying a room and taught by a teacher is about
fifteen, instead of the regular number of thirty to fifty. If, roughly 20 percent
of all pupils deviate from the typical so extremely as to require a considerable
amount of individual instruction for their welfare, it is difficult to see how
they may be well served without a considerable increase in the money cost of
education. (p. 207)

In the United States the theory was adopted that all men are created
equal. All children must, therefore, be required to take the same education.
Such a system violates individuality even more painfully and wastefully than
the despised caste system of the older countries does. (p. 210)

The writers and supporters of the 21st century's No Child Left Behind Act might take note.

Special education was described as a problem by John Horn in
1924: "There does exist a problem of special education. It is found in
the fact of variability among children to be educated" (Horn, 1924,
pp. 5–6). Horn noted that exceptional children could be classified into
three broad categories and seven subgroups:

I. *Children who are exceptional for reasons primarily mental*
1. *The most highly endowed group.*
2. *The most poorly endowed (but not feeble) group.*
II. *Children who are exceptional for reasons primarily temperamental*
3. *Incorrigibles and truants.*
4. *Speech defectives.*
III. *Children who are exceptional for reasons primarily physical*
5. *The deaf.*
6. *The blind.*
7. *The crippled.* (pp. 16–17)

The topic of this book is, primarily, children who fall into Horn's
category II, no. 3, whom he called incorrigibles and truants. Horn devoted a section of his book to such children and concluded: (a) There
is much misunderstanding of the problem because the prevalence varies
so markedly from one school system to another; and (b) many of the

children and youth who are incorrigible also have low intelligence. Although some of his conclusions are at odds with today's thinking, he certainly appears to have been astute in making those two observations.

The terms *emotionally disturbed* and *behaviorally disordered* had not yet been invented (*wayward* and *incorrigible* were more often the terms of choice). Particular labels aside, Horn's idea that variability is the basic problem of special education is, indeed, consistent with contemporary thinking (Kauffman & Hallahan, 2005b; Singer, 1988).

The first teacher training program in special education was begun in Michigan in 1914. By 1918, all states had compulsory education laws, and in 1919, Ohio passed a law allowing statewide care of children with handicaps. By 1930, 16 states had enacted laws allowing local school districts to recover the excess costs of educating exceptional children and youths (Henry, 1950). Educational and psychological testing was becoming widely used, and school psychology, guidance, and counseling were emerging as part of the general system of education. Mental hygiene and child guidance clinics became relatively common by 1930, and by that time *child* psychiatry was a new discipline (Kanner, 1973c). According to Dr. Leo Kanner, known as the father of child psychiatry, child guidance clinics of this era made three major innovations: (a) interdisciplinary collaboration; (b) treatment of any child whose behavior was annoying to parents and teachers, not just the severe cases; and (c) attention to the effects of interpersonal relationships and adult attitudes on child behavior (Kanner, 1973c, pp. 194–195).

In the 1920s, demand arose for mental hygiene programs in the schools, and some school systems established such programs. Thomas Haines, director of the Division of Mental Deficiency of the National Committee for Mental Hygiene, called for statutes governing the study and training of *all* exceptional children in the public schools, including the "psychopathic, the psychoneurotic, and those who exhibit behavior problems" (Haines, 1925). In an article in *The New Republic*, Dr. Smiley Blanton (1925), director of the Minneapolis Child Guidance Clinic and a practicing child psychiatrist, described the operation of mental hygiene clinics in the public schools of Minneapolis (see also Bremner, 1971, pp. 947–957, 1040–1057).

Blanton's clinical staff consisted of 1 psychologist, 3 psychiatric social workers (who had been teachers before they became social workers), 20 visiting teachers, and 10 corrective speech teachers. One of the functions of the clinic was to organize a course in mental hygiene for high school juniors and seniors. Another objective was to establish behavior clinics in kindergartens. The clinic took referrals from teachers and parents and also served preschool and juvenile court cases. After referral to the clinic, a child was studied carefully, and a staff meeting was held to determine a course of action. Typically, the staff talked things over with the parents and teacher and tried to change their attitudes toward the child. Specific instructions were given on behavior management, and a social worker would then go to the home or classroom to help carry out the program.

Two professional organizations that are particularly important to the education of children with emotional and behavioral disorders were founded in the 1920s. The Council for Exceptional Children (CEC) was organized in 1922. From its beginning, CEC members were primarily educators, but the membership included other professionals and parents. The group became a powerful force for the appropriation of monies and enactment of legislation concerning the education of all handicapped children. The American Orthopsychiatric Association (AOA), dominated by the professions of child psychiatry, clinical psychology, and social work but including education and other disciplines as well, was founded in 1924. The AOA did much to encourage research and dissemination of information regarding therapy and education for children and youth with emotional or behavioral disorders.

The CEC has been the dominant special education organization since its inception. From its origin, it has been an international organization, involving particularly members and officers from Canada as well as the United States. Many special interest divisions of the CEC have been organized over the years, including the Council for Children with Behavioral Disorders, which was founded in the 1960s.

The first annual meeting of the CEC was held in February 1923, in Cleveland, Ohio. Elizabeth E. Farrell, the inspector of "ungraded" classes (i.e., special education) in New York City was the CEC president (see Kirk & Lord, 1974, for her presidential address; see also MacMillan & Hendrick, 1993 for discussion of her role in early special education). In the published (but undated) *Proceedings of the First Annual Meeting of the International Council for the Education of Exceptional Children,* the aims of the CEC were listed:

- to unite those interested in the educational problems of the "special child"
- to emphasize the education of the "special child"—rather than his identification or classification
- to establish professional standards for teachers in the field of special education

The themes of the discussion and action at the first meeting of the CEC have continued over many decades: special education for all exceptional children, teacher characteristics and training, concern for legislation, vocational education and transition, gratitude for the service of teachers and officers, and excitement over the organization's activities and expansion. Like today, the proceedings reflect an earnest desire to do good things, a willingness to attack obvious practical problems, and a disregard of underlying questions of social policy and educational philosophy. The neglect of the more difficult underlying issues has never been a good omen for the fate of the CEC or for achieving substantive progress in special education (Kauffman, 1981).

During the 1920s, Freudian ideas found their way into work with children, and the assumption invariably was that children with emotional and behavioral disorders suffered some sort of unnecessary restriction at the hands of their parents. Among the first to articulate this notion was A. S. Neill, the educator turned psychologist (see Neill, 1927) who later wrote the book *Summerhill,* extolling the virtues of permissiveness (Neill, 1960). In the 1920s, Neill assumed that unhappiness was the root of all behavior problems of both children and adults: "All crimes, all hatreds, all wars can be reduced to unhappiness" (Neill, 1927, p. 11). His idea was simply that freedom from demands and restrictions produced happiness, the best antidote to childhood behavior problems. His idea of granting children with emotional and behavioral disorders the freedom to do as they wish became the basis for popular programs of the 1960s and 1970s granting children "freedom to learn."

1930 to the Postwar Era

The Depression and World War II necessarily diverted attention and funds from the education of students with disabilities. However, as we have already mentioned, President Hoover called the third White House Conference on Child Health and Protection in 1929 (the conference was held in 1930). More students with disabilities were receiving special education in 1940 than in 1930; and by 1948, 41 of the 48 states had enacted laws authorizing or requiring local school districts to make special educational provisions for at least one category of exceptional children (Henry, 1950).

The vast majority of special classes were for children with mild mental retardation, but college-level texts covering various exceptionalities and special education were available (e.g., Baker, 1944, 1953; Heck, 1940). Programs for students with emotional or behavioral disorders were relatively few and were designed primarily for acting-out and delinquent children and youth in large cities. Most of the texts of this era referred to the "socially handicapped" child (e.g., Heck, 1940) or "behavior adjustments" (e.g., Baker, 1944, 1953) or used some other moniker for the children we now say have emotional or behavioral disorders. Some of the books in psychology or psychiatry that were published in the 1930s focused on the behavior problems of children, including problems at school (e.g., Morgan, 1937; Richards, 1932), and a series of pamphlets published by the Woods School dealt with disordered behavior (e.g., Fay, 1935; Liss, 1935; Odiorne, 1934; Potter, 1935).

Hitler's rise to power in Europe provided several unanticipated benefits for the education of disabled children in the United States. Several people who were later to influence special education fled to America, including Bruno Bettelheim, Marianne Frostig, Alfred Strauss, and Heinz Werner. (We will touch on some of their contributions later; see also Hallahan & Cruickshank, 1973; Hallahan, Kauffman, & Lloyd, 1999.)

Several significant developments in child psychiatry occurred during this period. The first psychiatric hospital for children in the United States, the Bradley Home, was established in Rhode Island in 1931 (Davids, 1975). Leo Kanner of Johns Hopkins University contributed immeasurably to the field with the first edition of his text-book *Child Psychiatry* in 1935 and with his initial descriptions of early infantile autism (Kanner, 1943, 1973a, 1973b, 1973c). Here is his de-scription of his first experience with children who would later be said to have "Kanner's syndrome":

> *In October 1938, a 5-year-old boy was brought to my clinic from Forest, Mississippi. I was struck by the uniqueness of the peculiarities which Donald exhibited. He could, since the age of 2 ½ years, tell the names of all the presi-dents and vice presidents, recite the letters of the alphabet forwards and back-wards, and flawlessly, with good enunciation, rattle off the Twenty-Third Psalm. Yet he was unable to carry on an ordinary conversation. He was out of contact with people, while he could handle objects skillfully. His memory was phenomenal. The few times when he addressed someone—largely to satisfy his wants—he referred to himself as "You" and to the person ad-dressed as "I." He did not respond to any intelligence tests but manipulated intricate formboards adroitly.* (1973a, p. 93)

During the 1930s, Despert (as recorded in a 1968 collection of her papers) and Potter (1933), with Kanner and others, tried to clarify the characteristics of various categories of youngsters with severe emo-tional and behavioral disorders. Dr. Lauretta Bender pioneered the edu-cation of children with schizophrenia. After organizing the children's ward at Bellevue Psychiatric Hospital in New York City in 1934, she appealed in 1935 to the New York City Board of Education for teach-ers to staff special classrooms at Bellevue for children with severe emotional or behavioral disorders. The board responded by assigning two substitute teachers to teach ungraded classes (the category used for children with mental retardation or other exceptionalities) under the administration of the school for students with physical disabilities at Bellevue. Despite inadequate facilities and a complete lack of in-structional materials in the beginning, the program succeeded (Wright, 1967). The Bellevue school was to become a fertile training ground for future leaders, most notably Pearl Berkowitz and Esther Rothman (Berkowitz, 1974; Rothman, 1974).

Wanda Wright's (1967) description of the Bellevue Psychiatric Hospital School is rich in detail and surprisingly contemporary in many of its observations. Wright describes not only the school's program and curriculum but the kind of behavior exhibited by students enrolled (e.g., "bizarre, aggressive, incorrigible, withdrawn, passive, fearful, intolerable, violent, uncontrolled, impulsive," p. 87). She notes the characteristics that are needed in teachers of such children and that children little by little learn at the school that some adults can be trusted, learning can be enjoyable, personal strengths and weaknesses are to be acknowledged and accepted, they can function within the structure of the school, and getting along with others can be more satisfying than fighting or withdrawing. She also highlights the academic needs of the students:

One of the most consistent factors in a child's failure in school is related to reading ability. A large percentage of disturbed children cannot read or are seriously retarded in reading. Reading instruction and remedial reading are of utmost importance in educational planning for these children. (p. 109)

Children admitted to Bellevue on an average are retarded from two to six years. Some are total nonreaders, and teaching these children is a long slow process. (p. 111)

By the end of the 1930s, the literature on children's emotional and behavioral disorders had grown to sizable proportions (E. M. Baker & Stullken, 1938). Attempts had been made to define emotional disturbance and to delineate several subclassifications. Surveys of children's behavior problems and teachers' attitudes toward misbehavior had been completed (e.g., Wickman, 1929), and there had been efforts to estimate the prevalence of emotional and behavioral disorders (e.g., Martens & Russ, 1932). Various plans of special education such as special rooms, schools, classes, and consultative help had been tried (see Berkowitz & Rothman, 1967a).

The years leading up to and including World War II saw an emphasis on the perpetuation of American society and the importance of every citizen contributing whatever he or she could to the effort. The war, in particular, highlighted the importance of special education helping each exceptional individual to contribute in any way possible. The prevailing view was expressed by Martens (1941). It seems to reflect much of the spirit of the No Child Left Behind Act of the early 21st century, a federal law aimed at obtaining the maximum performance of every child in order to secure America's future:

> *There can be no strength and security for America unless there is security for her weakest citizens—the weak of body, the weak of mind, the weak in emotional stability. Nor, on the other hand, can America be strong unless there is strength and devotion on the part of her ablest ones—the gifted in intellect, in human relations, in the arts, who must give unselfishly of their best if the country they serve is to prosper.* (Martens, 1941, p. 37)

Before midcentury, it seems that all of the contemporary (and perhaps perpetual) issues in special education had been outlined. *Exceptional Children*, the journal of the CEC, began publication in 1934. Early volumes of the journal contain discussion of and comment on making education of children with disabilities (then called "handicapped children") "as nearly normal as possible" (Hefferman, 1935, p. 49). The importance of early intervention was noted (e.g., Brown, 1943). The question of "segregation" versus "integration" of children with disabilities was raised (e.g., Berry, 1936; Postel, 1937; Rautman, 1944; Tenny, 1944). Commonalities of special and general education were observed (e.g., H. J. Baker, 1934). The need for federal aid was mentioned (e.g., Berry, 1938). Education for social competence was discussed (e.g., Farson, 1940). Research and its effects on practice were highlighted (e.g., all of Volume 4 of *Exceptional Children*, 1938). Sex discrimination was raised as an issue (e.g., Spaulding & Kvaraceus, 1944).

In short, by midcentury, special education had become an identifiable and nearly ubiquitous part of American public education, at least in large cities, although relatively few of the special education programs were devoted to students with emotional or behavioral disorders. Much of the education of children with emotional and behavioral disorders was still undifferentiated from that of more general and typical categories, such as mental retardation. Some categories of special education (e.g., learning disabilities, traumatic brain injury) had not yet been identified. However, the foundation had been laid for the prodigious growth of special education in the 1960s and 1970s.

The Postwar Years and the 1950s

Following World War II, additional varieties of emotional and behavioral disorders were described by the psychiatric profession (for succinct summaries of the contributions of numerous individuals working in this era, see Haring & Phillips, 1962). Mahler (1952) delineated a form she called *symbiotic infantile psychosis* (overattachment to the mother); Rank (1949) introduced the term *atypical child* (a child with any severe disturbance of early development resulting from problems of relationship between mother and child); Bergman and Escalona (1949) described children with unusual sensitivity to sensory stimulation; and Robinson and Vitale (1954) wrote about children with circumscribed interest patterns. All of these children with severe disorders fit under the general category of *childhood psychosis*.

The 1940s and 1950s saw a rising wave of interest in the education of children with emotional or behavioral disorders. J. McV. Hunt edited a two-volume handbook on personality and behavior disorders, with chapters derived from experimental and clinical research (Hunt, 1944a, 1944b). These volumes contained chapters on how experiences in infancy, childhood, and adolescence affected personality development, but also chapters on cultural determinants of personality (Bateson, 1944) and ecological factors in human behavior (Faris, 1944). The behavior disorders of children were described by Kanner (1944), and Stevenson (1944) contributed a chapter on the prevention of personality disorders.

In 1944, Bruno Bettelheim began his work at the Sonja Shankman Orthogenic School at the University of Chicago. His concept of a *therapeutic milieu* (Bettelheim, 1950; Bettelheim & Sylvester, 1948) was used for decades in educational methods based on psychoanalytic thought (Bettelheim, 1961, 1967, 1970; Redl, 1959b, 1966; Trieschman, Whittaker, & Brendtro, 1969). During the 1940s, Fritz Redl and David Wineman began their work with hyperaggressive youngsters in Detroit. Basing their strategies on the ideas of Bettelheim and others who were psychoanalytic in their thinking regarding delinquency (Aichorn, 1935; Eissler, 1949; Freud, 1946), Redl and Wineman described their use of a therapeutic milieu and a technique called the *life space interview* at Pioneer House, a residential setting for young aggressive and delinquent boys (Redl & Wineman, 1951, 1952). The efforts and thoughts of Redl and Wineman influenced an entire generation of educators (e.g., Long, 1974; Morse, 1974).

The New York City Board of Education organized its "600" schools in 1946. These schools, arbitrarily numbered from 600 to 699 in an attempt to avoid labeling special schools and their students, were established specifically for the purpose of educating "disturbed" and "maladjusted" youngsters. Some were day schools located in regular school buildings; others were located in residential diagnostic and treatment settings (Berkowitz & Rothman, 1967a).

One of the most important publications of the 1940s was a book by Alfred A. Strauss and Laura E. Lehtinen titled *Psychopathology and Education of the Brain-Injured Child* (1947). This book summarizes the work of Strauss and his colleagues (especially Heinz Werner) and students at the Wayne County Training School in Northville, Michigan, and the Cove Schools in Racine, Wisconsin.

Although much of the work of Werner and Strauss was with children whose mental retardation was assumed to be exogenous (resulting from postnatal brain damage), Strauss and Lehtinen recognized that learning problems exist in some children of normal intelligence. They attributed these learning difficulties to brain injury; however, they recognized that emotional maladjustment is characteristic of such children:

> *The response of the brain-injured child to the school situation is frequently inadequate, conspicuously disturbing, and persistently troublesome. The following excerpts from a teacher's reports are illustrative.*
>
> *J. M., 7 years old: "... doesn't pay attention to any directions. He is unaware of anything said, yet at times he surprises me by noticing things that others don't."*
>
> *D. J., 7 years old: "... attention hard to hold. Asks constantly: 'When can I go? Can I go now?' etc. No initiative. Little self-control. Seems high strung and nervous...."*
>
> *D. H., 8 years old: "... has proven quite a serious problem in behavior. Has acquired the habit of throwing himself into tantrums at the slightest provocation...."*
>
> *J. K., 8 years old: "... has made scarcely any social adjustments in relationships with other children, he loses all self-control, becoming wild and*

uncontrollable; he is extremely nervous and excitable; his attention span is very short and he is unable to concentrate for more than a few minutes. During work periods he jumps from one activity to another." (Strauss & Lehtinen, 1947, p. 127)

For such children, Strauss and Lehtinen recommended a highly structured educational approach and a highly consistent, distraction-free environment (see also Strauss & Kephart, 1955). Besides general educational principles, they described special methods for teaching arithmetic, reading, and writing. Their work is particularly important because it provided the foundation for the later efforts of Cruickshank (Cruickshank, Bentzen, Ratzeburg, & Tannhauser, 1961) and Haring and Phillips (1962).

By the early 1950s, interest in special education for students with emotional or behavioral disorders gained considerable momentum. In fact, one could say that this area of special education came of age by the end of the 1950s, for one no longer had to be content with examining developments in psychiatry or with citing references in the field of mental retardation. Education of students with emotional or behavioral disorders had become a field of specialization in its own right. One early indication of mental health professionals' recognition of the importance of education was publication of a symposium on the education of emotionally disturbed children (Krugman, 1953). This issue was one of the first attempts by the *American Journal of Ortho-psychiatry* to devote an appreciable number of pages specifically to a collection of papers on the importance of schools and education. Among the papers of the symposium are those of Louis Hay (1953), detailing the Junior Guidance Class Program in New York City, and Dr. J. Cotter Hirschberg (1953), explaining the important roles of education in residential treatment. It is noteworthy that the second part of the *Forty-Ninth Yearbook of the National Society for the Study of Education* (NSSE), *The Education of Exceptional Children* (the first volume in its history devoted to special education, published in 1950), includes a chapter on the education of socially maladjusted children and youth (Stullken, 1950; the first NSSE yearbook on education of the gifted was published in 1920; the first on adapting schools to individual differences in 1925; the first on educational diagnosis in 1935; the first on delinquency and the schools in 1948). NSSE yearbooks are published only after a considerable amount of interest and research on a given topic has been observed.

Another landmark event of the early 1950s was Carl Fenichel's founding of the League School in 1953 (Fenichel, 1974; Fenichel, Freedman, & Klapper, 1960). The League School was the first private day school for seriously emotionally disturbed children in the United States. Fenichel, who had training in psychoanalysis, began the school using a permissive psychoanalytic orientation but soon gave that up in favor of a more directive, psychoeducational approach (Fenichel, 1966, 1974).

In 1955, the first book describing classroom teaching of children with emotional or behavioral disorders appeared. In *A Class for Disturbed Children: A Case Study and Its Meaning for Education,* Leonard Kornberg recounted his experiences in teaching 15 boys at Hawthorn-Cedar Knolls, a residential school near New York City. His teaching approach was based primarily on psychoanalytic thought and drew heavily on the interpersonal therapeutic process—"dialogue" and responding to "I" and "otherness." As he put it, "the essential classroom event is the transaction of meaning among more than two persons, as contrasted with the two-person contact of a therapy situation" (Kornberg, 1955, p. 132). This emphasis on interpersonal relationships and psychiatric-dynamic ideas is predominant in the literature of the 1950s, and it is a prominent feature of the later and better-known book by Berkowitz and Rothman, *The Disturbed Child: Recognition and Psychoeducational Therapy in the Classroom* (1960).

During the 1940s and 1950s, most thinking about children with emotional and behavioral disorders was dominated by psychoanalytic principles. Psychoanalytic, or psychodynamic, principles were articulated primarily by Sigmund Freud, his daughter Anna Freud, and their protégés. Psychodynamic theory includes the propositions that (a) behavior is predominantly a reflection of unconscious motivations; (b) behavior is controlled by the dynamic interplay of parts of the unconscious and conscious mind called the id, ego, and superego; and (c) behavior can be changed through therapy in which the unconscious becomes conscious. Some of the work in the 1950s emphasized primarily *ego psychology*, focusing on the conscious control of behavior. Some emphasized working with observable behavior directly. Behavior principles had been articulated much earlier, but the 1950s saw the beginning of their application to problems of individuals with serious emotional and behavioral problems (see Kazdin, 1978; Krasner & Ullmann, 1965; Ullmann & Krasner, 1965; Ulrich, Stachnik, & Mabry, 1966, 1970). The foundations of the conceptual models that guided practices were laid in this era (and articulated more clearly in the 1960s).

By the mid-1950s, researchers recognized that systematic procedures were needed to identify students with emotional or behavioral disorders in the public schools. Eli Bower and others began research in California that culminated in publication of the screening instrument devised by Bower and Lambert (1962), as well as other writings of Bower (e.g., Bower, 1960, 1980, 1981, 1982; Bower, Shellhammer, & Daily, 1960). Concern for teaching children and youths with emotional or behavioral disorders had grown by the late 1950s to the extent that an initial study of teacher preparation was reported by Mackie, Kvaraceus, and Williams (1957). Already in the 1950s (and earlier, as we have noted), some of the major controversies and issues in the field had been articulated—for example, general educators' management of children with emotional or behavioral disorders (Elkins, 1956; Hirschberg, 1956)

The last years of the decade were auspicious for the field because numerous individuals were attaining new vantage points in education: Pearl H. Berkowitz and Esther P. Rothman were collaborating in New York City; William C. Morse and Nicholas J. Long were working at the University of Michigan's Fresh-Air Camp; Frank M. Hewett was beginning his studies at the University of California at Los Angeles; Nicholas Hobbs and William C. Rhodes began conceptualizing new strategies at George Peabody College in Nashville, Tennessee; William M. Cruickshank and Norris G. Haring were conducting research projects in the public schools of Maryland and Virginia; and Richard J. Whelan was developing a directive, structured behavioral approach at the Menninger Clinic in Topeka, Kansas. These activities resulted in a wave of publications and research that burst upon the field in the 1960s and 1970s. In the remainder of this chapter we describe several institutions and the foundational work prior to the 1960s of several individuals who figured prominently in the later decades of the 20th century. We do not mention every individual whose work was important but highlight some of the individuals and institutions that played valuable roles in special education for children with emotional or behavioral disorders.

Wayne County Training School, Northville, Michigan

The Wayne County Training School became a training and research site for an entire generation of leaders in special education and psychology (including, among others, Sydney Bijou, William M. Cruickshank, Newell Kephart, Samuel A. Kirk, Alfred A. Strauss, and Heinz Werner). The experiences and research of these and other individuals at the school highlight the overlaps among the fields of mental retardation, brain injury, juvenile delinquency, behavioral disorders, emotional disturbance, and what Kirk and others were eventually to call learning disabilities (see Hallahan & Cruickshank, 1973; Hallahan & Kauffman, 1976; Kirk, 1976, 1984).

The Wayne County Training School brought together scientists from a wide array of disciplines related to child development and exceptionality. The influences of psychologists well known for their work in mental measurement and reading instruction are clearly evident in the reminiscences of Kirk (1976, 1984). Consider, for example, the influences of Harold Skeels, an important researcher in mental retardation, and Alfred Binet on Kirk's thinking:

> When I questioned Skeels about these results [dramatic IQ gains in an intervention study involving retarded children in an institution] he showed me a manuscript by Alfred Binet published in 1911, Modern Ideas About Children. In the chapter "The Educability of Intelligence" Binet presented a curriculum to develop memory, attention, reasoning, language, and other vectors of intelligence. In other words, Binet was not obsessed with the constancy of the IQ, but believed that it can be changed through educational intervention. (See a reprint in Kirk and Lord, 1974)
>
> That article and the work of Skeels had a profound effect on my future interests and activities. My experience at the Wayne County Training School also biased me toward a belief in the power of intervention. (Kirk, 1984, p. 35)

But it was not only the work of other scientists that gave Kirk and others at the Wayne County Training School a positive attitude toward the power of intervention: Their own experiences also created optimism:

> *Experience at the Wayne County Training School left me with the feeling that much more could be done with handicapped children than most people believed. The excellent case histories and diagnoses by clinics and schools in Detroit and by the staff of the residential school were for me an education in case analysis and procedures. The case conferences added much to my recognition that many children who were diagnosed as hopeless could be rehabilitated. One boy with whom I worked had an I.Q. of 56 on the Binet, was declared delinquent, and could not read; the only thing he could write was his name—and that he wrote backwards. As an experiment, I tried to teach him to read and found that in two years he could score seventh grade level (at the age of fourteen). Although he could score seventh grade on the* Gray Oral Reading Test, *his comprehension scores were at the fourth grade level. I worked with him a third year, but could not increase his comprehension scores substantially. At sixteen he tested in the borderline range of intelligence and was consequently paroled to his grandmother. Later I learned from a follow-up study that he had not only become a self-supporting citizen, but was also supporting his grandmother and his sister.* (Kirk, 1976, p. 247)

Suffice it to say that the Wayne County Training School served as a laboratory for many psychologists and educators who later turned their considerable talents to special education. Out of that setting came numerous individuals who brought a spirit of optimism and activism to special education in the 1960s and 1970s. It appears that many of the ideas later associated with the behavioral approach or conceptual model (e.g., work by Bijou, Cruickshank, Haring, and their students) grew out of the Wayne County Training School environment.

Bettelheim and the Orthogenic School of Chicago

Bruno Bettelheim worked for years in his family's lumber business in Austria, received his PhD degree in philosophical aesthetics from the University of Vienna, and in 1939 came to the United States, where he became a professor of psychology and psychiatry at the University of Chicago. He claimed to have studied psychoanalysis in Vienna with Sigmund Freud, although later that was called into question. Apparently, he had survived both Dachau and Buchenwald concentration camps. For many years he headed the Sonja Shankman Orthogenic School at the University of Chicago, which had been established in 1915. Perhaps his most controversial theory (now thoroughly debunked) was that mothers' indifference to or hostility toward their children caused them to be autistic. In 1990, Bettelheim committed suicide, and since his death he has been a figure of continuing controversy (e.g., Pollak, 1997; Sutton, 1997).

Bettelheim's writings became extremely influential both with professionals and with the general public (see Bettelheim, 1950, 1961, 1967, 1970, and Bettelheim & Sylvester, 1948, for examples of his writing for professionals). His pronouncements, always steeped in psychoanalytic theory, were taken seriously, no matter how bizarre. After his suicide, he was portrayed by former students, staff, parents, and biographers as a charlatan and a tyrant. His portrayal of himself had often been as a seeker of truth who was not like those who claimed superior wisdom. For example, he opened a 1970 address as follows:

> *Let's face it! All effort in education and child rearing is directed towards the modification of behavior, of course. The difference lies in the motives, the philosophical approach and how this is done. Do we modify behavior in terms of what we think, in our superior wisdom, is best for the other person or do we admit that we don't know? It seems that mankind divides itself into two unequal groups: those who always know what's best for other people (who are usually short on knowing what's best for themselves) and those who are struggling so very hard to know what's best for them and have such a tough time figuring that one out that they do not have the conviction that they know what is best for other people. I belong to the latter group, still trying to figure out what's good for me, and therefore have no superior knowledge of what's good for others.* (1970, p. 36)

In spite of comments like that, it is clear from Bettelheim's biographies that he did see himself as having superior knowledge and knowing what is best for others (Pollak, 1997; Sutton, 1997). He apparently was able to hide his own delusions behind a facade of psychoanalytic theory, fooling many into believing that he was, in fact, a scholar, a researcher, and an insightful, helpful therapist.

Redl, Wineman, and Detroit's Pioneer House

In 1946, the Junior League of Detroit adopted a project called Pioneer House, a residential home for aggressive preadolescent boys, located near Wayne University. The program served disturbed children from the Detroit public schools. The director of the program was Fritz Redl, and the executive director was David Wineman.

In this setting, Redl and Wineman based their work heavily on the writings of Anna Freud (1946), August Aichorn (1935), and Bruno Bettelheim (1950; see Redl & Wineman, 1951, preface). The writing of Redl and his associates (e.g., Redl, 1959a, 1959b; Redl & Wattenberg, 1951; Redl & Wineman, 1951, 1952) that grew out of their work at Pioneer House had a profound effect on the field, although Pioneer House served only ten 8- to 10-year-old boys and was in operation for less than two years (see Redl & Wineman, 1952, appendix).

Although they suggested a variety of techniques that should guide work with children (an advance over a purely permissive environment suggested by strict adherence to psychoanalytic principles), their work was decidedly in opposition to that of behavioral psychologists. They rejected the notion of using rewarding and punishing consequences in what they considered the manipulation of surface behavior:

> *In summary, we can say that, strange as it may seem, with children of our type of disturbances "promise and reward" is not a feasible technique. In a wider meaning of the term, of course, the pleasurableness of an experience would be occasionally used as a "propaganda item," to soften the necessity of an unavoidable step. We might fight their disgust with the job of packing bedrolls by reminding them of the fun they would have as soon as we got going. Or we might try to get them over some of the wildness during a "planning session" around a trip or party by dangling before their eyes the fun of the final event and the need to get there. But this would always be done casually, not as a condition on which the future event would depend. As specific techniques to start or stop behavior, the two techniques could not be used.* (Redl & Wineman, 1952, p. 230)

Like later writers who rejected the application of behavior principles in education (e.g., Kohn, 1993), they portrayed rewarding consequences as likely to corrupt motivation, punishment as too complex for the children to understand and likely to be ineffective in the long term, and substantial behavior change to be dependant on a change in thinking—hence their emphasis on verbal interaction (i.e., interviews) with children designed to help them understand their motivations. What came to be known as the life space interview (LSI) was first implemented in Redl and Wineman's work at Pioneer House. Redl and Wineman (1951, 1952) tried to establish a "therapeutic milieu" and to provide teachers and child care workers with tools for managing the *surface behavior* (i.e., observable conduct) of children with emotional and behavioral disorders. The techniques were described in considerable detail for the first time in *Controls from Within* (Redl & Wineman, 1952). Among those techniques, described in Redl's colorful language, were: Planned Ignoring, Signal Interference, Hypodermic Affection, Tension Decontamination Through Humor, Hurdle Help, and Antiseptic Bouncing.

The ideas of the therapeutic milieu, LSI, and manipulation of surface behavior survived the closing of Pioneer House and were implemented in other settings by those trained or influenced by Redl and Wineman. In fact, as we shall discuss, these ideas became important aspects of what was later to be called the psychoeducational approach, or conceptual model.

Morse, Long, and Michigan's Fresh-Air Camp
The University of Michigan's Fresh-Air Camp provided training for many of the important leaders of special education in the late 20th century, including Nicholas Long and William Morse (see Long, 1974; Morse, 1974). Morse, who received his BA, MA, and PhD degrees from the University of Michigan, directed the university's Fresh-Air Camp from 1945 to 1961. He describes his initiation into the camp as follows:

> As a young education psychologist my primary interest was in the reading process, specifically in research on eye movement. My direction altered after going through "hell" with the Dean. The "hell" was Hell, Michigan, last stop on the way to the University of Michigan Fresh-Air Camp, which the Dean had decided should be my new assignment. The camp was a group therapeutic setting for disturbed boys and was coordinated with a university training program for graduate students. (Morse, 1974, p. 201)

In his recollections, Long, who had earned his undergraduate degree in preschool and elementary education from Wayne State University in 1952 and done work in special education for children with physical disabilities before attending the University of Michigan, explains further the nature of the Fresh-Air Camp and its conceptual debt to Pioneer House:

> *My first experience with emotionally disturbed children was at the … Fresh-Air Camp in the summer of 1953…. Two counselors were assigned to each cabin of eight emotionally disturbed boys…. We learned about psychopathology from the ground up. This intensive approach to learning was just what I needed…. The camp setting and the philosophy allowed us close contact with the directors, Bill Morse and Dave Wineman. We could see them in action, observe them in stressful situations, and marvel at the variety of techniques and skills they possessed. It was a common feeling among the graduate students that they were men of great compassion, joy, and resource. We admired them because of their ability and used them as our professional models for many years. In addition, Fritz Redl and Ralph Rabinovitch were visiting consultants who added another dimension of excitement and greatness to this program …*
>
> *In this camp atmosphere, we also had the comfort of being able to fail and the support of learning from our failures…. For example, I remember encouraging an anxious, withdrawn boy to express his anger until he became so furious that he punched me in the nose. Then there was the time I over-controlled my cabin group and intervened at the slightest ripple of trouble. While the other groups appeared chaotic, my group was a perfect example of goodness. During the last week of camp, one of the boys baited me into a shouting match by refusing to do a simple task. At the outburst of my anger, the entire group exploded in grand style. They started fights, broke windows, and climbed on the roof of the cabin where they shouted obscenities and suggested that all adults perform impossible anatomical tricks.* (Long, 1974, pp. 172–173)

Both Morse and Long went on to make many significant contributions to special education for disturbed children in later years. Their training and experience at the Fresh-Air Camp was undoubtedly extremely influential in their later work.

Nicholas Hobbs and the Re-ED Program

In the 1950s, Nicholas Hobbs, a community psychologist, laid the groundwork for a significant educational program for children with emotional and behavioral disorders, which became known as Re-ED (for reeducation). Hobbs visited European nations in which *educateurs* worked with children in special schools, combining the roles of teacher, psychologist, and social worker. When he brought the basic idea to the United States, he described the educateur as a teacher-counselor (see Hobbs, 1965, 1974). Teacher–counselor training in the United States was initially provided by the Department of Special Education at Peabody College, now part of Vanderbilt University in Nashville, Tennessee.

The Re-ED program grew out of studies of children's mental health needs in the south, and two residential Re-ED schools were initially established: the Cumberland House Elementary School in Tennessee and the Wright School in North Carolina. In those schools, two teacher-counselors were responsible for each group of eight children. Emphasis was placed on formal schoolwork, adapted to the needs of individual students, and family contact. School and family were assumed to be the two most important concerns of children. Connections were maintained between children and their families and communities, and the children returned home most weekends.

Hobbs clearly saw Re-ED schools as only one of the types of services needed by children with emotional and behavioral disorders, not as a cure-all or single best approach for all children. He saw Re-ED as one of a complex array of services needed by children with emotional or behavioral disorders, which includes consulting for general education classroom teachers, special classes, day care centers, child guidance services, residential schools like Re-ED, treatment centers for those who need acute and intensive interventions, and long-term care facilities for those who are unresponsive to other forms of treatment (see Hobbs, 1965, p. 289). The complete details of the Re-ED plan are beyond the scope of this book, but the goals of the program are noteworthy in their grounding in the known and knowable realities of children's lives rather than assumed hidden motivations or problems. Hobbs saw the goals of Re-ED schools as purposely limited, not intending to yield a complete or radical reorganization of the child or the community. The objectives of the program were simply to help children become more successful in their schools, homes, and communities. Hobbs (1965) listed seven specific goals of Re-ED schools:

1. *Restoring to the child some trust in adults, some competencies to meet demands of family, school, and friends, some confidence in self, and some joy in the morrow.*
2. *Helping a child maintain normal progress in school when possible and providing him with remedial work in reading, arithmetic, and other subjects as needed to arrest the downward trend in school achievement so often observed in disturbed children.*
3. *Mobilizing resources in the child's home community in the interest of the child, especially by giving assistance to his family.*
4. *Assisting the staff of the child's regular school to understand his problem and to make such reasonable adjustments in the school program as may be required to make possible an early and successful return of the child to his own school.*
5. *Helping the child to unlearn some specific habits that cause rejection by family, school, and friends, and to acquire some specific habits that make him more acceptable to the people who are important in his life.*
6. *Helping the child gain some cognitive control over his behavior by helping him identify specific goals and reviewing each day as it is lived to identify sources of satisfaction and dissatisfaction and ways of behaving likely to bring more success to the next day.*
7. *Helping a child to achieve a sense of belonging in his home community, to perceive favorably and respond to the institutions provided by society to assist him in growing up: the schools, churches, libraries, health services, parks, museums, recreational areas, theaters, youth programs, and other similar agencies.* (pp. 291–292)

The Re-ED project is one of the most significant programs of the 20th century for children with emotional and behavioral disorders. Like all programs, it has its limitations and failures, but it is remarkable for its sound integrative design and relatively high rate of success (see Lee, 1971; Weinstein, 1969).

Berkowitz, Rothman, Fenichel, and the New York City Schools

Pearl Berkowitz, Esther Rothman, and Carl Fenichel are among the most prominent leaders of the 20th century in special education for children with emotional and behavioral disorders. Their descriptions of programs in New York City rank among the most influential in affecting how others conceptualized and addressed the emotional and behavioral problems of children.

Individually, Berkowitz and Rothman contributed immeasurably to the field. Berkowitz, originally trained as a musician (with a BA and an MA in music), became a psychologist, teacher, and principal at Bellevue Psychiatric Hospital (see Berkowitz, 1974). Rothman taught in both public New York City schools and at Bellevue and was a psychologist at a variety of schools and institutions in New York and Washington, DC (Rothman, 1974; see also Rothman, 1970). Both were colorful characters who enriched the field immensely with their personal recollections and professional observations.

Berkowitz recalls her early teaching experiences at Bellevue. The Mrs. Wright to whom she refers is Wanda Wright, whom we mentioned earlier in this chapter as an early educator of children with emotional and behavioral disorders:

> *If you could look back and focus on my most vivid memory, you might see me, now the teacher in Mrs. Wright's former classroom, futilely hovering over two hyperactive twelve-year-old girls who are fighting about which one should use the free half of an easel, while on the other side of this easel, a big, burly, belligerent boy is calmly painting, secure in the knowledge that no one would dare question his right to do so. Standing near the window is a small, thin-faced, pale, remote-looking boy who is staring at the fish tank, apparently just watching the fish swim around. Next to him, another boy is sitting on the rocker tickling himself under the chin with the mink tails he has just cut off the collar of the school secretary's new spring coat. Two children, a boy and a girl, perched on the old dining table, are playing a loud game of checkers, while another boy is silently resting, stretched out atop an old upright piano which I had inveigled into my room. Sporadically, in the midst of this magnificent atmosphere for learning, some child says to another, "Your mother," and the entire class seems to leap together and land in a football pile-up on the floor, while I stand helplessly by ...*

Of course I made many mistakes, but I hope I also learned something from each. Let me share just one of these early mistakes with you. I was doing my weekly planning when a brilliant idea occurred to me. I decided that the greatest contribution I could make that week would be to bring some culture into the lives of those poor, deprived, disturbed children at Bellevue. To start on this enriching experience, I elected to read to them a favorite poem from my own elementary school days, "The Owl and the Pussycat." Imagine my consternation at the chaos I caused when I reached the lines, "What a beautiful pussy you are, you are. What a beautiful pussy you are." The children actually tumbled out of my room with noisy screaming and guffawing. Within minutes, I was left alone in the classroom, bewildered and unaware of what had caused the difficulty. I had a lot to learn. (Berkowitz, 1974, pp. 30–31)

Rothman recalls not only her teaching career but her own early experiences in school:

From the start, I hated school, deeply, irrevocably, and silently.

Kindergarten was an anathema. Rather than take me to the doctor every other day with sore throats and stomachaches that were strictly school-induced, my mother finally capitulated and let me stay at home. First grade was no better, however, and as my sore "threats" would no longer work, and as the compulsory school laws prevented my mother from withdrawing me, I had no alternative but to start off for school daily and then divert myself to the rocks and crevices that then underlay the Hellsgate Bridge in the new and growing suburb of Queens, twenty minutes away by subway from the lower East Side where I was born.

I wonder if teachers really appreciate how overwhelmingly frightening it is to be a truant. Fear possessed me completely—fear of ridicule by school-loving seat-mates, each of whom was smarter than ten of me put together; fear of God, who was certainly going to punish me by striking my parents dead; but, most of all, fear of tongue-lashings by arm-twisting teachers, who were going to debase me by "leaving me back." Which indeed they did. I was a "holdover." My teacher didn't bother to explain to my mother why I was left back, but she clearly told everyone else. I couldn't read. And I couldn't read because I played hooky—or so she said. The fact that I was already reading Hebrew and the exotic adventures of Dickie Dare in my friend Lilly's third-grade reader was totally unknown to my teacher, yet I am certain, even now, that if she had known it, she would not have altered her decision.

My teacher was what I knew she was—anti-Semitic—because my mother told me so. This was a word I learned very early in life, and I accepted it casually as I accepted being an alien, one of only four Jewish children in the entire school. I felt special—not a bad feeling, but not completely good either.

I was never permitted to hold the American flag in front of the class for our morning class salute—a sacrosanct ceremony in every classroom in the entire school. My shoes were never clean enough. Once I was told I had lice. Or sometimes I did not have a handkerchief safety-pinned to the lower shoulder of my dress; this handkerchief always had to be in that exact same spot—never elsewhere. I never figured out how it was that we were supposed to blow our noses, and I never asked. I settled it myself. I had a handkerchief for showing and a handkerchief for blowing. And usually I forgot one or the other or both deliberately because I firmly believed that good little girls should never need to blow their noses at all. It was too crass. Instead, I stuffed pencil tip erasers up my nostrils. As for boys, I never even wondered what they did. Handkerchiefs were not within their generic classification.

These memories come flooding over me as I write—the hurt of being labeled a liar by a seventh-grade teacher who did not believe I had written a composition using the word chaos *because I could not give him a definition of it. Did he never understand that I knew the word* chaos *down to my very toes because I felt it deeply every day of my life in school? Then there was the day my fifth-grade teacher threw into the garbage can the chocolate cake my mother had baked for a class party and which the children had voted to give to the teacher because it was the prettiest cake of all. And going farther back, I remember staring at the school map that hung—large, frightening, and overwhelming—from the border of the chalkboard and trying desperately to find New York State while not another child spoke—every eye, especially the teacher's, was glued to me. But worst of all was the indignity, fear, and humiliation of having to cheat on a test because I could not remember whether four-fifths equalled 80 percent. (Rothman, 1974, pp. 221–222)*

With such vivid descriptions of what it is like to be an "outsider" or to be rejected by one's childhood peers and teachers and what it is like to teach such children, it is little wonder that Berkowitz and Rothman influenced generations of special educators.

Also working in New York City before the 1960s was Carl Fenichel, founder (in 1953) and director of the League School. Before founding the League School, he had been a teacher of "normal" children in New York City schools and had noticed that some of his students had serious emotional or learning problems. He also had been a teacher of severely emotionally disturbed children at the psychiatric division of the Kings County Hospital. His early training was in Freudian approaches to mental illness, and his early years at the League School were attempts to apply psychoanalytic theory to the education of children with emotional and behavioral disorders. However, Fenichel also saw the need to maintain children with such disorders in their communities and keep them with their families. Hence, he founded a day school and later described his early experiences with the school as follows:

> Early in 1953, with the financial support of a few friends and a newly formed parent group called the League for Emotionally Disturbed Children, I was able to convert a little Brooklyn brownstone into a three-room schoolhouse. This was the modest beginning of the League School, the first day school in the country to work exclusively with severely disturbed children who had been turned down by every school and agency except state mental institutions.
>
> Keeping the school door open and the day school idea alive wasn't easy. Like any pioneering program operating without professional acceptance, community support, or government assistance, our school was plagued by debts and deficits. Our only resource was the unwavering determination of a handful of parents, trustees, and friends to break through some of the doom and despair that surrounded childhood mental disorders.
>
> We opened with one teacher and two children. Before a year had passed, the school had reached full capacity and was bursting at the seams with twelve children, including three whose families had uprooted themselves and moved to Brooklyn from other states so that their children could be in a day-school program. The staff at that time consisted of myself, six teachers, a psychiatric consultant, a part-time social worker, and a music therapist. (Fenichel, 1974, pp. 55–56)

The League School and other programs in New York City, as well as those in other parts of the nation, broke new ground. In the early 21st century, we have the benefit of tested educational strategies that were nonexistent when the League School was founded. As Fenichel explains,

> At the time the League School began, efforts at educating severely disturbed children were professionally ignored and unexplored. There were no existing programs or tested educational strategies or techniques to guide us. **Nearly everything significant that I have learned about our children has come, not from the books I have read, the courses I have taken, or the degrees I have earned, but from working closely and intensively with a few hundred of these children over the past twenty years.** (Fenichel, 1974, p. 57)

There is still no substitute for firsthand experience in working with troubled and troubling children, but a half century after the League School was founded, we do have more reliable information about what works and what does not (e.g., Cullinan, 2002; Jones, Dohrn, & Dunn, 2004; Kerr & Nelson, 2002). Books and courses now can and often do provide reliable guidance to prospective teachers. Such information and guidance were simply not available prior to 1960.

Prior to 1960, the New York City schools became aware of the issue of stigma and tried to avoid the problem by beginning, in 1946, to designate schools for emotionally disturbed children by a number (Berkowitz & Rothman, 1967a). As mentioned previously, such schools were known as "600" schools because their numbers were all in the range 600-699. Nineteen years later, the numbering was abandoned, for reasons Berkowitz and Rothman (1967a) explain in the following passage:

> These schools were created to provide a therapeutic school environment for children who could not be taught effectively in the regular schools, and whose behavior, whether aggressive, bizarre or withdrawn, could not be tolerated in the ordinary classroom. The "600" school program was an experiment in rehabilitation, directed towards altering undesirable behavior and designed to exploit the potentialities of each individual child.
>
> In the years that the "600" schools have been in existence, this basic philosophy has remained unchanged. That effective education is possible for

even the most severely disturbed youngster is a conviction which has been repeatedly reinforced.

From an initial group of seven schools, the "600" division has been expanded to well over forty separate units with a total population of over 6,000 youngsters ranging from five to twenty-one years of age. The teaching staff numbers over 600. Moreover, this staff is supplemented by professional workers in related areas, such as guidance counselors, psychologists, social workers and psychiatrists.

There are a number of different types of "600" schools. Some are in the community and function as day schools for children who can live at home but cannot adjust to their neighborhood schools. The rest are primarily residential settings for both boys and girls and include psychiatric hospitals, treatment centers, court remand centers, child care centers and correctional institutions.

In 1965, after deciding that the "600" appellation had stigmatized many of the students, the Board of Education decided to use names and random numbers instead of the "600" numbers for these special schools. (1967a, pp. 18–19)

Stigma has been an ever present concern in special education. The history of special education in New York City suggests that the stigma arises not from the label we use to designate problems but from the public perception of the meaning of those problems (see Kauffman, 2003a).

Bower and Early Identification in California

Eli Michael (Mike) Bower was among the first to conduct large-scale studies of the problem of emotional and behavioral disorders in schools in California. Most of his work was published after 1960 (e.g., Bower, 1960; Bower & Lambert, 1962; Bower, Shellhammer, & Daily, 1960). He was also among the first to offer a coherent, school-based definition of emotional and behavioral disorders (usually called "emotional handicaps" in his writings).

Bower's work prior to 1960 is especially noteworthy for two reasons. First, he was among the first in the nation to highlight the problem of early identification and prevention. Second, his definition of "emotionally handicapped" was used, with some nefarious alterations that we discuss in the next chapter, by federal education agencies (and some state and local education agencies, as well) in describing the category of "emotionally disturbed" (until the late 20th century, "seriously emotionally disturbed," or SED).

Hewett, Lovaas, and Behavioral Interventions in Los Angeles

The writings of Frank M. Hewett and O. Ivar Lovaas became well known in the 1960s, although the two men began their work with disturbed children before 1960. Both were guided in that work primarily by behavioral theory or behavior modification principles. Hewett and Lovaas were psychologists by training, but Hewett, in particular, directed his efforts toward school-based programs. His undergraduate degree was in theater arts. He began teaching in the 1950s, however, and his early experiences involving students with learning and behavior problems were something like those described by Pearl Berkowitz:

The lesson plan was simple enough. I was going to demonstrate a tape recorder and how it worked to a class of boys with behavior and learning problems during my turn as a "teacher" while I was enrolled as a student teacher in the Clinic School training program at UCLA. Since it was 1952 and the marvels of the electronic age had not arrived to a full enough extent to overshadow the rather tame excitement surrounding recording your own voice on tape and hearing a playback, I had the interest of the class. As I stood in front of the room and pointed out each feature of the tape recorder, some fifteen pairs of eyes were riveted on me and my machine. This wasn't so bad after all, I thought. Teaching was a snap. But as I announced that each boy was to have a chance to record and hear his own voice, the wiggling and buzzing began among my audience. I realized I didn't have a plan of how to conduct fifteen recording sessions in a systematic and orderly fashion. Everyone wanted to be first. When I finally selected a student, there were groans from the others. The first boy failed to follow my instructions to state his name and regular school and launched into an imitation of a popular crooner of the day, thereby succeeding in breaking up the class and inspiring several other boys to run to the front of the room. In moments, we had a quartet instead of a solo. Settling this group down and getting them back to their seats took most of the time I had left for my presentation, and the demonstration ended with an unhappy, frustrated group of boys and that uneasy classroom climatic state known as "out-of-controlness." (Hewett, 1974, pp. 117–118)

Lovaas had begun his work with children with autism at the University of Washington before moving to UCLA in 1961. He concentrated his efforts on teaching language and social skills to children with autism, whereas Hewett made his most significant contributions educating children with other disorders. Autism became a separate category under the Individuals with Disabilities Education Act (IDEA) in 1990 and thereafter was not considered in federal regulations to be an "emotional disturbance." The "autistic" children Lovaas and Hewett worked with are now said to have some form of "autistic spectrum disorder" (see National Research Council, 2001). In the history of education for children with emotional or behavioral disorders, work with children with autism plays a significant role, simply because these children typically exhibit extremely problematic behavior and social skill deficits.

Hewett also conducted important research and demonstration projects with students who were not diagnosed with autism, and the results of his projects were widely disseminated in special education. Both Hewett and Lovaas became mentors to generations of special educators, and we discuss their work further in the next chapter.

Cruickshank, Haring, and Research Projects in Maryland and Virginia

You may recall that William M. Cruickshank was one of the individuals who spent time at the Wayne County Training School. He had become a faculty member at Syracuse University in 1946 (see Cruickshank, 1976). In the 1950s, he and one of his early students, Norris G. Haring, were conducting projects in educating children with what today would probably be called learning disabilities and emotional or behavioral disorders. Cruickshank's Montgomery County (Maryland) project was later described in a volume on teaching "brain-injured and hyperactive children" (Cruickshank, Bentzen, Ratzeburg, & Tannhauser, 1961), and Haring's Arlington County (Virginia) Project was described in the first special education text in emotional and behavioral disorders that was clearly based on behavior theory (Haring & Phillips, 1962).

Cruickshank had been influenced by former teachers and colleagues, including William C. Morse, Fritz Redl, Alfred Strauss, and many others (see Cruickshank, 1976). However, in his Montgomery County Project, his emphasis was on routine, structure, and reduction of distracting stimuli. Haring took the idea of structure further for emotionally disturbed students and emphasized the essential elements of structure: clear directions, firm expectations, and consistent follow-through in applying consequences. In the following years, his work greatly influenced many special educators, including his students at the University of Kansas Medical Center, where he was an associate professor of pediatrics and director of the Children's Rehabilitation Unit from 1960 to 1965 (see Haring, 1974a).

Whelan, the Southard School of the Menninger Clinic, and the University of Kansas

Richard J. Whelan began working with emotionally disturbed children at the Menninger Psychiatric Clinic in Topeka, Kansas, in the 1950s. He was first a recreational therapist and childcare worker, later a teacher, and finally director of education and principal of the Southard School, which was part of the children's division of the Menninger Clinic (Whelan, 1974). At Southard, Whelan had found that permissive education based on psychoanalytic theory was not very successful and that students made much more academic and behavioral progress under a highly structured, directive program. He was among the first to recognize the value of behavioral psychology in educating students with emotional or behavioral disorders.

In 1962, Whelan left the Menninger Clinic to begin doctoral study at the University of Kansas with Norris G. Haring. He continued to develop his ideas (e.g., Whelan, 1963, 1966), but he and Haring also collaborated in further refining a structured, directive, or behavioral approach to teaching students with emotional or behavioral disorders (e.g., Haring & Whelan, 1965).

Whelan went on to become a distinguished professor of child development and special education at the University of Kansas Medical Center. For many years, he directed the Children's Rehabilitation

Unit, where he trained generations of special educators of children with emotional and behavioral disorders.

....

Prelude to the Late 20th Century

The early history of special education was a neglected topic in the mid-20th century. The leading textbooks of that era in the psychology of exceptional children and special education provided no historical sketch of the field at all (e.g., Baker, 1953; Cruickshank, 1955; Dunn, 1963; Garrison & Force, 1959; Kirk, 1962) or were brief and dismissive in their treatment of the history (e.g., Cruickshank & Johnson, 1958; Frampton & Gall, 1955a, 1955b, 1956). A *Guide for the Study of Exceptional Children*, published in 1955, included no historical notes (Abraham, 1955). No book provided anything approaching an in-depth discussion of the history of special education. Even specific chapters on emotional disturbance or social maladjustment (e.g., McCandless, 1956; Morse, 1958; Pate, 1963; Stullken, 1950) gave little or no indication of the rich historical background of the topic.

We have mentioned only a few of the researchers and writers whose work before 1960 was necessary to the outpouring of publications, legislation, advocacy, and program development during the last four decades of the 20th century. By necessity, our discussion has left out many individuals, particularly psychologists and psychiatrists whose work was applied by special educators. For example, Gerald R. Patterson's work with difficult children in school and with families of aggressive children at the Oregon Research Institute (see Kazdin, 1978; and, e.g., Patterson, 1965a, 1965b, 1973, 1975, 1980, 1982, 1986; Patterson & Forgatch, 1987; Patterson, Reid, & Dishion, 1992; Patterson, Reid, Jones, & Conger, 1975) greatly influenced the work of many, including Hill Walker and his associates (e.g., Walker, 1995; Walker, Reavis, Rhode, & Jenson, 1985). What is now clear is that a great deal of groundwork had been laid before 1960 for what was to emerge in the latter part of the century.

4 1960s to the End of the Century

S UBSTANTIAL attention was not paid to the history of special education until the late 1960s and 1970s, although histories of the recognition and educational treatment of mental retardation were published earlier (e.g., Doll, 1962, 1967). Cruickshank (1967), among the first to recognize the importance of the historical roots of the whole field of special education, contributed a chapter on the field's development to an introductory special education textbook.

In their introductory text on special education, Hewett and Forness (1974) paid serious attention to its history. Their first chapter covered the following periods: primitive and ancient (up to 500 B.C.), Greek and Roman (500 B.C.–A.D. 400), Middle Ages (A.D. 400–1500), 18th century, 19th century, and 20th century. They also saw historical determiners of treatment of children with disabilities as including survival (e.g., harsh physical environment and treatment, infanticide, eugenics), superstition (e.g., torture, trephining, exorcism, demonology), science (e.g., categorization, mental measurement, psychological theory, research), and service (e.g., humane treatment, custodial care, education, societal acceptance). However, even this source did not suggest the rich and extensive literature of the field of special education in the 19th and early 20th centuries.

Berkowitz and Rothman (1967b), Kauffman (1976, 1977), and Kauffman and Lewis (1974) were among the first to highlight the importance of early work in the field of emotional and behavioral disorders. We do not find this neglect of history very surprising for the simple reason that many students express impatience with and distaste for historical information, preferring current information under the assumption that *current* implies greater utility and relevance.

As we mentioned previously, until the 1970s, discussion of the history of the care and treatment of children with emotional and behavioral disorders tended to be superficial and dismissive. Perhaps reflection on earlier decades and centuries signals a certain level of maturity of the profession. In any case, the groundwork for the proliferation of special education after 1960 had long been laid.

Overview

By the 1960s, the mental health of children and adolescents was receiving more intensive attention than it had been afforded in earlier decades. Child psychiatry had become well established as a field of specialization, and concern about disordered behavior in schools and communities edged toward center stage in American consciousness. The report of a conference held in 1960 on prevention of children's mental disorders (Caplan, 1961) included chapters on mental health and schooling (Biber, 1961) and primary prevention in a school setting (Bower, 1961; see also Bower, 1962). Reading Bower's (1961) comments on prevention is in some ways eerily like reading comments on prevention written in the early 21st century. For example, Bower asked rhetorically, "Who put the public in the public schools?" (p. 353), a comment related to the absurdity of supposing that the academically diverse students served by public schools should be expected to study the same curriculum and learn it all to the same level:

> *Often, the notion of standards that reaches down from sacrosanct collegiate halls to the elementary and high schools tends to make "good" public schools those with high average achievement scores, and "poor" schools those with low average achievement scores. Presumably, good schools can become better by raising standards, i.e., dispatching with greater rapidity the slow, inadequate, or unwilling academic learner.* (Bower, 1961, p. 354)

Bower also noted that a previous researcher had concluded, "A disturbed childhood is likely to be reflected in learning difficulties; children who do poorly in school are likely to develop emotional problems" (1961, p. 355) and made the following observation:

> *Except in unusual circumstances, the school and the community are oriented to wait for the delinquent act, the school dropout, or the fully developed illness before being enjoined to help. Any program of prevention must contend with these and other conflicts in the primary preventive role of the school.* (p. 357)

Almost half a century after Bower's observation, we seemed no closer—in fact, perhaps further from—a society in which primary prevention is routinely practiced (see Kauffman, 1999c, 2004a, 2004b). The notion persisted in the early 21st century that all children can and must learn the same things regardless of their characteristics, that no child will be "left behind" in achievement, and that all students can achieve to the same "acceptable" standard with the same instruction—and by the same chronological age. The untenability of that assumption, however, is the very basis for special education (see Kauffman & Hallahan, 2005b; Kauffman & Wiley, 2004).

Special education came into its own as a discipline and as a social policy in many ways in the 1960s. In 1965, the Bureau of Education for the Handicapped (BEH) was established in the U.S. Office of Education (the Office was later to become the Department of Education, a cabinet-level enterprise, and BEH was later to become the Office of Special Education Programs, or OSEP, under the Office of Special Education and Rehabilitative Services, or OSERS). The increasing visibility and presence of federal agencies in special education played an important role in the growth of special education in public schools across the nation.

By 1960, there was great diversity of theory and practice in the education of students with emotional or behavioral disorders. Much of the groundwork was laid before 1960, but after that point specific classroom practices were more clearly articulated. Bower (1960, 1962, 1981) published his seminal work on definition and identification of California schoolchildren. Special classes in the public schools became so common that Hollister and Goldston (1962) published planning guidelines and Morse, Cutler, and Fink (1964) conducted and published a nationwide survey of special classes. Professionals banded together in 1964 to form a new division of the Council for Exceptional Children: the Council for Children with Behavioral Disorders (CCBD; see Wood, 1999, for details).

Various curriculum designs were outlined after 1960 (e.g., Kauffman, 1974a; Rhodes, 1963), and curricula to teach specific social-interpersonal skills were developed (Fagen, Long, & Stevens, 1975; Walker, Hops, & Greenwood, 1981; Walker et al., 1983). A series of three annual conferences on the education of emotionally disturbed children was held at Syracuse University, bringing together educators and psychologists of divergent viewpoints (Knoblock, 1965, 1966; Knoblock & Johnson, 1967). Preparation of personnel to work with children with emotional or behavioral disorders received federal support in 1963 with the enactment of P. L. 88-164 (amending P.L. 85-926 of 1958). The Autism Society of America (initially called the National Society for Autistic Children) was founded in 1965, and the national mental health and special education coalition was launched in 1987 (see Forness, 1988). What was later known as the Individuals with Disabilities Education Act (IDEA) was first passed in 1975 and signed into law by President Gerald Ford (as P.L. 94-142, the Education for All Handicapped Children Act).

Reviewing all the important events and trends that took place between 1960 and the turn of the next century is impossible. We offer brief summaries of some of the more critical developments, which we have organized around conceptual models and projects because distinctly different and competing concepts of emotional and behavioral disorders and intervention were further elaborated during this era and important projects were conducted.

....

Conceptual Models

Conceptual models are the ideas that guide teaching practices. Another way of stating this is that conceptual models are assumptions about the nature of a problem and what to do about it. A conceptual model provides the basic assumptions or ideas about how students learn, and an educational approach is the way those assumptions are put into practice in instruction. A conceptual model is a theory or way of conceptualizing why teachers should do what they do—a way of thinking about problems and their resolution. Conceptual models are useful for several reasons, given by Hallahan, Lloyd, Kauffman, Weiss, and Martinez (2005):

- *They provide general guidelines for education and foster specific practices.*
- *They help clarify similarities and differences between educational strategies.*
- *They promote consistent descriptions and approaches to teaching.*
- *They encourage research.*

In the 1960s, Morse et al. (1964) described variations in programs across the nation that had been initiated by adherence to different conceptual models ranging from psychoanalytic to behavioral. They noted that one of two basic ideas or continua guided most programs—either psychoanalytic principles or behavioral psychology. They found that some of the classrooms they visited had a "psychiatric-dynamic" orientation, and some were "psycho-educational" (i.e., based on the primacy of the ego or ego psychology). The worst classrooms they saw that used psychoanalytic ideas as a foundation were what they called "chaotic," because they assumed only an attitude of permissiveness toward misbehavior. On the other continuum they found programs that implemented behavior principles (a "psychological-behavioral" approach) and "educational" programs (emphasizing traditional academic work). The worst programs based on psychological-behavioral notions were what they called "primitive," because they used harshness and intimidation to keep behavior under control. At the meeting of these two continua (i.e., programs based on psychoanalytic principles and those based on behavioral psychology), they found programs they called "naturalistic," because they represented an ad hoc approach in which teachers tried to implement any useful ideas they could find from any source (see Morse et al., 1964, pp. 28–31, for a description of program types).

In the early 1960s, Morse and his colleagues reported that site visitors categorized the 74 classrooms they visited as follows: psychiatric-dynamic (14%), psycho-educational (26%), psychological-behavioral (4%), educational (29%), naturalistic (15%), primitive (7%), and chaotic (1%). The site visitors provided no classification data on 4% of the classrooms. But the most striking feature of this study was perhaps the conclusion, "The research reveals an amazing lack of specific patterns and uniformity of approach.... Approaches are much less systematic and more intuitive than had been expected" (Morse et al., 1964, p. 130).

The importance of conceptual models was first highlighted by the Conceptual Models Project, which we discuss below. Description of such models became a standard expectation in textbooks on special education for students with emotional or behavioral disorders (e.g., Cullinan, 2002; Kauffman, 2005a). Conceptual models were also the topic of a volume edited in the 1980s by McDowell, Adamson, and Wood (1982).

Conceptual Models Project

Various conceptual models of working with emotionally disturbed children had become so well articulated by the 1970s that William C. Rhodes and his colleagues conducted a major project resulting in four volumes describing alternative theories, interventions, and delivery systems and speculating about the future (Rhodes, 1975; Rhodes & Head, 1974; Rhodes & Tracy, 1972a, 1972b). The idea was to commission a series of descriptions of the various conceptual models, bring synthesis to the models, provide training in analyzing cases from the models, and provide direction for predicted future developments of foundational ideas in the field.

Rhodes (1972a, 1972c, 1975) provided a view of what was to become known in the late 20th century as "postmodernism." In the early 1970s, he described what he saw as the "crisis of theory" in his introduction to the Conceptual Models Project (Rhodes, 1972a):

> A bewildering and contradictory development has occurred in Behavioral Science. There has been a wide-scale and profuse growth of information about human behavior. We have an over-whelming richness of knowledge about the origins, development, influences, variations and outcomes of behavior. And yet, the very foundation of our behavior thought seems to be collapsing under the weight of this wildly flourishing accumulation of data and fact. (p. 13)

Rhodes did not seem to anticipate the extraordinary acceleration of knowledge in subsequent decades (we return in the last chapter to his view of the future from the 1970s). Suffice it to say, that by the early 1970s, the various conceptual models were fairly clearly drawn, but the information then available was meager by standards of the early 21st century.

In the first volume of *A Study of Child Variance* (Rhodes & Tracy, 1972a), a product of the Conceptual Models Project, six conceptual models were described: biophysical (Sagor, 1972), behavioral (Russ, 1972), psychodynamic (Rezmierski & Kotre, 1972), sociological (Des Jarlais, 1972), ecological (Feagans, 1972), and counter theory (Tracy,

Reimer, & Bron, 1972). In the second volume (Rhodes & Tracy, 1972b), interventions from five perspectives were summarized: be-havioral (Kameya, 1972a), biophysical (Kameya, 1972b), psycho-dynamic (Cheney & Morse, 1972), environmental (Wagner, 1972), and counter theoretical (Burke, 1972).

In his introduction to Volume 2 on interventions, Rhodes (1972b) made exceedingly clear his rejection of conceptual models other than counter theory and his commitment to what he described as the revolt against (a) "care giving metaphors," (b) "care receiving investiture," (c) "care givers," (d) "the economics and politics of care," (e) "care taking institutions," (f) "the melting pot myth of caretaking" and (g) "underclass revolt." He described "the gathering force" of revolt that he believed would bring a "renaissance of caring" and a "cultural resurrection." He stated that "the legal attacks upon 'special' education, and the rights of 'exceptional children,' are typical of these scattered counter-attacks upon our present forms of caretaking" (p. 70), and concluded,

> No matter where you look in the society today, there is this new awareness of the consciousness of caring, and of its significance in counteracting the forces of technical destruction let loose in the world by the perfection of a nuclear holocaust. This has led to a total examination of the right relation-ship between men and between men and community; and in the process the whole fabric of our caring apparatus and assumptions is under scrutiny. Any thought about future interventions has to take this force into account. (p. 70)

Volume 3 (Rhodes & Head, 1974; see also Rhodes & Sagor, 1974) took up service delivery models. In *A Study of Child Variance*, "service delivery model" referred to the social agency or system pro-viding intervention, not to the special class *versus* the general class (i.e., inclusion) controversy of later decades of the 20th century (see Kauffman & Hallahan, 1995, 2005a). A history of the response of each social agency or system to social deviance was provided, fol-lowed by the structure of the agency's response, and a case study illustrating the system's treatment. Treatment of deviance by the educational system was described by Hoffman (1974a, 1974b), and the case example was provided by Ellis (1974). The legal–

correctional system was discussed by Atkinson (1974a, 1974b), and a case study was written by Neff (1974). The history of the mental health system's response to deviance was described by Fraser (1974), its response by Sagor (1974), and a case study by Kantor (1974). The social welfare system was also described (Ravlin, 1974; Unger, 1974a, 1974b), as was treatment by religious institutions (Pekarsky, 1974a, 1974b). Volume 3 ended with descriptions of counterinstitutional and countercultural alternatives to modern institutions (Moore, 1974a, 1974b) and a case study of an apparently hypothetical (fictional) description of what alternative service delivery systems might look like in a town called Noah, Euphrates (Nemetz-Carlson, 1974). In the case study description, Noah is said to offer alternatives to all of the major service delivery systems: educational, legal–correctional, social welfare, mental health, and religious.

Volume 4 was Rhodes's predictions of future conceptual models and interventions (Rhodes, 1975). He revealed his own affinity for countercultural views and explanations, again (as in his introduction to Volume 2) citing Thomas Szasz, Ivan Illich, Carlos Castenada, and many others associated with the countercultural movement of the 1960s in support of his rejection of the other conceptual models his project described and adding the icon of postmodernists, Michel Foucault. He maintained that reason is not superior to idiosyncratic experience or to counter theory. Counter theory is a rejection of all other theories, under the guise of the assumption that no theory is more correct than any other as a means of understanding the world (counter theory being the exception).

Although Rhodes (1975) decried labeling, he nonetheless described a separation of the "thesists" (those who embrace a particular conceptual model other than counter theory) from the "antithesists" (those, of which he is one, opposed to any theory other than counter theory). Ironically, his separation of "thesists" from "antithesists" was an obvious exercise in labeling. His view was that multiple realities exist and should be embraced as equally valid. He suggested that any other view is an attempt to control people against their will or to co-opt their will. Only multirealists see reality as it is, he intimated:

> *Many multirealists see the end of the Control Era as the beginning of the Human Era: not chaos, but discovery of the Self and of the Other await us*

on the other side of the nightmare of Western history. It is into this life that we must induct the child. (p. 18)

> *The ultimate goal of the new multirealists is the celebration of being in the multivarious forms in which it will reveal itself. Although deviance is not "being," to affirm and celebrate deviance in the current situation is to negate the ultimacy of existing definitions of being and reality. Just as, for the normal man, deviance is a symbol of nonbeing, for the antithesist it offers the one real glimpse of being that is available to us. Although the variant person may not recognize himself as the power behind the reality he inhabits, his reality is a different one from our own. He thus imitates the forgotten image of man in his real capacity as the subject of his existence.* (p. 28)

> *The multirealists affirm, however, that what cries out for expression is not dark and evil chaos, but our own subjectivity, our own repressed longings to realize a constellation of potentialities which we have learned to disavow. Our characterization of these potentialities as evil "not me's" is a repudiation of our own subjectivity, of our unique personhood, and is thus a feature of our alienation from ourselves. The problem of variance, in the antithesist view is the problem of being human, of self acceptance, self appreciation, and self realization.* (p. 59)

Some of the predictions made by Rhodes (1975, pp. 92–99; e.g., "Major changes in the next decade will result in experiencing ourselves and others to new depths," p. 94, and "There will be a beginning erosion of the belief in 'normality' as used in the area of child variance," p. 95) have apparently not come to pass. Moreover, the rejection of reason, logic, and scientific evidence in favor of idiosyncratic experience and ideology are inconsistent with some historians' evaluations of 20th-century Western history and with contemporary perspectives on the nature of doubt and reliable evidence (e.g., Conquest, 2000; Hecht, 2003; Ruscio, 2002). Rhodes's later work (e.g., Rhodes, 1987, 1992; Rhodes & Doone, 1992; Rhodes & Paul, 1978) revealed a continuing commitment to ideas running contrary to the dominant understanding of human conduct.

The bias of Rhodes (1975) for what later became known as postmodernism (e.g., Danforth & Rhodes, 1997) aside, the Conceptual Models Project was important in highlighting various views of human behavior, social deviance, and the response of different service agencies to troublesome behavior. The project did help to foster the coalescence of thinking about emotional and behavioral disorders into clusters of alternative views.

The Biological or Biogenic Model

The biological or biogenic model has had adherents for many generations. The basic idea of this model is that emotional and behavioral disorders have a biological basis, that they represent brain injury or dysfunction or some imbalance of biochemistry. In the late 19th and early 20th centuries, the predominant idea was that mental illness was just that—a malfunction of the brain. However, scientists at that time understood little of how various diseases (e.g., syphilis) affected the brain. Scientists of the early 20th century understood that there probably was a link between genetics and mental illness, but they understood little of its nature.

By the late 20th century, especially with progress toward the conclusion of the Human Genome Project, it was clear that genetic research was "moving away from establishing the *fact* of heritability and toward explaining the *how* of heritability" (Carey & Goldman, 1997, p. 250). Before the beginning of the 21st century, it had become clear that many personality characteristics and behavioral predispositions were transmitted by genes (cf. Weiner, 1999), but some scientists and the news media oversold what gene therapy could accomplish (D. Brown, 1995). Still, the Human Genome Project, the mapping of all the genes in human chromosomes, seemed by the 21st century to hold the promise of revolutionary therapies for both physical and mental illnesses (Collins, Green, Guttmacher, & Guyer, 2003).

Various psychosurgeries for most emotional and behavioral disorders (e.g., cutting neural pathways, implanting devices in the brain to stimulate certain regions, or removing brain tissue) were largely unsuccessful or abandoned in the 20th century. Moreover, diet and "orthomolecular psychiatry" (i.e., megavitamin therapy, the ingestion of very large quantities of certain food substances) did not prove to be effective (see Kameya, 1972a).

Pharmacology made great strides in treating mental illnesses beginning about midcentury. In 1962, Rosenblum stated, "If 1953 can be considered the beginning of the tranquilizing age in America and up to 1957 the period when this new approach was received with most enthusiasm and credited with most dramatic results—1958, 1959, and 1960 can be called the years of sober assessment, when there has been a swinging away from subjective bias to more objective attempts at gauging the worth of these agents" (p. 655). We now know that psychopharmacology can be helpful in treating a variety of emotional and behavioral disorders, although overselling what these chemical agents can accomplish will likely always be possible (see Konopasek, 1996; Konopasek & Forness, 2004).

Until about 1960, medication was not very effective in combating any major mental illnesses such as schizophrenia. However, the invention of antipsychotic medication in the middle of the 20th century radically altered expectations for people with major mental illnesses, and many were deinstitutionalized. Gadow (1979) was among the first in the 1970s to provide explicit information and guidance for teachers on the nature and effects of medication on exceptional children. By the late 20th century, some special educators were calling for a "new medical model" in the light of improved understanding of the biological bases for many emotional and behavioral disorders and improved medicines to treat such disorders (Forness & Kavale, 2001).

The Psychoanalytic or Psychodynamic Model

A variety of labels have been devised for the model we discuss here (see Cheney & Morse, 1972). The basic feature of this model, however, is Freudian ideas about the mind and mental illness: that emotional and behavioral disorders are the result of an imbalance of the parts of the mental apparatus (id, ego, superego) or something gone wrong in their dynamic interplay. It is the notion that education should be based on the same principles as psychoanalysis. Although teachers deal more with the "ego" function than with the unconscious processes of the id and superego, they need to understand and acknowledge that they are dealing with only "surface" behavior, according to this approach.

Anna Freud, Bruno Bettelheim, Fritz Redl, and David Wineman were, as we noted in Chapter 3, among the foremost early proponents of applying Freudian ideas to education. Bettelheim, in particular, was noted for florid and obtuse interpretations based on psychoanalytic theory. His fanciful ideas included such tales as the following:

> When I tried to teach understanding deviant behavior to my students, I suggested to them that they should give me any number that came to their mind. One student said 784 and I wrote on the blackboard 748, reversing the figure. Of course the class laughed and so did I because we were talking about errors and I had committed the error of writing, instead of 784, the number 748. If we believe that human behavior makes sense we must know that we learn much more from faulty performance. The title of Freud's book is Psychopathology of Everyday Life, which is changed from the original German title. For Freud, there did not exist such a thing as psychopathology of everyday life because this implies faulty performance. Typically we think all our emotionally disturbed children engage in faulty performances but what Freud tried to show us in this book and in his work is that there are no faulty performances. There are only performances which show less or more originality, less or more complicated thinking. Therefore, after I had changed 784 to 748, it behooved me to tell the class why I had made such a mistake. I told them that I had an instinctive reaction to that 84 because it reminded me of Orwell's 1984. The student who had given me 784 announced that indeed she had thought in her own mind of the incredible manipulation of human beings which characterizes modern mass society and that teachers, administrators, and politicians try to impose their way of thinking and doing things on everyone just as Orwell predicted in 1984. Her thinking was that the only protection against 1984 was for people to think more psychoanalytically as I tried to teach them. She was astonished when I explained to her that in changing 784 to 748, I too had reacted to 1984 and had changed it to 1848, the year of great liberation in my country. The revolution of 1848 let loose great liberating forces, including those that made Freud possible. It took me to the end of the hour to explain why I had anxiously changed 84, which to me also had some bad connotations, to 48 which to me had some good connotations. And the class rather liked that but I still got stuck with 784, so I had to do some homework and think a little about why a student would have selected 784. When the next class began, I wrote on the blackboard 784, and added these numbers up to equal 19. Then I turned to the girl and said, "I guess you're 19 years old." From this I got a round of applause from these usually very negative students. But that wasn't very difficult because

college students after all, are from 18 to 22 so I had a 25% chance that 19 would be the correct age. I suggested then from 784, that when she was 7, her older brother or sister, I did not know, was 8 and the youngest was 4. This was only a blind suggestion, but it happened to be correct. After that, I explained to them that in common parlance number 1 is me. This is part of the American vernacular, number one, so the first number, therefore, had to be she. I also suggested that she selected the age of 7 because something important must have taken place then. And it turned out that when she was seven and her brother was 8 and her little brother was 4, her parents got a divorce. We then arrived at why she had selected a three rather than a five digit figure. At this time the family did not consist of a five digit number because with the divorce of the parents, the three children were really left to their own devices. (Bettelheim, 1970, pp. 40–41)

Apparently, Bettelheim did not consider that if the number of digits were to represent the number of individuals in the whole family (in this case, five digits), then his student's parents would have to have been younger than 10 years! But in Bettelheim's world of psychoanalysis, things do not have to "add up":

Let's take another example from the area of arithmetic: 2 × 2 makes 9. By now you should be well able to understand what happens here. What happens is that if two people multiply (remember the scriptures: you shall multiply) the results are 9, by which you can readily see there must be seven children in this family. If two parents multiply two times two, the result is four, but as the child knew, the result is nine. Let me give you another simple arithmetic example from emotionally disturbed children. Five is less than three. If we accept that the numbers refer to what is most important to one, we recognize that three are indeed more than five if you are the oldest child. When there are only three in the family, you and your parents, you have a lot more than after the arrival of two more children; and therefore, three is more than five, and five is less than three. I tried to suggest that if you just listen carefully to what children tell us through their behavior, you will understand them, and after we demonstrate to them that we can understand them, they are willing to listen to us. (Bettelheim, 1970, p. 42)

Such fanciful explanations did little, of course, to help teachers know how to manage or instruct children with emotional or behavioral disorders. Others with a psychoanalytic view of special education (e.g., Ack, 1970) avoided such flights of fancy but, nevertheless, emphasized Freudian notions of the importance of teacher–pupil relationships for teaching and assumed that underlying cognitive and emotional problems had to be resolved before skills could be learned.

In 1960, Berkowitz and Rothman published their now classic book, *The Disturbed Child: Recognition and Psychoeducational Therapy in the Classroom*. After describing various classifications of children, they devoted four chapters to the teacher's role and classroom procedures. Based on psychoanalytic theory, they suggested a highly permissive approach to education. But the permissive approach suggested by Freudian theory, the Freudian emphasis on resolving underlying mental conflicts before teaching, and the Freudian insistence on relationship-building before instruction led to the disappointment of many (e.g., Fenichel, 1966, 1974). Eventually, the bizarre psychoanalytic notions of Bettelheim as well as the more rational psychoanalytic notions of the others were seen as counterproductive, and they have been largely abandoned.

The Psychoeducational Model

"Psychoeducational" implies a combination of knowledge of "underlying" or unconscious motivations for behavior and management of observable behavior in an educational setting. It is the recognition that psychoanalytic principles alone have limited usefulness for teachers and that practical techniques for managing the way a student behaves are important. It became a conceptual model frequently embraced by those whose basic training and early interventions were psychoanalytic in orientation but who saw the need for more than listening to and understanding children (e.g., Fenichel, 1966, 1974).

For example, Berkowitz's and Rothman's later publications (after their 1960 volume) reflected their movement from a strictly psychoanalytic perspective toward a more pragmatic stance (e.g., Berkowitz & Rothman, 1967b). The work of Morse and others at the University of Michigan in the 1960s showed a similar tendency to emphasize practical considerations and ego development. In 1965, Long, Morse, and Newman published the first edition of a landmark volume, *Conflict in the Classroom*. This book included disparate viewpoints but brought together the ideas of Redl and Morse regarding the life space interview (LSI).

The LSI grew out of Redl's work at Pioneer House in Detroit in the 1940s and 1950s, which had a psychiatric-dynamic (psychoanalytic) foundation but emphasized working with "surface behavior" (see Heuchert & Long, 1980; Long & Newman, 1965). It is a particular way of talking with children about their behavior, typically using the techniques for management of surface behavior described by Redl and Wineman (1951, 1952; see also Chapter 3) or any other tactic described by Redl and his colleagues (e.g., "massaging numb value areas"). The idea of the LSI is that at or shortly after a behavioral crisis, the teacher (or other child worker) conducts an interview to strengthen the youngster's ego, help the student understand his or her motivations, and help the interviewee correctly interpret the problems he or she has just encountered (James & Long, 1992; Long & Newman, 1965; Morse, 1953, 1965b; Morse & Wineman, 1965; Redl, 1959a; Wood, 1990). The LSI was later renamed life space crisis intervention (LSCI; see Long, Fecser, & Brendtro, 1998), but the basic idea remained essentially the same.

In the 1960s, Morse explained his idea of the crisis teacher—a teacher skilled in LSI techniques and remedial teaching who would be prepared to take over the management and teaching of a difficult student for a short period of time (during a behavioral crisis) and to obviate the need for full-time special class placement (Morse, 1965a, 1971a, 1971b). The crisis teacher became a very popular notion and helped form the basis for the idea of the resource or consulting teacher.

The psychoeducational model also led to the development of special curricula for teaching social skills. For example, Fagen et al. (1975) presented a psychoeducational self-control curriculum, and Fagen (1979) described psychoeducational methods for adolescents (see also Dembinski, Schultz, & Walton, 1982; Rezmierski, Knoblock, & Bloom, 1982; Rich, Beck, & Coleman, 1982; Wood & Long, 1991).

The psychoeducational model has great intuitive appeal because it acknowledges the publicly popular notion of unconscious motivation and, simultaneously, provides a more practical and reality-oriented view of teaching. Fenichel's (1966) observations about the uselessness of psychoanalytic theory for classroom teachers and on what he and others learned about teaching are among the clearest and most appealing comments on the psychoeducational model:

> *We learned that disorganized children need someone to organize their world for them. We began to recognize that disturbed children fear their own loss of control and need protection against their own impulses; that what they needed were teachers who knew how to limit as well as accept them. We learned the need for a highly organized program of education and training that could bring order, stability, and direction to minds that are disorganized, unstable, and unpredictable.* (Fenichel, 1966, p. 9)

Fenichel not only challenged the permissiveness encouraged by psychoanalytic theory but questioned the idea of "symptom substitution" as well. Symptom substitution is the idea that observable behavior is only a symptom of underlying psychological problems and that removing a symptom is useless, as another will merely take its place. In fact, as the following passages show, Fenichel (1966) confronted many psychoanalytic notions, including the idea that problems represent deeply hidden, unconscious conflicts, with reasonable skepticism and realistic conclusions about teaching:

> *Many will insist that sufficient ego strength can come only after inner emotional conflicts have been resolved through psychiatric intervention and individual psychotherapy....*
>
> *We have found far too many immediate reasons for the overwhelming problems and deviant behavior of our children without having to dig and search for them in deeply buried conflict.... I strongly believe that the pathology of our children—their disorganization, withdrawal, disorientation and confusion—is more closely related to serious learning disorders and language handicaps than to the repression of traumatic childhood memories or unresolved intrapsychic conflicts.* (p. 10)
>
> *No matter what the primary cause of a child's disturbed behavior, we believe the teacher cannot afford to wait until first causes are dug up, "worked through" and resolved. Something must be done NOW to correct the confusion, impulsivity, anxiety and other secondary symptoms that disrupt and overwhelm him today....*

96

*Many may question the lasting value of alleviating or correcting symp-
toms since "it isn't getting to the heart of the problem." They assert that all
we are doing is to suppress or repress the symptoms, and that unless we un-
cover and eliminate the primary conflict, other symptoms will arise to replace
the repressed ones. All that we would accomplish therefore is to substitute
one symptom for another.*

*We believe that quite the reverse is true: that the removal of one symp-
tom is more likely to facilitate the removal of other symptoms by reducing the
child's overall anxiety and confusion and improving his feelings of well-being
and self-esteem.* (p. 11)

The psychoeducational model and associated educational approaches have become more reality oriented and less fanciful over
time. Although teachers may have an understanding of the psychological conflicts of their pupils, psychoeducational procedures have
become ever more focused on the here and now, on the consequences
of behavior, and on providing effective instruction.

Humanistic Education and the Counter Theory Model

As E. W. Martin (1972) noted, individualism and humanism
were the forces shaping special education in the 1960s and 1970s.
In that era, there was concern for the particular educational needs
of African American and other youngsters from ethnic minority
groups, especially those from inner-city areas and economically im-
poverished backgrounds (Dennison, 1969; Dokecki, Strain, Bernal,
Brown, & Robinson, 1975; Johnson, 1969, 1971; Rothman, 1970,
1974).

For students with emotional or behavioral disorders, it was suggested that radical departures from past educational practices were
needed. Counter theorists, who departed markedly from tradition,
and many of whom were not accepted as fellow professionals by established authorities in their fields, became a strong force in the mid-
1960s. Many who were part of this counter theory group considered
themselves humanists and subscribers to the freedom and openness
called for by Carl Rogers (1983), Herbert Kohl (1970), Jonathan
Kozol (1972), A. S. Neill (1960), and others of the era (see Rhodes,
1972a, 1972b, 1972c, 1975). We have already commented on and

provided excerpts from the work of Rhodes and his colleagues on counter theory.

In addition to the ideas of Rhodes, pleas for freedom, openness, and humanism were made by Dennison (1969), Grossman (1972), Knoblock (1970, 1973, 1979, 1983), Knoblock and Goldstein (1971), and Trippe (1966, 1970). Humanistic education tended to emphasize the affective side of learning and teaching (see Morse, Ardizzone, MacDonald, & Pasick, 1980; Schultz, Heuchert, & Stampf, 1973).

The humanistic and counter-theoretical models are difficult or impossible to characterize in terms of recommended instructional or behavior management strategies or techniques, other than those of postmodernism, holism, and whole language. For example, Burke's (1972) proposals for change based on counter theory were later developed into the ideas known as "whole language," "holistic teaching," and "child-centered" education (see Hallahan et al., 2005; Hirsch, 1996). Counter theory seems to be a rejection of existing theories or other theoretical frameworks without the proposal of more than very general or vague recommendations. Here is Burke's (1972) explanation:

> *"Counter theory" is not clearly a separate body of theory. The writers discussed here disagree with each other, as well as with other, established writers. In fact, the most satisfactory definition of "a countertheorist" seems to be a definition by extrusion: a countertheorist is someone whose work, though derived from a recognized tradition, is not generally accepted as "part of the field" by the authorities in that area. For example, A. S. Neill bases his work on a psychoanalytic framework, but is not accepted by most psychoanalytic authorities.*
>
> **Counter theory is what countertheorists say and do.** *Usually it begins with the school or the child and works back to the theory from there. It means a bent toward the humanistic ideas of writers like Abraham Maslow. It is a tendency toward freer education, more in the hands of the student and less determined from above than in most models. Often it means a spirit of rebelliousness and innovation. And it is not so much a body of theory as it is a praxis.* (p. 577; emphasis added)

Many of the ideas propounded by counter theorists are now promoted as "postmodern" (see Kauffman, 2002; Sasso, 2001). But from an historical point of view, what is called postmodern may in some sense represent a return to earlier ideas, perhaps without the intent of mimicking earlier philosophers. Hecht (2003) has described philosophical positions similar to those held by counter theorists or postmodernists that were put forward in the 3rd century by Sextus Empiricus:

> *Skeptics of this period went about their arguments by dividing any notion into two possible, oppositional ideas, and then positing a dependent notion for each side until they found something contradictory or absurd, at which point they would dismiss the original proposition. In so doing, they sought not to isolate the truth, but rather to prove that certainty, on any issue, made bad sense.... It was the philosophy of "no," and it reigned for centuries at the Academy.... The relativism is a lofty aim, but taking a subject and arguing against all opinion on it is a very strange way to proceed and makes for weird reading.* (p. 163)

> *There is a beautiful tedium to it. The argument has an almost liturgical singsong quality, such that in the deficit of knowledge Sextus posed, this song and its debunking scythe could perhaps soothe its own wound, its own harsh claim that we can know nothing.* (p. 164)

Or consider the late 11th- and early 12th-century Muslim author Abu Hamid al-Ghazzali. "He managed to demonstrate how all rational belief may be reduced to confusion" (Hecht, 2003, p. 236). The consequence of taking al-Ghazzali's teaching seriously was disastrous. "Henceforth, until modernity, Muslim theology would be based in authoritative texts and in mysticism" (Hecht, 2003, pp. 236–237).

The Ecological Model

Concern for ecological factors in emotional and behavioral disorders was expressed at least as early as the 1940s (e.g., Faris, 1944). However, the 1960s also saw the rise of interest in and application of the ecological approach. Based primarily on the writing of Hobbs (1965, 1966, 1974) and Rhodes (1963, 1965, 1967, 1970), this approach called for intervention not only with the child or youth but also with the student's home, school, and community. Wagner (1972) described the ecological or sociological model as involving environmental interventions—community, family, school, and so on.

The most important project associated with the ecological approach was Project Re-ED, which we described in Chapter 3. After working extensively in the mental health field in this country and having observed the European educateur programs, Hobbs, along with William C. Rhodes, Matthew J. Trippe, Wilbert W. Lewis, Lloyd M. Dunn, and others, began Re-ED programs in Tennessee and North Carolina in the early 1960s. Re-ED schools focused on health rather than illness, teaching rather than treatment, learning rather than fundamental personality change, the present and future rather than the past, and on the child's total social system rather than his or her intrapsychic processes exclusively (Hobbs, 1965).

In the initial Re-ED schools, youngsters were served in a residential setting during the week but returned home on weekends. A central aspect of Project Re-ED was the selection and training of the teacher-counselors, who carried out the moment-to-moment and day-to-day work with youngsters, and the liaison teachers, who maintained communication and coordination with the home and regular school class (Hobbs, 1966, 1974). Most evaluations of the Re-ED model appear to support the efficacy of an ecological approach (Daly, 1985; Lee, 1971; W. W. Lewis, 1982; Votel, 1985; Weinstein, 1969). Furthermore, the initial work of Hobbs and Rhodes apparently gave impetus to the research and writing of others who emphasized ecological concepts (Apter & Conoley, 1984; Graubard, 1976; Graubard, Rosenberg, & Miller, 1971; Rosenberg & Graubard, 1975; Swap, 1974, 1978; Swap, Prieto, & Harth, 1982).

The ecological model emphasized working with various aspects of the child's environment, not a particular set of assumptions about the causes and cures of emotional or behavioral problems. It thus remained open to strategies and techniques that could be demonstrated to work and to the application of all reality-oriented, empirically verifiable interventions. Hobbs (1974) explains further the value of ecological concepts:

> *The formulation of the disturbed child's problem in ecological terms led naturally to the emergence of a new generalized role, variously called the liaison teacher-counselor, the child advocate, the child development specialist, and*

the liaison specialist. Ecological concepts sprang from the practical necessity of working with parents, siblings, teachers, agency representatives, and others, if the Re-ED school was to be effective. In fact, one of the reasons the Re-ED schools have been so successful is the amount of attention that has been given to restoring to effective functioning the several components of the ecological system defined by the child. It soon became manifest that many of the kinds of children who were brought into the Re-ED school could, in fact, be helped very substantially by the liaison specialists without being removed from their homes and regular schools. One of the cardinal principles of the Re-ED idea is that the disturbed child should be removed the least possible distance from his home, school, and community—in time, in geographical space, and in the psychological texture of the experience provided. Logically extended, this concept leads to keeping children out of Re-ED schools whenever possible and seeking, instead, to work with the child and significant other people in his life in their natural settings. Special residential placement would thus be indicated only when a child needs intensive, around-the-clock re-education or when the family is so fragile as to be unable to sustain him. (p. 163)

The ecological model appears to be one open to grafting with other conceptual models, such as the behavioral model. Trends of the late 20th and early 21st centuries suggest behavioral interventions in the broader sense described by Wagner (1972) (see Landrum & Kauffman, in press; Malone, 2003; Strand, Barnes-Holmes, & Barnes-Holmes, 2003).

The Behavioral Model
In the late 1950s and early 1960s, some special educators began to make explicit use of basic behavior principles and behavior modification techniques (cf. Cullinan, Epstein, & Kauffman, 1982; Forness & MacMillan, 1970; Kazdin, 1978). The behavior modification frame of reference was derived primarily from B. F. Skinner's (1953) basic research and writing. However, its initial application to the education of students with emotional or behavioral disorders was the work of many individuals, a number of whom were influenced by the work of Heinz Werner, Alfred Strauss, Laura Lehtinen, Newell Kephart, and others who devised methods of teaching brain-injured children at the Wayne County Training School in the 1940s (see Chapter 3).

William M. Cruickshank and his colleagues conducted an experimental public school program for brain-injured and hyperactive
children (many of whom had emotional difficulties) in Montgomery County, Maryland, in the late 1950s. The report of this project
(Cruickshank et al., 1961) described a highly structured program
similar in many ways to that outlined earlier by Strauss and Lehtinen
(1947). The report emphasized control of extraneous stimuli and use
of a consistent routine and consistent consequences for behavior.

Shortly after the Montgomery County project, Norris G. Haring
and E. Lakin Phillips extended the concept of structure to work with
students with emotional or behavioral disorders in the public schools
of Arlington, Virginia (see Haring, 1974a; Haring & Phillips, 1962,
1972; Phillips, 1962, 1967; Phillips & Haring, 1959). Their major
hypothesis was that these youngsters lacked order, predictability, and
consistency in their environment and needed the stability and consistent demands of Cruickshank's program. They particularly emphasized
the use of consistent consequences for behavior (a basic behavior
modification principle). A structured approach as defined by Haring
and Phillips consists of three primary elements: clear directions, firm
expectations that the child will perform as directed, and consistent
follow-through in applying consequences for behavior.

Later in the 1960s, Haring collaborated with Richard J. Whelan
at the University of Kansas Medical Center to refine and extend the
concept of structure (Haring & Whelan, 1965; Whelan & Haring,
1966), which was extended even further in the late 1960s and into
the 1970s by Haring and Phillips to include the behavior modification
technology of direct daily measurement of behavioral rates (Haring,
1968, 1974b; Haring & Phillips, 1972). Whelan had previously developed a structured approach to teaching at the Southard School of
the Menninger Clinic in Topeka, Kansas (Whelan, 1963, 1966).
Whelan has since expanded and refined the concept of structure
and the use of behavior principles (Whelan, 1974, 1998, 1999;
Whelan & Gallagher, 1972).

Others were also pioneering the behavioral approach. The report
of Zimmerman and Zimmerman (1962) was a prelude to an outpouring of behavior modification research in the late 1960s and 1970s.
Their simple anecdotal reports of how they resolved two behavior
problems—temper tantrums and refusal to write spelling words—by

systematic use of consequences was followed by a spate of technically sophisticated reports in the behavior modification literature. Many behavioral psychologists, including those interested in special education, made tremendous strides in therapeutic endeavors in this era (Goodall, 1972). For example, Herbert C. Quay and his associates contributed immeasurably to the classification of disordered behavior (e.g., Quay, 1975, 1977). Lloyd Homme articulated a behavioral approach to education (Homme, 1970) and initiated the use of contingency contracts in the classroom (Homme, 1969). Gerald R. Patterson and his colleagues studied the families of aggressive children and contributed many insights into the coercive processes that operate in such families, as well as effective techniques for managing aggression (e.g., Patterson, 1965a, 1965b, 1973, 1975, 1980, 1982, 1986; Patterson & Forgatch, 1987; Patterson, Reid, & Dishion, 1992; Patterson, Reid, Jones, & Conger, 1975). Hill Walker and colleagues, often working with Patterson's research group, applied behavior principles to managing acting-out behavior in the classroom and teaching social skills (e.g., Walker, 1995; Walker & Buckley, 1973; Walker, Colvin, & Ramsey, 1995; Walker, Hops, & Fiegenbaum, 1976; Walker et al., 1983; Walker, Reavis, Rhode, & Jenson, 1985).

Frank Hewett was among the most influential and prolific behavioral psychologists working in special education in the late 20th century. Two of his areas of activity are particularly noteworthy. First, in the mid-1960s, he designed an *engineered classroom* that employed a token (point) system as well as special curricula and centers of activity. The Santa Monica Project and his Madison Plan, early trials of his behavioral program, were widely cited and emulated (see Hewett, 1967, 1968). As part of his research and training activities, Hewett also proposed a hierarchy of educational tasks (Hewett, 1964a) and a hierarchy of competencies for teachers (Hewett, 1966). He continued to write about his research and training using behavioral methods (Hewett, 1970a, 1970b, 1971, 1974). His second area of interest was teaching children with severe disorders. Through systematic use of operant conditioning (reinforcement) techniques, he found that he was able to teach speech and reading skills to a boy with autism (Hewett, 1964b, 1965).

Finally, during the 1960s and 1970s, there was a dramatic increase in interest and effort to educate children and youth with severe disabilities, including those with severe emotional or behavioral disorders. The intervention techniques that gained widest acceptance in this era and proved to be most effective with students having severe disabilities were behavior modification methods. Although the professionals who made contributions in this area are too numerous to name, the work of O. Ivar Lovaas is particularly notable. First at the University of Washington and later at the University of California at Los Angeles, Lovaas and his colleagues researched the teaching of language and daily living skills to autistic and schizophrenic children (Devany, Rincover, & Lovaas, 1981; Lovaas, 1966, 1967, 1987; Lovaas & Koegel, 1973; Lovaas, Koegel, Simmons, & Long, 1973; Lovaas, Young, & Newsom, 1978). His work, along with that of others who employed operant conditioning techniques, demonstrated that students with severe disabilities can learn when appropriate conditions are arranged and that one need not wait for this learning to occur spontaneously. However, his work was not without its critics (Gresham & MacMillan, 1997a, 1997b; see also Smith & Lovaas, 1997).

Before the end of the 20th century, it was clear that the behavioral model made use of much of the research that could be characterized as social learning theory. The best-known proponent of social learning theory is the psychologist Albert Bandura (e.g., Bandura, 1973, 1977, 1978, 1986). Bandura's social learning theory combined the recognition of internal states (thinking and emotions) with the demonstrated power of external consequences (reinforcement and punishment) in shaping behavior. His theories were applied by other psychologists working with children who have emotional or behavioral disorders (e.g., Kazdin, 1994, 1995, 1998), as well as by special educators (e.g., Cullinan, 2002; Jones et al., 2004; Kauffman, 2005a; Kerr & Nelson, 2002; Walker, 1995; Walker, Ramsey, & Gresham, 2004).

The 1997 amendments to the Individuals with Disabilities Education Act seemed to embrace at least certain aspects of a behavioral model. Functional behavioral assessment (FBA) seemed clearly to be based on behavioral concepts (see Fox & Gable, 2004). Furthermore, positive behavioral support (PBS) seemed to be based primarily on behavioral concepts and empirical evidence (see Jones, Dohrn, & Dunn, 2004; Kerr & Nelson, 2002; Lewis, Lewis-Palmer, Newcomer, & Stichter, 2004), although some have claimed that PBS can be seen as something other than behavioral or empirical (Sailor & Paul, 2004). Likewise, school-wide discipline is based primarily on behavior principles (see Liaupsin, Jolivette, & Scott, 2004; Martella, Nelson, & Marchand-Martella, 2003). In short, the behavioral model seemed at the end of the 20th century to be the basis for some of the provisions of special education law and for many of the most practical and successful strategies for teaching children and youth with emotional and behavioral disorders (see Landrum & Kauffman, in press; Peacock Hill Working Group, 1991; Rutherford et al., 2004).

....

Projects and Organizations of the 1970s, 1980s, and 1990s

Many special projects with long-range implications for children and youth with emotional or behavioral disorders were conducted in the 1970s, most under the sponsorship of federal agencies. We described the Conceptual Models Project in the previous section for two reasons: First, its origins are rooted in the late 1960s, although its reports were published in the 1970s, and the controversy about conceptual models is ongoing; second, it is most relevant to our discussion of conceptual models. In this section, we briefly describe other projects and organizations of the late 20th century that are relevant to special education for students with emotional or behavioral disorders.

Leadership Training

The federal government addressed the need for leadership training in the early 1960s by amending P.L. 85-926 with P.L. 88-164 (extending grants to institutions of higher education to support doctoral-level personnel training in all categorical areas of special education). Many, if not most, of the university faculty who in the 1960s and 1970s began preparing classroom teachers of students with emotional or behavioral disorders completed their doctoral study with the help of grants under P.L. 88-164. That law also provided support for many classroom teachers obtaining their undergraduate or master's degrees in special education in the 1960s and 1970s.

In the early 1970s, the University of Minnesota obtained funding for a grant to establish an Advanced Training Institute directed by Frank H. Wood, who described the history of the institute as follows:

In the early 1970's, several of us who were active in CCBD **[the Council for Children with Behavioral Disorders]** had conversations with Herman Saettler, who at that time carried the EBD portfolio for the Bureau of Education for the Handicapped. Many colleges and universities were developing programs for training teachers in this area with the number of new programs tending to run well ahead of the number of trainers with actual experience in the field graduating from Ph.D. programs. BEH **[the Bureau of Education for the Handicapped]**, under Herman's leadership, had supported the Conceptual Project in Emotional Disturbance at Michigan as one way of providing advanced training in the field. BEH supported a single conference at George Peabody College in 1971, and I think others may have been proposed that were not funded.

Beginning in 1961, Bruce Balow, who headed a psychoeducational diagnostic clinic at the University of Minnesota, planned a series of annual conferences for teachers, psychologists, special education administrators, etc., in Minnesota and the surrounding region which featured presentations by guest speakers such as Bill Morse and others, as well as some of us who were working in the schools. In 1962, Frank Wilderson, who had been a student of Morse's at Michigan, joined the Minnesota faculty and helped plan the conferences. Similar conferences were being held in Michigan and other places at this time. Some of our conferences were co-sponsored with the University of Wisconsin–Madison. At one of these, I first heard Dick Whelan speak. He was still a graduate student at KU at the time, if I remember correctly. Several of the conferences were followed by the publication of a proceedings including papers contributed by the speakers. After Frank Wilderson moved to the Dean's Office, I took over more responsibility for the conferences.

In 1972–73, Herman Saettler and I discussed the idea of a national training and dissemination effort which would include conferences with invited speakers who would also commit to contributing a paper to a proceedings which would be printed and distributed to the field. I wrote up a proposal which was funded as the Advanced Training Institute for Trainers of Teachers for Seriously Emotionally Disturbed Children and Youth. (SED was the federal label at the time. A number of the proceedings titles incorporated the EBD label.) Our overall hope was that the Institute would be a forum to continue the discussion of theoretical perspectives begun by the Conceptual Project while emphasizing the dissemination of information about best practices to the field. There were three components to the program: First,

106

the conferences themselves; second, the dissemination of the sets of papers; third, post-doctoral fellowships to support training program faculty who would come to the University of Minnesota for a quarter.

A statement of purpose printed at the front of some of the Institute's publications says: "The Advanced Institute has as its purpose to provide information to trainers of teachers for seriously emotionally disturbed children and youth on important topics in this field through conferences, internships and publications."

The first two years, the Institute was very generously supported. In addition to covering the costs of the speakers, publications, and post-doc fellows, stipends were provided to help defray some of the cost incurred by those attending the conferences. As BEH grant funds decreased or were diverted to other priorities, some parts of the program such as the stipends and the fellowships had to be dropped so that funds would be available to support the broadened publications program.

A great deal of work was involved in carrying out the Institute program. Success was achieved only with the support of a great many people in the field. At Minnesota, I had the support of two outstanding assistants who lent a hand while completing their doctoral programs: first, Bob (Robert H.) Zabel, and later, Charlie (Kenneth C.) Lakin. A number of the conferences were co-sponsored by scholars at other institutions: University of California–Los Angeles, University of Kentucky, the R. R. Moton Memorial Institute in Washington, DC, and of course, you there at the University of Virginia. The papers were disseminated widely and contributed to a national discussion of issues such as labeling, the use of aversive procedures, and teacher competencies. We had remarkable success with our invited speakers. Not only were the oral presentations well done, but over all those years, very few speakers failed to provide the requested paper. We did provide a stimulus/support in several cases by providing a transcript of the oral presentation. (F. H. Wood, personal communication, June 15, 2004)

Among the major publications of the Institute were Coppock and Wood (1980), Nelson (1978), Wood (1977a, 1977b, 1977c, 1978, 1980), Wood and Lakin (1982a, 1982b), and Wood, Zabel, and Uhlemann (1977). In the late 20th and early 21st centuries, Wood was a major figure in special education for children with emotional or behavioral disorders, influencing the training of many doctoral students and providing postdoctoral experience for many through the Advanced Training Institute (see also Wood, 1987, 2004; Wood, Smith, & Grimes, 1985).

Special Conferences

Numerous conferences of professional organizations have featured sessions on the emotional and behavioral disorders of children and youth. However, two annual professional conferences focused entirely on special education and related services for such children and youth were begun in the 1970s.

In 1977, an annual conference on severe behavior disorders of children and youth was started at Arizona State University (Robert B. Rutherford, personal communication, May 2, 2004). These conferences have been jointly sponsored by Teacher Educators for Children with Behavioral Disorders (TECBD), the Council for Children with Behavioral Disorders (CCBD, a division of the Council for Exceptional Children), and Arizona State University. A monograph series based on the conferences was established in 1978. The first monographs were published by CCBD, but the 1987 and 1988 volumes were published by College-Hill Press as books edited by Rutherford, Nelson, and Forness (1987, 1988). CCBD resumed publishing the monographs from 1989 until 1994, when the journal *Education and Treatment of Children* began publishing the monographs as an annual special issue. By the end of the 20th century, the TECBD conference (as it came to be known), held each year in Arizona in November, attracted a national audience and group of presenters, with foreign registrants and presenters as well.

The Midwest Symposium for Leadership in Behavioral Disorders (MSLBD) was founded in 1982 (Reece Peterson, personal communication, May 6, 2004). In 1983, the first of its annual conferences was held in Kansas City. The MSLBD was in part an outgrowth of earlier Kansas symposia on behavior disorders, which began in 1979. It was organized by faculty members from various midwestern universities (representing initially, besides Kansas, the states of Iowa, Missouri, and Nebraska) who worked cooperatively to provide programs they felt would be of interest to special educators like themselves, and it was generally aligned in purpose with CCBD. By the end of the 20th century, the MSLBD conference typically had a registration of more than 1,000 participants and attracted speakers and registrants from many states in the nation and some foreign countries as well. An outgrowth of the MSLBD was a small, invitational "think tank" conference featuring speakers and discussion on various topics. The first such meeting was on the topic of family and behavior disorders and was held in 1996 in Nebraska. The MSLBD also established annual awards and a scholarship program.

The MSLBD was also involved in various publication efforts. From 1987 to 1989, individuals who attended the conference or were members of CCBD in the four-state region (Iowa, Kansas, Missouri, Nebraska) received a magazine called *Behavior in Our Schools*. Beginning in 1990, the MSLBD sponsored creation of the CCBD publication *Beyond Behavior*. In addition, a book on multicultural education (Peterson & Ishii-Jordan, 1994) grew out of one of the programs of the MSLBD.

Project on the Classification of Exceptional Children

The Project on Classification of Exceptional Children was directed by Nicholas Hobbs in the early 1970s. This project was conducted (at the request of the U.S. secretary of health, education, and welfare) to examine the consequences of labeling exceptional children of all categories, including those with emotional or behavioral disorders. The results (Hobbs, 1975a, 1975b) reflect the stigmatizing and damaging effects of an inadequate classification and labeling process, an issue of intense concern in the first half of the 1970s.

National Needs Analysis

Beginning in the late 1970s, a federally funded project on national needs analysis and leadership training was launched at the University of Missouri. The work of Judith Grosenick and Sharon Huntze documented the unmet needs of children with emotional or behavioral disorders in the nation's schools and outlined many unanswered questions regarding educational programs (Grosenick & Huntze, 1979, 1983).

National Mental Health and Special Education Coalition and Federation of Families for Children's Mental Health

The prospect that all students with emotional or behavioral disorders will be served by special education and mental health remained dim at the turn of the century, as only about 20% of children with serious mental health needs were receiving mental health services in the late 1990s (U.S. Department of Health and Human Services, 2001). However, two important organizations formed in the late 1980s brought new hope of progress.

In 1987, the National Mental Health Association and the Council for Exceptional Children joined efforts to form the National Mental Health and Special Education Coalition (Forness, 1988). The coalition brings together the leadership of diverse groups, including parents, special educators, school psychologists, clinical psychologists, psychiatrists, social workers, and others involved in serving children and youth with emotional or behavioral disorders. It provides a forum for communication among various groups and encourages joint efforts to improve services. It has proposed a new definition and terminology (Forness & Knitzer, 1992), and its continuing efforts are geared toward improving mental health and special education legislation and increasing collaboration among disciplines.

Another important milestone in the field was the organization in 1989 of the Federation of Families for Children's Mental Health. The federation now offers support and advocacy for parents and families of children and youth with emotional or behavioral disorders.

National Juvenile Justice Coalition and National Center on Education, Disability, and Juvenile Justice

Many published works on special education contained chapters on delinquent youths prior to the 1960s. The first book devoted to special education in the criminal justice system, however, was not published until 1987 (Nelson, Rutherford, & Wolford, 1987). In 1989, the National Juvenile Justice Coalition was formed to address problems of education and treatment of youth involved with the juvenile justice system. It brought together a variety of organizations concerned with those young people for the purpose of obtaining a strong national voice for juvenile justice issues.

The curious exclusion of socially maladjusted children who are not emotionally disturbed from the federal definition made providing services to incarcerated youths particularly problematic (Murphy, 1986a, 1986b; Nelson et al., 1987). Incarcerated youths obviously exhibit disordered behavior, and antisocial youngsters are those with the worst prognosis (Kazdin, 1994, 1995, 1998; Patterson, 1986; Patterson, Reid, & Dishion, 1992). Moreover, antisocial behavior or social maladjustment is characteristic of many adolescents with emotional or behavioral disorders (Braaten, 1985). Fortunately, studies of the needs of incarcerated youths for special education and efforts to define appropriate education for youths in prisons and detention centers were funded by the federal government in the 1980s (Rutherford, Nelson, & Wolford, 1985, 1986).

One century after the establishment of the first juvenile courts (that is, in 1999), the National Center on Education, Disability, and Juvenile Justice (EDJJ) was established (see www.edjj.org). EDJJ is a collaborative research, training, and technical assistance and dissemination organization linking the University of Maryland (with a focus on policy studies), the University of Kentucky (focus on prevention), Arizona State University (focus on transition), the PACER center in Minneapolis (focus on parent and family training), and the American Institutes for Research in Washington, DC (focus on policy studies and dissemination). Its funding and activities are overseen by both the Office of Special Education Programs (in the U.S. Department of Education) and the Office of Juvenile Justice (in the Justice Department).

National Agenda

Partly in response to recognition that the outcomes for students with emotional or behavioral disorders were unsatisfactory, the federal government launched a project in the early 1990s to establish a national agenda for education. At that time, it was noted that students with emotional or behavioral disorders typically have low grades and other indications of unsatisfactory academic outcomes, have higher dropout and lower graduation rates than other student groups, are often placed in highly restrictive settings, are disproportionately from poor and minority families, and frequently encounter the juvenile justice system (Chesapeake Institute, 1994; U.S. Department of Education, 1994). The national agenda consisted of the following seven interdependent, strategic targets (notice that the terminology used is that of federal legislation of the era—"serious emotional disturbance," or SED):

Target 1. *Expand Positive Learning Opportunities and Results: To foster the provision of engaging, useful, and positive learning opportunities.*

111

These opportunities should be result-driven and should acknowledge as well as respond to the experiences and needs of children and youths with a serious emotional disturbance.

Target 2. Strengthen School and Community Capacity: *To foster initiatives that strengthen the capacity of schools and communities to serve students with serious emotional disturbance in the least restrictive environments appropriate.*

Target 3. Value and Address Diversity: *To encourage culturally competent and linguistically appropriate exchanges and collaborations among families, professionals, students, and communities. These collaborations should foster equitable outcomes for all students and result in the identification and provision of services that are responsive to issues of race, culture, gender, and social and economic status.*

Target 4. Collaborate with Families: *To foster collaborations that fully include family members on the team of service providers that implements family-focused services to improve educational outcomes. Services should be open, helpful, culturally competent, accessible to families, and school-based as well as community-based.*

Target 5. Promote Appropriate Assessment: *To promote practices ensuring that assessment is integral to identification, design, and delivery of services for children and youths with SED. These practices should be culturally appropriate, ethical, and functional.*

Target 6. Provide Ongoing Skill Development and Support: *To foster the enhancement of knowledge, understanding, and sensitivity among all who work with children and youths who have or who are at risk of developing SED. Support and development should be ongoing and should aim at strengthening the capacity of families, teachers, service providers, and other stakeholders to collaborate, persevere, and improve outcomes for children and youths with SED.*

Target 7. Create Comprehensive and Collaborative Systems: *To promote systems change resulting in the development of coherent services built around the individual needs of children and youths who have or who are at risk of developing SED. These services should be family-centered, community-based, and appropriately funded.* (U.S. Department of Education, 1994, pp. 119–120)

The national agenda was an ambitious statement, and it remains to be seen whether sufficient resources will ever be allocated to make achievement of those targets possible. Also at issue since the targets were published is whether the agenda is sufficiently specific to guide needed changes. It has appeared to some to be a prescription for virtually certain failure because it addresses a little of everything but nothing in sufficient depth to achieve substantive change (Kauffman, 1997).

At the End of the Twentieth Century

At the end of the 20th century, it appeared that the same sad story was repeating itself again and again: We need to be preventive, to intervene early and effectively in the problems that become, eventually, severe emotional and behavioral disorders. The rhetoric is old, and so is the evasion of what is required to replace rhetoric with action to achieve substantive change. Talk is cheap, and talk in vague generalities is particularly inexpensive because anyone who suggests such out-of-focus objectives will never be held accountable for failure to meet them. No one can be held accountable for failure to achieve ill-defined goals or objectives that are not clearly tied to realities. The forces working against preventive programs remained overwhelmingly strong at the end of the 20th century in spite of reliable knowledge that early identification and intervention save money and grief in the long run (Kauffman, 1999c).

5 Perpetual Issues and Their Historical Roots

A T the turn of the 20th century, many difficult issues dogged special education for students with emotional and behavioral disorders. All of the critical issues have deep historical roots. In reviewing several of those issues, we begin with their presentation in the late 20th century, cite references or give examples of earlier (sometimes much earlier) concern for the issues, and return to late 20th-century and early 21st-century perspectives and unresolved problems.

In our view, the issues we discuss are perpetual. They are never likely to be completely resolved, although we believe they can be addressed better or more fully with time. In many cases, the history of our field has shown progress in understanding and addressing important problems. The lack of an ultimate resolution should not be used as an excuse to avoid struggling with an issue.

Definition

In 1997, the language of IDEA changed from the term *seriously emotionally disturbed* to *emotionally disturbed*. This may have represented progress, but the federal definition and terminology remained far from that recommended by the National Mental Health and Special Education Coalition (Forness, 1988; Forness & Knitzer, 1992). Apparently, the definition and terminology suggested by the coalition raised fears of a substantial increase in the number of students identified as having emotional or behavioral disorders, although all indications were that many students with these disorders remained unidentified and unserved (Kauffman, 2005a, 2005b; U.S. Department of Health and Human Services, 2001).

One aspect of the federal definition that made little sense to commentators of the 1980s was the specific *exclusion* of children with autism and the specific *inclusion* of those with schizophrenia. The exclusion of autism and the inclusion of schizophrenia make no sense in the context of Bower's (1960) definition, which is the basis for the federal definition; a rational reading of Bower's definition includes both (see Bower, 1982; Kauffman, 2005a).

Even more bizarre, in the context of Bower's work on identification and the nature of emotional and behavioral disorders, is the federal definition's exclusion of children and youth who are said to be "socially maladjusted but not emotionally disturbed" (see Bower, 1982; Cline, 1990). Nevertheless, controversy regarding the inclusion versus exclusion of socially maladjusted students (which, as far as we can tell, is another way of referring to antisocial behavior or conduct disorder) in the special education category "emotionally disturbed" continued into the 21st century, as did concern for students considered delinquent and adjudicated by juvenile justice (Kauffman, 2005a; Nelson, Leone, & Rutherford, 2004).

The definition of the population of students now typically said to have emotional or behavioral disorders has always been problematic. Regardless of the terminology used to designate these students— *incorrigible, wayward, socially handicapped, socially maladjusted, unstable, emotionally disturbed, delinquent, difficult, atypical,* for example—their clear definition was difficult and depended, to some degree at least, on the profession or agency providing services to them (see Cullinan & Epstein, 1979). We recall Battie's (1758) conclusion that a useful definition (of madness—but we may say of emotional or behavioral disorder) must say precisely what an emotional or behavioral disorder is and what it is not. Stullken (1950) stated the problem for special education succinctly—a problem that has existed as long as the issue of educating children with emotional and behavioral disorders:

> *This chapter is concerned with those who are "exceptional" because of their notable failure to adjust themselves to the behavior pattern of ordinary school situations. There is somewhat greater confusion of terminology in this phase of special education than in those dealing with physically and mentally handicapped children.... The handicaps of children with physical and mental deviations are more distinct and clear-cut than are those which characterize the socially maladjusted.* (p. 281)

Indeed, there is no "test" for emotional and behavioral disorders comparable to the intelligence test for mental retardation, the vision test for partial sightedness or blindness, or the audiogram for definition of hearing loss. The definition and identification of emotional and behavioral disorders are inevitably judgmental matters, in spite of the data one might obtain from observations, rating scales, and other measures (Kauffman, 2005a). Some definitions may be better than others, and some definitions contain obvious absurdities, but none is—or probably can be—entirely objective and nonarbitrary. One of the great unresolved problems of early 21st century special education is how to define emotional and behavioral disorders such that (a) deviance is not confused with legitimate, culturally norma-tive behavior, (b) students are not excluded from the definition based on irrelevant criteria, and (c) false positives (i.e., false identification as having a disorder) and false negatives (i.e., false identification as *not* having a disorder) are both minimized (Merrell & Walker, 2004).

....

Conceptual Models

Some conceptual models of the 1970s were said to be more helpful than others in particular ways (Cullinan, Epstein, & Lloyd, 1991). But conceptual models became more sophisticated, integrative ap-proaches during the 1980s and later decades (Van Hasselt & Hersen, 1991a, 1991b). Based on a melding of behavioral and cognitive re-search, many leaders in the field embraced intervention strategies variously called *cognitive-behavior modification*, *social learning theory*, and *individual psychology* (see Bandura, 1986; Mahoney, 1974; Meichenbaum, 1977; Morse, 1985). These strategies take into consideration how individuals think and feel about their behav-ior as well as how their social environments influence it.

The Conceptual Models Project (Rhodes, 1975; Rhodes & Head, 1974; Rhodes & Tracy, 1972a, 1972b), which we discussed in Chapter 4, summarized the major models of the 1960s and cap-tured their evolution through that decade. However, all of the models underwent considerable additional elaboration and experimentation after the 1960s.

In short, many of the seemingly simplistic notions of earlier de-cades—that behavior can always be modified effectively merely by manipulating its consequences, or that behavior cannot be changed until the student gets insight into the nature of the problem—had

117

been put to rest before the end of the 20th century. By the beginning of the 21st century, many researchers and practitioners understood that best practices ignore neither the realities of human affective and cognitive experiences nor the reality that people's behavior is powerfully influenced by its consequences. Biological, or medical, models of mental illness became much more relevant as brain imaging and genetic studies became increasingly sophisticated (Forness & Kavale, 2001). However, the essence of teaching or instruction and building human relationships is never likely to be fully explained by biological studies. A major problem is the creation of a conceptual model that excludes no essential feature of emotional and behavioral disorders but includes no inessential feature and provides a guide to effective treatment. Conceptual models present, in essence, the same problems as definition does (Kauffman, 2005a).

Inclusion in General Education

During the 1980s and 1990s, some called for a closer working relationship between special and regular education for *all* students with disabilities, almost as if the issue were new. In fact, some proposed a merger or "integration" of regular and special education (e.g., Goodlad & Lovitt, 1993). Some called for abandonment of pullout programs in which students are taught in any setting other than the regular class, calling separate programs "segregated" (e.g., Stainback & Stainback, 1991). These calls for radically integrating or merging were known first as the Regular Education Initiative (REI) (Braaten, Kauffman, Braaten, Polsgrove, & Nelson, 1988; see also Lloyd, Singh, & Repp, 1991). Some immediately recognized and described the problems inherent in proposals to merge special and regular education (e.g., Lieberman, 1985; Mesinger, 1985). Others took longer to point out that problems lay ahead if the proposed merger was to be taken seriously (e.g., Kauffman, 1989, 1991; Walker & Bullis, 1991).

In later years, similar calls for radical reform were called the *full inclusion movement* (Fuchs & Fuchs, 1994, 1995). The probable effects of the REI and full inclusion on teachers, students with emotional or behavioral disorders, and students without disabilities are matters of considerable controversy; and many special educators appear to be

118

skeptical of the outcome (Braaten et al., 1988; Kauffman, 1989, 1991, 1993, 1995, 1999a, 1999f; Kauffman & Hallahan, 1993, 2005b; Kauffman, Lloyd, Baker, & Riedel, 1995; Walker & Bullis, 1991). Although mainstreaming, inclusion, or increased integration may indeed be desirable and feasible for many students, there are questions about the limits to which the concept of integration can be pushed without becoming counterproductive, especially in the case of students with emotional or behavioral disorders (Kauffman et al., 1995; Kavale & Forness, 2000; MacMillan, Gresham, & Forness, 1996; Walker & Bullis, 1991). Some have argued that special classes or schools for students with emotional or behavioral disorders can also be better than regular classes or schools for these students (e.g., Brigham & Kauffman, 1998; Carpenter & Bovair, 1996; Kauffman, Bantz, & McCullough, 2002). The problems of students with disabilities in secondary schools present particularly difficult questions for inclusion (see Kerr, Nelson, & Lambert, 1987; Kerr & Zigmond, 1986). Empirical investigations of the 20th century do not support the full inclusion of all students in general education (MacMillan et al., 1996; Simpson, 2004).

Some may be surprised to find that the concerns of late-20th-century advocates of inclusion have long historical roots. All of the basic issues of segregation versus integration and the relationship between general and special education were raised about a half century before Stainback and Stainback (1984) and Will (1986) brought the field the REI (e.g., Baker, 1934; Berry, 1936; Martin, 1940; Postel, 1937; Rautman, 1944; Tenny, 1944). Before the advent of universal public education and the widespread existence of special education, the issue was moot. But once all states had the expectation that all children would attend school and had special education for students with disabilities, then the relationship of general and special education and the "segregation" of children with disabilities became an issue.

The fundamental issues regarding placement of students with emotional or behavioral disorders have not changed. Our teminology has changed somewhat (from "incorrigible" to "disturbed," for example), but not the problems of how to accommodate differences among students. Horn's (1924) observation that the basic problem of special education is variability in the student population has not changed. Variability among students is a problem recognized by Singer

(1988) and Kauffman and Hallahan (2005b). Zigmond (2003) noted that *where* students should be taught is, perhaps, the wrong question to ask, the better or more important question being *how* they are taught.

Nevertheless, where students are placed for educational purposes, as well as for other forms of treatment, continued through the 20th century and into the 21st as a significant and controversial problem (Crockett & Kauffman, 1999). The problem of placement raises many important questions, but, as Kauffman et al. (1995) pointed out, especially important questions in the case of students with emotional or behavioral disorders include the following:

1. *What effects will the modifications of the regular classroom that are necessary to manage and teach these students have on non-handicapped students? Especially, how will the educational and social development of students who need far less classroom control and structure be affected?*

2. *How will schools justify to parents the placement of students known to be highly volatile, disruptive, and perhaps violent in regular classrooms? Will the physical and psychological safety of other students and the benefits of an orderly learning environment be jeopardized?*

3. *As special schools and classes are eliminated as placement options, what alternatives are most likely to be used for these students?*

4. *What will be the benefits to students with emotional or behavioral disorders of being included in regular classrooms? If they have not previously imitated appropriate peer models or benefitted from the instructional program in the regular classroom, what assurances can be given that they will now imitate prosocial models and benefit from instruction?*

5. *What training would be sufficient to allow regular classroom teachers to deal with these students? What training will regular classroom teachers be given, and when and by whom?*

6. *Which teachers will be asked to include more students with emotional and behavioral disorders in their classrooms? Will the most capable teachers be asked to assume disproportionate and unfair responsibility for these students?*

7. *What additional support services will be provided to regular classroom teachers?*

8. *How will the success of inclusionary programs be assessed? What criteria will be used to ascertain that inclusion is having positive effects on both nondisabled students and those with emotional and behavioral disorders?* (p. 545)

Questions about inclusion are many; reliable answers are few. It appears that the issue is robust, if not perpetual (see Kauffman & Hallahan, 2005a, 2005b).

....

Continuum of Alternative Placements

As we have discussed, inclusion was perhaps one of the most controversial and divisive issues in education in the 1990s (Crockett & Kauffman, 1999; Kauffman & Hallahan, 1995, 2005a; Mock & Kauffman, 2002, 2005). However, federal law (the Individuals with Disabilities Education Act) and regulations of the late 20th and early 21st centuries mandated a continuum of alternative placements (CAP).

Since the early 1960s, the CAP has included the following options:

- *Regular classroom with supports, including aides, counseling, or mental health services*
- *Crisis or resource teachers in regular schools, including consultation with regular classroom teachers and students spending minimum time in the resource room*
- *Self-contained special classes in regular schools, including mainstreaming for part of the school day*
- *Special day schools, including those organized on a cooperative or regional basis*
- *Day treatment or partial hospitalization programs attached to hospitals or residential centers, including those placing some students in regular classrooms in the community*
- *Residential treatment centers and inpatient hospitals, including those sending some students home on weekends and to regular classrooms in the community*
- *Homebound instruction, in which teachers visit students' homes to provide instruction*

- *Schools in juvenile detention centers and prisons.* (Kauffman & Smucker, 1995, pp. 36–37)

As we discussed in Chapter 3, alternative placements, including but not limited to regular classroom placement, have long been recognized as critical to the success of special education. In 1950, Stullken noted the alternatives then existing for "socially maladjusted" children (who today would be called children with emotional or behavioral disorders):

> *The different levels of operation from the simplest to the most complex type include the following personnel and services: (a) the work of the regular classroom teacher in preventing and correcting social maladjustment; (b) the employment of a counselor to assist the teacher when she fails or does not know what to do; (c) the professional services of visiting teachers, school psychologists, and medical consultants; (d) the organization of a special class to try new and different techniques; (e) the establishment of special schools, such as are found in large cities like Chicago, Detroit, and New York; and (f) the use of the custodial school, supported by the city or state.* (pp. 291–292)

Moreover, Stullken (1950) clearly saw the need for the full range of placement options. He noted two particularly relevant points as part of his 12 principles of good practice:

> 2. **Segregation as commonly defined is not a necessary concomitant of the education of socially maladjusted children.** *School administrators should realize that an exceptional child may be more harmfully segregated when kept in a regular class which does not meet his needs than when assigned to a special class which meets his needs much better.* (p. 299)

> 6. **The special-education program for socially maladjusted children should be a part of and not apart from the general educational program.** *The same general objectives for educating normal children hold for educating socially maladjusted children.* (p. 300, emphasis in original)

Others writing before 1960 described the need for a CAP. For example, Morse (1958) included descriptions ranging from regular classroom placement to institutional schools. He noted then what is true in the early 21st century: "Most disturbed children are to be found in regular classrooms" (p. 602). Moreover, many of those who are in regular classrooms are not identified as having emotional or behavioral disorders. In short, the CAP has historically been seen as essential to the education of children with emotional or behavioral disorders.

The suggestion of reformers that the CAP be abandoned in favor of a single placement option (i.e., regular classroom in the neighborhood school), or at least very few placement options, was seen by many special educators of the late 20th century as ill advised, unworkable, and detrimental to many students with disabilities, especially to many with emotional or behavioral disorders (e.g., Kauffman et al., 1995; Mock, Jakubecy, & Kauffman, 2003; Mock & Kauffman, 2005; Morse, 1994).

Throughout history, the purposes of specialized environments for students with emotional or behavioral disorders have been to create and control social ecologies conducive to desirable behavior and mental health. Kauffman and Smucker (1995) listed the following purposes (not necessarily in order of importance):

- *Protecting others (family, community, schoolmates) from children's uncontrolled or intolerable behavior*
- *Protecting children from themselves or others*
- *Educating or training children in academics and other life skills and appropriate emotional responses, attitudes, and conduct*
- *Educating or training children's families or teachers and peers in order to provide a more supportive environment*
- *Keeping children available and amenable to therapies—psychotherapy, pharmacotherapy, or behavior therapy*
- *Providing opportunity for observation and assessment of children's behavior and its contexts.* (p. 37)

It seems extremely unlikely that these purposes can be achieved without a CAP (cf. Gliona, Gonzales, & Jacobson, 2005). Furthermore, meta-analyses (i.e., systematic statistical comparison of evidence from many studies) of the 20th century indicated that students placed in self-contained classrooms have been more likely than those placed in general education to show improved achievement and decreases in disruptive behavior (e.g., Carlberg & Kavale, 1980; Stage & Quiroz, 1997).

....

Early Identification and Early Intervention: Prevention

The issue of special education's service to very young children with emotional or behavioral disorders was highlighted in the 1980s, and calls for early identification and intervention persisted in the decades after. In 1986, the U.S. Congress extended the requirements of Public Law 94-142 (now IDEA) to all children with disabilities between ages 3 and 5. The law applied even in states that did not provide free public education to nondisabled children in this age group. The law also included incentives for states to develop early intervention programs for infants with disabilities and infants at risk, from birth to age 36 months.

Regardless of the emphasis on early identification and intervention and data suggesting that earlier intervention is more effective (e.g., Walker et al., 2004), most children with emotional or behavioral disorders were not identified in schools and communities in the late 20th and early 21st centuries. In fact, students with emotional or behavioral disorders were typically known to have serious problems for years prior to their identification (Duncan, Forness, & Hartsough, 1995). Early intervention and prevention remained, in late 20th-century America, primarily a rhetorical reality (Kauffman, 1999c, 2005b), in spite of our knowledge that letting emotional or behavioral problems fester until they become serious or dangerous is self-defeating.

The problems inherent in early identification and prevention have been well understood for many years (e.g., Bower, 1960; Caplan, 1961; Ingram & Schumacher, 1950; Martens & Russ, 1932; Stevenson, 1944; Stullken, 1950), yet few measures to address the problems of prevention on any widespread basis have been taken. Stullken recommended in his principles of good practice that *"school systems should provide for early identification and early diagnosis of children who are mal-adjusted"* and recommended early intervention as well "to prevent problems from becoming acute" (p. 300, emphasis in original). In his Chapter 32, which included a section on prevention of "social handicap," Heck (1940) stated,

> society is much more willing to provide for the immediate and observable needs of children than to spend money on programs of prevention, which would ultimately mean far more to society and to our children; distant values seem hard to visualize. (p. 495)

Not much changed in the following 65 years, and the statement still had currency in the early 21st century (cf. Kauffman, 1999c; 2004a, 2004b, 2005b). We know that the early signs of emotional and behavioral disorders can be detected through careful observation or use of reliable screening instruments (Bierman et al., 2002; Conroy, Hendrickson, & Hester, 2004; Denham, Blair, Schmidt, & DeMulder, 2002; Ialongo, Vaden-Kiernan, & Kellam, 1998; Loeber, Farrington, Stouthamer-Loeber, & Van Kammen, 1998a, 1998b; Loeber, Green, Lahey, Christ, & Frick, 1992; Strain & Timm, 2001; Tobin & Sugai, 1999; Walker, Kavanagh, et al., 1998; Walker & Severson, 1990; Walker, Severson, & Feil, 1994). In summarizing the implications of their massive longitudinal study of antisocial boys, Loeber et al. (1998a) stated,

> interventions should deal with early problem behaviors in an attempt to prevent their escalation to serious levels. Particular candidates are physical fighting, covert behaviors, and chronic disobedience, which we assume ... are keystone behaviors in the development of more serious acts. (p. 267)

Walker and Sprague (1999) and Kingery and Walker (2002) detailed how antisocial behavior develops and what we can do about it. However, the fact that educators know the path to long-term negative outcomes does not mean that they or anyone else will intervene early to change the child's course. For decades, educators and psychologists have known that intervention should be early in two ways: (a) early in the child's life and (b) in the early stages of misbehavior regardless of the person's age (Hester & Kaiser, 1998; Kamps & Tankersley,

125

1996; Kauffman, 1999a, 1999c, 2003a, 2005b; Strain & Timm, 2001; Walker, Ramsey, & Gresham, 2004; Walker & Sprague, 1999). Early intervention—both types—is the essence of prevention; yet early identification, intervention, and prevention remain unresolved problems in the early 21st century.

Will schools use the knowledge and tools we have to identify students early, before problems become very serious? Having identified the students, will schools take preventive action? These are the same questions raised by Bower in 1960 and by many others in the intervening years. The answers are in doubt in the early 21st century for reasons both readily apparent and exasperating (Kauffman, 1999c, 2003a, 2003b, 2004b, 2005b).

One sure way to thwart prevention is to deny the student's deviance. The denial of deviance has been common among people of all colors, both sexes, adults and children, and people of vastly different political persuasions. In the late 20th and early 21st centuries, it was politically unacceptable to define as deviant any behavior viewed as merely "cultural" or typical of a given group (Hendershott, 2002). Furthermore, "what is judged to be 'mild' deviance is often ignored, while those acts viewed as 'very deviant' elicit demands for severe sanctions" (Hendershott, 2002, p. 82).

Mild deviance is a clear warning sign that trouble lies ahead. However, warning signs are often ignored, and minor deviance is allowed to escalate to hurtful if not lethal levels before action is taken. "Better safe than sorry" is a bromide not often applied to the questionable behavior of children and youth. Although early identification and prevention are compelling ideas embraced by many special educators and psychologists of the 21st century (see Bierman et al., 2002; Eddy, Reid, & Curry, 2002; Walker & Shinn, 2002), turning these ideas into coherent, consistent, sustained action will require scientific and political finesse that past generations could not muster.

....

Transition to Work or Post–High School Education

In the late 1980s, programs at the secondary level, particularly the transition from school to work, became a national priority in special education. Many students with serious, if not severe, disabilities, particularly those with emotional or behavioral disorders and learning disabilities, were known to drop out or be elbowed out of high schools (Bullis & Cheney, 1999; Edgar, 1987; Edgar & Siegel, 1995; Wagner, 1991). Most of these students, in addition to being disabled, were found to be poor minority males.

Since its inception, however, special education has been concerned with preparing students for the world of work after the typical school years, simply because public education has been rife for decades with controversy about whether secondary education should be preparation for work or higher education—or both (see Miller, Ewing, & Phelps, 1980; see also MacMillan & Hendrick, 1993). Miller et al. noted that the vocational education movement has had its staunch supporters and ardent opponents since the early 20th century. Those emphasizing the liberal arts curriculum and preparation of high school students for college, even in the 1920s, 1930s and 1940s, saw vocational education as breaking down standards and selling students short. Students with emotional or behavioral disorders, whether called "truants," "incorrigibles," "delinquents," or some other label, were often considered problematic in both vocational and liberal arts curricula. Morgan (1937) observed,

> *Vocational guidance based on ability alone will always be subject to the drawback that it does not consider emotional outlets for buried mental conflicts. One may have the intelligence to do a certain type of work, but if that work is constantly bringing to the foreground some mental disturbance, the individual will loathe his work and never make a success of it.* (p. 326)

Should we make greater efforts to integrate students with emotional or behavioral disorders into high school academic programs that do not meet their needs and in which their continued presence or success is highly unlikely? Or should these students be offered a special curriculum, a separate educational track? Edgar (1987) stated the difficult choices succinctly:

> *What a dilemma—two equally appalling alternatives, integrated mainstreaming in a nonfunctional curriculum which results in horrendous out-*

*comes (few jobs, high dropout rate) or separate, segregated programs for
an already devalued group, a repugnant thought in our democratic society.*
(p. 560)

The primary controversy about transition involves the curriculum
and the placement options that should be available at the secondary
level to students with disabilities (Bullis & Cheney, 1999; Cheney
& Bullis, 2004; Edgar & Siegel, 1995). Plans for the transition of students with emotional or behavioral disorders may become especially
controversial because of the problems Edgar (1987) noted. First, the
curriculum for college-bound high school students may be inappropriate for the interests, life goals, and abilities of some students with
disabilities, even with special supports in regular classes. Forcing all
students into classes of either type not only fails to prepare them for
technical education or work but also creates an environment in which
students are likely to misbehave, fail, and drop out. Second, any alternative curriculum or placement option makes the student vulnerable
to stigma, neglect, and second-class status. Any alternative to inclusion in the regular, college-bound curriculum is bound to bring charges
of discrimination, tracking, and abuse.

In the early 1990s, the reports of the National Longitudinal Transition Study (NLTS), a major effort to assess the outcomes of secondary
education for students with disabilities, were filed. As summarized by
the U.S. Department of Education (1995),

> *the NLTS shows that secondary school programs can produce post-school
> benefits for students with disabilities—but only for students who can suc-
> ceed in them. Perhaps the greatest positive contribution schools can make
> to the post-school success of students with disabilities is to contribute to the
> in-school success of those students, regardless of their placement. As the
> inclusion movement gains momentum, great care must be paid to issues of
> quality and support.* (p. 88)

Individualized or differentiated education is always controversial
simply because not all students are treated the same. If all students
are not treated the same, then we assume that some are treated un-
fairly. We have great difficulty reconciling difference and equality

in spite of our commitment as special educators to individualization (Johns, 2003).

The dilemmas inherent in helping secondary students plan for life after school are not easily resolved. Maybe they are perpetual and unresolvable. In any event, they are likely to be issues with which people of every generation will have to struggle throughout their professional lives. Answers to the problem will differ, depending on the individual student's abilities, preferences, and disability. Decisions based on the student's categorical label are manifestly illegal and are not supported by special education's premise of individual planning.

....

Education of Antisocial, Violent, and Delinquent Students

In late-20th-century American culture, youth violence became a major problem demanding intervention on multiple fronts (American Psychological Association, 1993; Flannery, 1999; Flannery & Huff, 1999; Furlong & Morrison, 1994; Kauffman, 1994; Kauffman & Burbach, 1997; Walker et al., 2004). In fact, the education of antisocial and violent students became a central issue in both general and special education in the 1990s, in part because of high-profile school shootings. The education of incarcerated and delinquent youth was also highlighted (Leone, Rutherford, & Nelson, 1991; Nelson, Leone, & Rutherford, 2004; Nelson et al., 1987).

However, antisocial, delinquent, and violent behavior in schools and communities has been a perplexing issue for a very long time (Achenbach, 1975; Dorney, 1967; Graubard, 1976; Healy, 1915; Healy & Bronner, 1969; Kreuter, 1967; Nelson, Rutherford, & Wolford, 1987; Rothman, 1971). Juvenile delinquency has been a concern of educators and psychologists for well over a century, and it has played a major role in special education for students with emotional or behavioral disorders for decades. In fact, in Volume 3 of their massive work *Special Education for the Exceptional*, Frampton and Gall (1956) included a chapter on juvenile delinquency (Suerken & Bloch, 1956).

Youth violence remains a great concern in the early 21st century, although violent crime in general is on a downward trajectory

(Furlong, Morrison, & Jimerson, 2004). Usually, children and youth show warning signs that they are likely to exhibit violent behavior, so research and recommendations sometimes emphasize looking for the precursors of violent acts. Precursors are usually such things as aggressive talk, talk of aggression, threats, intimidation, and various forms of bullying. Best practices include intervention to stop such precursors of more serious problems (e.g., Lerman & Vorndran, 2002; Smith & Churchill, 2002). Violent behavior and its precursors are complex and demand that we struggle with difficult questions. For example, one might consider the following:

- When is antisocial, violent behavior legitimately declared a disability, and when should it be considered criminal or delinquent behavior for which special education is inappropriate?
- What level of antisocial and violent behavior can be tolerated in a general education classroom?
- If students cross the line of what is tolerable in a classroom or school, then where and how should their education be continued?
- What means of controlling violent and antisocial behavior are legitimate?
- How can schools best function as a part of a larger community effort to lessen antisocial and violent behavior?

Decades of research suggest how some of these questions might be addressed (American Psychological Association, 1993; Kazdin, 1998, 2001; McMahon & Wells, 1998; Walker et al., 2004). However, the educational treatment of students who bring weapons to school, threaten and intimidate their peers or teachers, disrupt the education of their classmates, or are incarcerated will likely be controversial for decades to come. Discipline of students with disabilities, especially those with learning disabilities or emotional or behavioral disorders, is a controversial and critical issue involving IDEA and other education laws (Dupre, 1996, 1997, 2000; Huefner, 2000; Yell, 1998; Yell, Rogers, & Rogers, 1998; Yell & Shriner, 1997).

Comprehensive, Collaborative, Community-Based Services

A strong trend of the late 20th century was the integration of a variety of services for children and families. Such integrated services were often considered "wrapped around" children in their homes and communities. "Wraparound" services were thought to have the advantage of serving children in their typical environments rather than sending them to a succession of intervention programs in other places. These attempts to coordinate and improve the effectiveness of multiple social service programs such as special education, child protective services, child welfare, foster care, and so on were built on the observation that individual programs are seldom sufficient to meet children's needs and that a closer working relationship of all service providers is required (Clark & Clarke, 1996; Clarke, Schaefer, Burchard, & Welkowitz, 1992; Eber & Keenan, 2004; Epstein, Kutash, & Duchnowski, 1998; Nelson & Pearson, 1991; Quinn, Epstein, & Cumblad, 1995; Zanglis, Furlong, & Casas, 2000).

Making the school a center for social welfare programs of all kinds is an idea that originated long ago (Rothman & Berkowitz, 1967b). As we pointed out in Chapter 3, even in the 1920s, some people had the idea of providing mental health services in schools (e.g., Blanton, 1925). Rothman and Berkowitz (1967a) described a clinical school that included professional training for teachers, research, welfare, therapy, dental and medical services, legal services, and a citizens' group program in addition to teaching (see pp. 356–369). This is the kind of "one-stop shopping" or coordinated, integrated service program envisioned by many advocates thought to be "innovative" in the late 20th and early 21st centuries.

The idea of comprehensive, coordinated social services, including general and special education, delivered through the neighborhood school is compelling. It is particularly appealing in the case of children whose lives are in great disarray, as is the case with many children who have emotional or behavioral disorders and are also in foster care. However, implementing the ideas and demonstrating that the service delivery system is effective are far from simple. The idea of wraparound services is confronted with several practical problems.

First, simply combining inadequate services will not solve many problems. Many communities have a variety of social services that are insufficient to meet children's needs. If individual agencies have too few resources, then the combined or integrated service delivery system, too, will leave many children ill served.

Second, creating the needed expertise to offer integrated services is expensive, and voters in many states and communities appear unwilling to fund them. If wraparound services are going to be adequate in the long run, they must have highly trained personnel who can coordinate a sufficient number of adequately trained direct-service personnel. Serving difficult children and youth is highly personnel intensive, and there is no shortcut or cheap path to the goal.

Third, the idea of providing varied services through local schools inevitably becomes enmeshed in controversies about what schools are for. In many communities, schools are poorly funded even to accomplish their academic goals for students, and those who control the schools seem reluctant to expand their mission to include collaborative work with other social agencies.

Whether wraparound services become a reality in many American communities will depend on how Americans come to view their schools and value their children. Barring a dramatic change in the political will of the nation, the promise of the ideal will remain unfulfilled, at least well into the 21st century. There is a huge gap between rhetoric and practice on this issue, just as there is in early identification and prevention. Many American children still live in poverty, and many who are emotionally disturbed do not receive mental health services (Knitzer, 1982; Knitzer & Aber, 1995; U.S. Department of Health and Human Services, 2001). Dwyer and Bernstein observed that in the late 20th century, "In reality, services are often provided in a series of uncoordinated, unmeasured interventions.... Schools tend to rely on interventions that are short-term and narrowly focused when responding to students who create disruptions or experience serious problems and disabilities" (1998, p. 278).

Focus on Academic and Social Skills

Following the report of Knitzer, Steinberg, and Fleisch (1990) indicating that special educators of children with emotional or behavioral disorders tended to focus on behavioral control and neglect academic instruction, there was increased concern about the quality of instruction in special education programs for these students. Knitzer and her colleagues suggested that in far too many classrooms serving these students, the emphasis is almost exclusively on controlling acting-out behavior, meaning that students were being given neither the academic proficiency nor the social skills they need to be reintegrated into general education or become employable adolescents and adults.

However, special educators of the 1950s and 1960s understood that excellent academic and vocational instruction, as well as improvement in social skills, were important for students with emotional or behavioral disorders (e.g., Fenichel, 1966; Haring & Phillips, 1962; Hewett, 1968; Morse, 1958; Motto & Wilkins, 1968; Rothman & Berkowitz, 1967c; Wright, 1967). True, social-interpersonal behavior and general intelligence were always assumed also to be important issues, but academics and vocational training were not forgotten. In 1958, Morse commented about curriculum and teaching methods for "emotionally disturbed" children:

> In over-all perspective, the curriculum for the disturbed child follows a modern, well-planned educational program. The skills of reading, language, numbers, and social relationships are always vitally important. The arts, social studies, and science studies are major concerns. More separation of content takes place throughout the junior high school level where material may be organized around unified studies, English and social studies on the one hand, and science and mathematics on the other.... With older adolescents vocational preparation assumes major importance. Again, following the philosophy of modern education for normal children, a broad range of play activities, physical education, and extracurricular programs round out the picture.
>
> In short, the educational birthright of the normal certainly belongs to the special pupil as well. The old idea that, since they were different, one must

wait until they are in good mental health before they can be taught has been left behind. (pp. 584–585)

From its inception, special education as an enterprise has been concerned with teaching academic and vocational skills to those students who have extraordinary difficulty with the standard curriculum (cf. MacMillan & Hendrick, 1993). There are clear indications from the historical literature that academic achievement was of concern to special educators of students with emotional and behavioral disorders, although social learning and adjustment and preparation for work were also critical issues. Perhaps Knitzer et al. (1990) highlighted a lost priority (see also Colvin, 1992), but concerns for special instruction and academic achievement were not absent from special education's beginning.

By the early 21st century, special educators clearly recognized and stated that effective instruction is at the heart of both special education and behavior management (e.g., Kauffman, Mostert, Trent, & Pullen, 2006; Kerr & Nelson, 2002; Lane, 2004; Walker et al., 2004; Witt, VanDerHeyden, & Gilbertson, 2004). In fact, researchers of the 1990s devised procedures in which teachers approach predictable misbehavior as an instructional problem and devise teaching procedures for desirable behavior similar to those used for academic instruction (e.g., Colvin, Sugai, & Patching, 1993; Walker, Colvin, & Ramsey, 1995). Emphasis on teaching seems likely to continue indefinitely for at least two reasons. First, good instruction has been shown by researchers to be the first line of defense in behavior management. That is, a good instructional program prevents many behavior problems from arising, and an emphasis on instruction is compatible with the clearest mission of public schools. Researchers are helping teachers understand how the classroom conditions they create and the instructional procedures they use may contribute to behavior problems and their resolution (e.g., Kauffman et al., 2006; Kerr & Nelson, 2002; Walker et al., 2004). Second, empirical evidence to support an instructional approach to behavioral problems is accumulating, and a clear consensus may be reached that teaching appropriate behavior explicitly is a central mission of special education programs (Landrum & Kauffman, in press). Given that teaching both academics and appropriate social behavior is seen as the central role of schools, there may be less tolerance for programs in which the objectives are merely behavioral containment. Mere suppression of misbehavior has never been a sufficient outcome for those who take special education seriously.

Multicultural Special Education

The rapidly changing age, social class, and ethnic demographics of the United States brought multicultural concerns to the forefront of educators' and psychologists' thinking in the 1990s. Serving students with any type of exceptionality demands understanding of multicultural issues (Gay, 1998; Gibbs & Huang, 1997; Hallahan & Kauffman, 2006). Teaching students with emotional or behavioral disorders requires particularly keen attention to the distinctive cultural aspects of behavior and behavioral change as well as to the principles that are common to all cultures (Kauffman, 2005a; Peterson & Ishii-Jordan, 1994).

There seems to be little in the historical literature that parallels the late 20th- and early 21st-century concept of multicultural education. The cultural factors discussed prior to the late 1960s and early 1970s tended to be class distinctions, socioeconomic levels, family problems, and other social issues rather than ethnic identity (cf. Morse, 1958; Stullken, 1950).

Beginning in the late 1960s and early 1970s, however—and concomitant with the civil rights movement—there was emphasis on the relationship between ethnicity and special education (e.g., Johnson, 1969, 1971). Johnson (1969) seemed to suggest that at least in some cases, African American students were misidentified as having emotional or behavioral disorders when they did not have such problems. This concern seems to have developed into the heightened concern of the late 20th and early 21st century with disproportional representation of ethnic groups in special education (see Donovan & Cross, National Research Council, 2002; Hosp & Reschly, 2004; Osher et al., 2004). The concern does not appear to have been prompted by the conceptual models of the 1960s (see the relative absence of discussion of ethnic issues in Rhodes, 1975; Rhodes & Head, 1974; Rhodes & Tracy, 1972a, 1972b).

Historically, multiculturalism in special education is a relatively recent phenomenon. However, it raises questions of historical significance, among them the following:

- How can emotional or behavioral disorders be identified or assessed without any cultural bias?
- What emotional expressions and social behavior are normative and what is considered deviant in the student's culture?
- If emotions or behavior of given description are normative in a particular culture, does that mean they are acceptable in U.S. culture?
- What interventions are acceptable in the student's culture?
- If an intervention is effective across all cultural groups, should it be avoided if it is considered unacceptable or inappropriate in the student's culture?
- How might deviance be attributed in part to racism, sexism, and other forms of discrimination?

The challenge of multicultural education is not new. Americans have always faced the daunting task of dealing with cultural diversity (National Research Council, 2002). Historically, the U.S. has failed, as have most if not all other nations of the world, to provide an overarching or general culture that is inviting to and supportive of all of the desirable subcultures it comprises. To have a general culture that welcomes differences, multiculturalism must focus primarily on the common humanity of all people who constitute the larger culture regardless of their cultural heritage, as giving greater attention to differences than to commonalities will merely perpetuate the cultural conflicts of the nation (see Kauffman, 1999b, 2002; Singh, 1996). Fostering a common culture in a multicultural society in one nation is an enormous task. But perhaps, as Cohen (2004) suggests, bridging the cultural chasms that divide some nations of the world is considerably more difficult.

Personnel Preparation

Training, attracting to the task, and retaining highly competent personnel, including teachers, have always been problematic. Working with disturbed individuals, including students who have emotional or behavioral disorders, is difficult and sometimes frightening or dangerous. The working conditions of many teachers of children with emotional or behavioral disorders have been considerably less than ideal (Billingsley, 2004; McManus & Kauffman, 1991). Furthermore, teaching such students in any setting, but especially in an environment in which there is little support for or understanding of the task, is not one for which many individuals have much stamina.

But these are not new problems. In Chapter 2, we quoted Ray's (1852) comments on the difficulty of finding good attendants for institutions, as well as Hobbs's (1966) description of the ideal teacher-counselor. In fact, nearly all of those who have written seriously and extensively about special education for students with emotional or behavioral disorders have commented on the difficulty of finding and training good personnel. Stullken (1950) noted that teachers who work with socially maladjusted children need to have a good personality and that no amount of training can make up for personal problems of teachers. He also expressed the belief that this means the teacher must not be "irritable, fussy, or infantile" (p. 298). The teacher must be able to teach by example, respect the child's personality and show respect to the child as an individual, have a good sense of humor, have the knack of placing people and events in proper perspective, be adaptable and flexible, and have both a normal range of human contacts outside of school and a wholesome approach to life. But, of course, finding enough such individuals, who are what Ray (1852) called "shining ornaments of the [human] race" and want to be teachers of students with emotional or behavioral disorders, is an extraordinary challenge.

Stullken's principles of good practice included the following:

Any program of education for the socially maladjusted will be conditioned by the selection of properly qualified and trained personnel.

The teacher must have personal qualifications suitable for the task in hand and should have training which is particularly adapted to the requirements of working with problem children. Also, sufficient experience to be able to handle maladjusted children without becoming confused because of lack of familiarity with the mere mechanics of teaching is important. (1950, pp. 300–301)

Morse (1958) remarked that the educational consequences of any system design cannot be greater or better than the teacher. He concluded,

There are times when a difficult child receives more help from the regular classroom than from the special service. So much depends upon the teacher. Is there a way of selecting those who will make the good teachers in this area? What types of training are necessary? What is the function of self insight? … It is obvious that special teachers must obtain satisfactions of a somewhat different nature than the regular teacher. Since the emotional demands of this type of work are greater, how can these teachers be given support on the job? (p. 603)

In the late 20th and early 21st centuries, identifying teachers who will be successful with students who have emotional or behavioral disorders remains a puzzle, and specifying the training they should have to be considered well qualified is still controversial (see Bullock & Gable, 2004; Gelman, Pullen, & Kauffman, 2005). The field remains uncertain about how to prevent entry into it or rid itself of teachers whose mentalalth is precarious or worse (McGee & Kaufmann, 1989). The reauthorization of IDEA in late 2004 did not adequately address the issue of "highly qualified" teachers of students with emotional or behavioral disorders.

6 Postscript

AFTER reviewing the history of our field, we might reasonably ask, "Where do we go from here?" You may be reading this long after our writing, and so you may have a vantage point that we do not have. The "here" to which we refer is the middle of the first decade of the 21st century. Soon, this era, too, will be written about as history (see Cole, 2005). We can only speculate about the verdict on our era. Kauffman, Brigham, and Mock (2004) suggested the following from their early-21st-century location in time:

> *Progress may be possible, but so is regression. We hope that the future of research in behavior disorders will be marked by a renewal of interest in and commitment to scientific investigation. That is the only hope we see of advancement or progress, which we believe means learning more about the nature of emotional and behavioral disorders and getting better at teaching students with such disorders.* (p. 26)

Kauffman et al. (2004) expressed grave concerns that the slow but steady progress promised by science has been routinely denigrated and might well be completely derailed by promises of quicker fixes or simply faddish thinking. Examples of unscientific and even antiscientific thinking abound throughout our history, with so-called postmodern thought providing the most recent example of the abandonment of science at the outset of the 21st century:

> *Research in behavior disorders may continue on the path of scientific discovery or be sidetracked or hijacked by ideologies. In this respect, the field of behavior disorders is no different from other fields of study, such as psychology. As one writer noted of postmodernism, "All it can offer, by its own admission, is word games—word games that lead nowhere and achieve nothing. Like anthrax of the intellect, if allowed into mainstream psychology, postmodernism will poison the field" (Locke, 2002, p. 458). Sasso (2001) described postmodern ideology as a retreat from knowledge. Kauffman (2002) noted how postmodernism can poison the well of knowledge.*

> *Heward (2003) and Heward and Silvestri (2005) detailed how the ideas associated with postmodernism harm the effectiveness of special education. Ideas have consequences, and the field of behavior disorders must come to grips with the extremely negative consequences of postmodernism and related ideologies.* (p. 26)

Kauffman et al. (2004) may well be wrong in their assessment of the direction of the field and the influence of postmodernism and other ideologies. Objectivity about the past is difficult, and such objectivity can never be absolute. However, prediction contains even greater sources of error, and it must be offered with great trepidation.

Rhodes's 1970s speculation that "there will be the beginning of profound and radical changes in caring, caretaking, and human services in the next decade" (1975, p. 92) seems to have missed the mark by a considerable margin, unless he foresaw the undoing of human services. He also predicted that "within the next decade, a new perception of human services will emerge" (Rhodes, 1975, p. 93), but it seems not to have occurred to him that the change could be in a negative direction and that human services would come to be viewed as a waste of public money and a failed government effort to improve citizens' lives (see Edelman, 2001; Kauffman, 1996, 2003b). In short, Rhodes's predictions from the perspective of the mid-1970s seem to have been profoundly wrong. But, in fairness, it would have been extremely difficult, if not impossible, to anticipate in that era, based on the events of the 1960s and early 1970s, the conservative drift of government beginning in about 1980 or the radical religious, political, and social conservatism of the late 20th and early 21st centuries.

We are now faced with the consequences of substantial disinvestment in the social welfare programs of government, including education. Jails, detention centers, and the streets are the primary residences of most adults and many children with serious mental illness, just as in the mid-19th century when Dorothea Dix was working to found social institutions. In our view, this is regressive change, not progressive change. But in the early 21st century, we saw regressive action combined with seductive, dissembling language that promised one thing and delivered the opposite. For example,

Prominent casualties [of the George W. Bush administration's policies]
include child care assistance for working mothers and federal aid for needy
college students. The latest victim appears to be Section 8, the government's
main housing program for the poor. The program provides rent subsidies for
two million of the country's most vulnerable families and encourages private
developers to build affordable housing.

Section 8 subsidies go primarily to families that live at or below the
poverty level, in households that include children, disabled people or the el-
derly.... Having paid lip service to the goal of ending chronic homelessness,
the Bush administration is now threatening to kill off the only program that
could possibly achieve it. ("Killing Off Housing," 2004)

Similar rhetoric masked unsympathetic policy decisions that
threatened special education in the early 21st century (Kauffman,
2004b, 2005c; Kauffman & Wiley, 2004). With reference to the
George W. Bush administration's policy toward women and public
health, Cocco (2004) wrote, "Its cloak is the language of compassion.
Its core is reactionary and extreme" (p. A6). But cloaking policy in
euphemism and other pretense had become common practice in special education and related fields by the early 21st century (Kauffman,
2003a).

Perhaps our only chance of making any predictions that are not
wildly inaccurate is to note that optimism and pessimism about social deviance seem to follow waves or cycles, as noted by Achenbach
(1974). Very likely, there are ups and downs in constructive social
welfare programs, just as there are in business cycles. We do not know
when the next turn in direction will occur or in which direction public policy will turn. We profoundly hope that things will not turn out
eventually as Rhodes (1975) predicted regarding counter theory (although we do hope that human services will become more humane and
more effective). We do not think that a return to pre-Renaissance understanding of and responses to social deviance would result in kinder
or gentler or more effective responses to social deviance. If history
suggests anything with certainty, it is that the abandonment of rationality, empiricism, and scientific inquiry are followed by vicious ideologies, mysticism, and persecutions (see Conquest, 2000; Gould, 1997a;
Hecht, 2003). Thus we are not sanguine about the antithesis point of

view suggested by Rhodes (1975), which "accepts nonrational states of being, experiences, and perceptions as equal with rationality" (p. 88), or about suggestions that all ideas should be treated equally (e.g., Danforth, 2001).

Nearly any scenario is possible to imagine, including a return to prescientific attitudes toward and "treatment" of social deviance in a theocracy or, alternatively, the resurgence of Enlightenment ideas and a flowering of government social welfare programs in which best practices are based to the greatest extent possible on scientific evidence. Our personal preference is for the latter, but we make no predictions.

Those of us engaged in the education of students with emotional or behavioral disorders often see the dark side, the ugly side of social deviance—both the deviance of people with the disorders and, sometimes, the deviance of the people offering "treatment." The late Stephen Jay Gould (1997a) offered a caution about the abandonment of rationality:

> Only two possible escapes can save us from the organized mayhem of our dark potentialities—the side that has given us crusades, witch hunts, enslavements, and holocausts. Moral decency provides one necessary ingredient, but not nearly enough. The second foundation must come from the rational side of our mentality. For, unless we rigorously use human reason both to discover and acknowledge nature's factuality, and to follow the logical implications for efficacious human action that such knowledge entails, we will lose out to the frightening forces of irrationality, romanticism, uncompromising "true" belief, and the apparent resulting inevitability of mob action. Reason is not only a large part of our essence; reason is also our potential salvation from the vicious and precipitous mass action that rule by emotionalism always seems to entail. Skepticism is the agent of reason against organized irrationalism—and is therefore one of the keys to human social and civic decency. (p. x)

Much of what happens depends on economic and political conditions, and it is difficult to know how these factors will affect science and social welfare. In the early 21st century, there was a resurgence of fundamentalist religion (Armstrong, 2000), much of it inimical to modern science. As one writer put it, "Tribalists and fundamentalists have identified cosmopolitanism and modernity as their arch-enemy" (Neier, 2001, p. A29). All fundamentalist religions, whether Christian, Islamic, Judaic, or other, are deeply suspicious of many modern, scientific ideas and of the skepticism of scientists (Armstrong, 2000).

In late-20th-century and early-21st-century special education, there was a resurgence of nihilism and the multirealist notions embraced by Rhodes and others in the 1960s (e.g., Brantlinger, 1997; Danforth & Rhodes, 1997; Gallagher, 2004; Sailor & Paul, 2004; P. Smith, 1999, 2001). As we noted in Chapter 4, similar anti-empirical and anti-rationalist ideas were expressed by ancient philosophers as well (Hecht, 2003), so it is clear that these notions about the nature of reality and rationality are not new. Several writers have pointed out the absurdity of these notions for educators (e.g., Kauffman, 2002; Mostert, Kauffman, & Kavale, 2003; Ruscio, 2002; Sasso, 2001). Ruscio commented,

> Genuine belief in the nonexistence of external reality also renders education meaningless. If there is no reality—nothing "out there" to know about—then one cannot "teach" or "learn" anything aside from direct personal experience. Given that the relatively few individuals who claim to endorse this extreme version of postmodernism are employed by academic institutions, this situation is both amusing (because they appear to have chosen a futile direction for their lives' work) and troubling (because they are exposing students to such unfounded ideas).
>
> The tolerance for logical contradictions presents another puzzle. If it is the case that "truth is relative," that what is true for one person might be false for another, how can a society function at all?...
>
> In fact, the fuzzy thinking that embraces contradictions breaks down in any real-world scenario. The attempt to relieve the sting of error by elevating all ideas to an equally acceptable status through sheer force of will is a reckless practice with dangerous consequences. (pp. 99–100)

Some special educators have warned of reckless practices and dangerous consequences associated with the multirealist (postmodern) views (e.g., Mostert et al., 2003; Sasso, 2001). According to multirealism, what is real or true cannot be determined objectively, as there are equally real or true or valid assertions based on subjective realities. The consequences of the multirealist view for special education, no matter whether under the banner of counter theory, postmodernism, holism, or anything else, are severe and negative (Mostert et al., 2003). Such an approach denigrates knowledge and makes impossible any reliable distinction of fact from fiction (Sasso, 2001).

If truth is variable, "floating," not objectively verifiable, then calls for social justice are merely calls for power or dominance. The truth is the first casualty of multirealist philosophy, simply because what is ostensibly the truth is determined only by the dominant power's calling something "truth." In spite of calls for moral judgment and social justice by those who promote multirealist philosophies, neither moral judgment nor social justice can be attained using such philosophies. Multirealism corrupts not just special education but the political process on which it depends. Writing in *defense* of liberal ideals, Reich (2004) observed that in politics,

> many liberals have adopted a kind of moral relativism; no single version of morality is superior to any other. By this view, abuses of power may violate legal or economic principles, but they don't raise moral issues.
> This is a dangerous cop-out. (p. 54)

Thus have supposedly liberal ideas been allowed to undermine liberal ideals. Whether such warnings will be dismissed as hyperbole and be ignored, be overwhelmed by multirealist (postmodern) philosophy, bring renewed commitment to reliable evidence derived from scientific investigation, or none of these is anyone's guess.

The problems of special education cannot be resolved without improving instruction, which means recruiting the best individuals possible and training them appropriately. Historically, as we discussed in Chapter 5, this is a perpetual and key issue. Late-20th- and early-21st-century proposals to train all teachers to deal effectively with all students who have emotional or behavioral disorders (i.e., to train all teachers for the full inclusion of all students with disabilities) appeared to be facile solutions to serious, long-standing problems (Mock & Kauffman, 2002). Although all teachers need good behavior management skills, the idea that all teachers can be trained to deal with the most difficult of students seems naive in the extreme.

In early-21st-century America, special and general education seemed to us to be on a collision course. General education was expected to conform to the No Child Left Behind Act of 2002 (NCLB), which set as a goal eliminating any gaps in achievement between various subgroups of the general populations (e.g., gaps between rich and poor, male and female, disabled and nondisabled, various ethnic groups, and those fluent in English and those not). According to the President's Commission on Excellence in Special Education, which was appointed by President George W. Bush in 2001 and completed its report in 2002, special education can be seen as valuable only to the extent that it closes the gap between students with and without disabilities in academic achievement test scores. But, of course, that is an impossible expectation, one that education of no description can meet, an expectation sure to make special education always look like a failure (Kauffman, 2004b, 2005c; Kauffman & Wiley, 2004). One special education teacher describes the Act's effects as follows:

> *"We will always fail," said Melissa Gogel, a sixth-grade special-ed teacher, whose students include several nonreaders and several reading on a third- or fourth-grade level. "The government is trying to put everybody in one melting pot and say that everybody has to pass the same test." She says she is teaching her students demonstrative pronouns when she should be teaching them life skills.*
>
> *In theory, Gogel's students spend four and sometimes five hours a day on reading and math. In practice, it is hard to retain their attention for more than a few minutes. On a recent day, one student was playing video games on a computer at the back of the classroom while Gogel was threatening to send another to the principal for disruptive behavior. (Dobbs, 2004, p. A12)*

Furthermore, NCLB and IDEA call for different approaches to variability among students. Aligning IDEA with NCLB would, as Johns (2003) points out, eliminate the special treatment of those with disabilities: "IDEA focuses entirely on the individual. NCLB focuses entirely on the group (on all those with disabilities)" (Johns, 2003, p. 89).

147

In late 2004, IDEA was reauthorized as the Individuals with Disabilities Education Improvement Act, now known as IDEA 2004. The language used to describe the reauthorization was, predictably, positive. It described the reauthorization as improving education by increasing accountability for outcomes, reducing paperwork, reducing conflicts between parents and schools, and giving schools more flexibility in implementing the basic provisions of IDEA. Nevertheless, IDEA 2004 was aligned with NCLB in ways that reduce special education's emphasis on individualization (Johns, 2003). Moreover, it appears to us that the reauthorization weakened special education in other respects, making it easier for schools to exclude misbehaving students and reducing the demands on schools for serving students with disabilities and writing short-term objectives. A key issue related to this book—the definition of "emotional disturbance"—was not changed. In short, we suspect that IDEA 2004 has undermined special education while purporting to improve special instruction for students with disabilities, including those with emotional or behavioral disorders. Future histories will record whether our suspicion is justified.

Most trainers of special education teachers emphasize teaching at a level based on the possibility of the individual student's success rather than merely teaching at grade level. However, at least some general educators—particularly those deemed credible in the education reform movement of the early 21st century under the promotion of NCLB—believe that teaching on a student's level is bad practice if the student is not on grade level. Mitchell (2004) expressed this point of view:

> *Teachers say they have to teach the students where they are, which means at sixth-grade level in high school if they can't read well. Their attitude may be compassionate, but it is misguided. There's ample evidence that accelerating instruction works better than retarding it in the name of remediation. Observations made in the Dallas Unified School District show that students who score well have teachers who cover the curriculum appropriate to the grade level. These teachers spend little time on drill and practice, and don't remediate in the classroom but rather get help for students outside of class.* (p. A21)

Hecht's (2003) history of doubt is but one thing that leads us to express our skepticism about many current proposals for reforming education, including special education. The history of our field as we have read it also prompts our expression of doubt that reform proposals of the late 20th and early 21st centuries are on the right track. Perhaps expecting students to do what they cannot do is the answer to improving their achievement, but we doubt it. Perhaps all students will achieve at grade level if they are expected to do so, but we doubt it. Perhaps those who cannot perform at grade level simply do not belong in our schools, but we doubt it. Perhaps we should train teachers to expect grade-level or higher performance of all students and train teachers not to attempt remediation, but we doubt it. Perhaps acceleration of instruction (i.e., teaching at a more advanced level) is the best option for all students, including those whose performance is low, but we doubt it. Perhaps heterogeneous grouping for instruction is best for all students regardless of their level of performance, but we doubt it. Perhaps remedial education should be excluded from teacher training and from our schools, but we doubt it. Perhaps the key to successful preparation of competent special educators is simply making certain that every teacher knows the subject matter he or she is teaching, but we doubt it. Perhaps uniformly high expectations of performance will increase the acceptance of students with disabilities in regular schools and classes and minimize the separation of special and general education, but we doubt it. In short, we doubt that NCLB, the full inclusion movement, and changes in schools associated with these initiatives are the keys to improving special education. The evidence to date seems to support the opposites of proposed reforms. But, of course, in time, empirical evidence obtained through research could prove us wrong and make our doubts about current reform proposals look misguided, if not silly.

The history of the education and treatment of those with emotional or behavioral disorders, especially the admittedly cursory overview provided here, does not provide answers to the questions that continue to plague special education, or even offer clear direction on specific measures that must be taken to improve the futures of children with EBD and their families. But the cyclical nature of movements and the ebb and flow of ideas that have characterized the treatment of EBD are apparent. Such cycles are evident in periods of humane treatment and progress, as well as in periods of inhumanity and regression. The notion of perfect prediction remains elusive, but the course of our history does leave us with the general sense that the best hope for progress lies in the continued accumulation of knowledge derived from scientific thought and action, coupled with sustained efforts to apply that knowledge.

References

Abeson, A., Burgdorf, R. C., Casey, P. J., Kunz, J. W., & McNeil, W. (1975). Access to opportunity. In N. Hobbs (Ed.), *Issues in the classification of children* (Vol. 2, pp. 270–292). San Francisco: Jossey-Bass.

Abraham, W. (1955). *A guide for the study of exceptional children.* Boston: Porter Sargent.

Achenbach, T. M. (1974). *Developmental psychopathology.* New York: Ronald Press.

Achenbach, T. M. (1975). The historical context of treatment for delinquent and maladjusted children: Past, present, and future. *Behavioral Disorders, 1*(1), 3–14.

Ack, M. (1970). Some principles of education for the emotionally disturbed. In P. A. Gallagher & L. L. Edwards (Eds.), *Educating the emotionally disturbed: Theory to practice* (pp. 1–14). Lawrence: University of Kansas.

Aichorn, A. (1935). *Wayward youth.* New York: Viking.

Alexander, F. G., & Selsnick, S. T. (1966). *The history of psychiatry: An evaluation of psychiatric thought from prehistoric times to the present.* New York: Harper & Row.

American Psychological Association. (1993). *Violence and youth: Psychology's response: Vol. 1.* Summary report of the American Psychological Association Commission on Violence and Youth. Washington, DC: Author.

Annual Reports of the Court of Directors of the Western Lunatic Asylum, 1836–1850. (1870). Staunton, VA: Kenton Harper.

Apter, S. J., & Conoley, J. C. (1984). *Childhood behavior disorders and emotional disturbance.* Upper Saddle River, NJ: Merrill/Prentice Hall.

Armstrong, K. (2000). *The battle for God.* New York: Knopf.

Atkinson, L. (1974a). The treatment of deviance by the legal-correctional system: History. In W. C. Rhodes & S. Head (Eds.), *A study of child variance: Vol. 3. Service delivery systems* (pp. 167–189). Ann Arbor: University of Michigan.

Atkinson, L. (1974b). The treatment of deviance by the legal-correctional system: Structure. In W. C. Rhodes & S. Head (Eds.), *A study of child variance: Vol. 3. Service delivery systems* (pp. 191–215). Ann Arbor: University of Michigan.

Baker, E. M., & Stullken, E. H. (1938). American research studies concerning the "behavior" type of the exceptional child. *Journal of Exceptional Children, 4,* 36–45.

Baker, H. J. (1934). Common problems in the education of the normal and the handicapped. *Exceptional Children, 1,* 39–40.

Baker, H. J. (1944). *Introduction to exceptional children.* New York: Macmillan.

Baker, H. J. (1953). *Introduction to exceptional children* (rev. ed.). New York: Macmillan.

Baker, H. J., Crothers, B., McCord, C. P., & Stullken, E. H. (1931). Behavior problem children. In F. J. Kelly (Chair), *Special education: The handicapped and gifted, Committee on Special Classes: Section 3. Education and training* (pp. 491–534). New York: Century.

Ball, T. S. (1971). *Itard, Seguin, and Kephart: Sensory education—A learning interpretation.* Columbus, OH: Merrill.

Balthazar, E., & Stevens, H. (1975). *The emotionally disturbed mentally retarded.* Upper Saddle River, NJ: Prentice Hall.

Bandura, A. (1973). *Aggression: A social learning analysis.* Upper Saddle River, NJ: Prentice Hall.

Bandura, A. (1977). *Social learning theory.* Upper Saddle River, NJ: Prentice Hall.

Bandura, A. (1978). The self–system in reciprocal determinism. *American Psychologist, 33,* 344–358.

Bandura, A. (1986). *Social foundations of thought and action: A social cognitive theory.* Upper Saddle River, NJ: Prentice Hall.

Barrett, R. P. (Ed.). (1986). *Severe behavior disorders in the mentally retarded.* New York: Plenum.

Barrows, I. C. (Ed.). (1893). *Proceedings of the National Conference of Charities and Correction.* Boston: G.H. Ellis.

Bateman, B. D. (1994). Who, how, and where: Special education's issues in perpetuity. *The Journal of Special Education, 27,* 509–520.

Bateson, G. (1944). Cultural determinants of personality. In J. McV. Hunt (Ed.), *Personality and the behavior disorders: A handbook based on experimental and clinical research* (Vol. 2, pp. 714–735). New York: Ronald Press.

Battie, W. (1758). *A treatise on madness.* London: Whiston & White. (Republished in facsimile 1969.) New York: Brunner/Mazel.

Beers, C. W. (1908). *A mind that found itself: An autobiography*. New York: Longmans, Green.

Bergman, P., & Escalona, S. (1949). Unusual sensitivities in very young children. *Psychoanalytic Study of the Child, 3–4*, 333–352.

Berkowitz, P. H. (1974). Pearl H. Berkowitz. In J. M. Kauffman & C. D. Lewis (Eds.), *Teaching children with behavior disorders: Personal perspectives* (pp. 24–49). Upper Saddle River, NJ: Merrill/Prentice Hall.

Berkowitz, P. H., & Rothman, E. P. (1960). *The disturbed child: Recognition and psychoeducational therapy in the classroom*. New York: New York University Press.

Berkowitz, P. H., & Rothman, E. P. (1967a). Educating disturbed children in New York City: An historical overview. In P. H. Berkowitz & E. P. Rothman (Eds.), *Public education for disturbed children in New York City* (pp. 5–19). Springfield, IL: Thomas.

Berkowitz, P. H., & Rothman, E. P. (Eds.). (1967b). *Public education for disturbed children in New York City*. Springfield, IL: Thomas.

Berry, C. S. (1936). The exceptional child in regular classes. *Exceptional Children, 3*, 15–16.

Berry, C. S. (1938). Federal aid for the education of physically handicapped children. *Exceptional Children, 5*, 38–41, 44.

Bettelheim, B. (1950). *Love is not enough*. New York: Macmillan.

Bettelheim, B. (1961). The decision to fail. *School Review, 69*, 389–412.

Bettelheim, B. (1967). *The empty fortress*. New York: Free Press.

Bettelheim, B. (1970). Listening to children. In P. A. Gallagher & L. L. Edwards (Eds.), *Educating the emotionally disturbed: Theory to practice* (pp. 36–56). Unpublished manuscript, University of Kansas at Lawrence.

Bettelheim, B., & Sylvester, E. (1948). A therapeutic milieu. *American Journal of Orthopsychiatry, 18*, 191–206.

Biber, B. (1961). Integration of mental health principles in the school setting. In G. Caplan (Ed.), *Prevention of mental disorders in children: Initial explorations* (pp. 323–352). New York: Basic Books.

Bierman, K. L., Coie, J. D., Dodge, K. A., Greenberg, M. T., Lochman, J. E., McMahon, R. J., & Pinderhughes, E. E. (2002). Using the Fast Track randomized prevention trial to test the early-starter model of the development of serious conduct problems. *Development and Psychopathology, 14*, 925–943.

Billingsley, B. S. (2004). Special education teacher retention and attrition:

A critical analysis of the research literature. *The Journal of Special Education, 38*, 39–55.

Blanton, S. (1925). The function of the mental hygiene clinic in schools and colleges. *The New Republic, 122*, 93–101.

Blatt, B. (1975). Toward an understanding of people with special needs. In J. M. Kauffman & J. S. Payne (Eds.), *Mental retardation: Introduction and personal perspectives* (pp. 388–427). Columbus, OH: Merrill.

Blatt, B., & Kaplan, F. (1966). *Christmas in purgatory: A photographic essay on mental retardation*. Boston: Allyn & Bacon.

Bockoven, J. S. (1956). Moral treatment in American psychiatry. *Journal of Nervous and Mental Disease, 124*, 167–194, 292–321.

Bockoven, J. S. (1972). *Moral treatment in community mental health*. New York: Springer.

Bower, E. M. (1960). *Early identification of emotionally handicapped children in school*. Springfield, IL: Thomas.

Bower, E. M. (1961). Primary prevention in a school setting. In G. Caplan (Ed.), *Prevention of mental disorders in children: Initial explorations* (pp. 353–377). New York: Basic Books.

Bower, E. M. (1962). Comparison of the characteristics of identified emotionally disturbed children with other children in classes. In E. P. Trapp & P. Himelstein (Eds.), *Readings on the exceptional child: Research and theory* (pp. 610–629). New York: Appleton-Century-Crofts.

Bower, E. M. (Ed.). (1980). *The handicapped in literature: A psychosocial perspective*. Denver, CO: Love.

Bower, E. M. (1981). *Early identification of emotionally handicapped children in school* (3rd ed.). Springfield, IL: Thomas.

Bower, E. M. (1982). Defining emotional disturbance: Public policy and research. *Psychology in the Schools, 19*, 55–60.

Bower, E. M., & Lambert, N. M. (1962). *A process for in-school screening of children with emotional handicaps*. Princeton, NJ: Educational Testing Service.

Bower, E. M., Shellhammer, T. A., & Daily, J. M. (1960). School characteristics of male adolescents who later became schizophrenic. *American Journal of Orthopsychiatry, 30*, 712–729.

Braaten, S. R. (1985). Adolescent needs and behavior in the schools: Current and historical perspectives. In S. R. Braaten, R. B. Rutherford, & W. Evans (Eds.), *Programming for adolescents with behavioral disorders*

(Vol. 2, pp. 1–10). Reston, VA: Council for Children with Behavioral Disorders.

Braaten, S. R., Kauffman, J. M., Braaten, B., Polsgrove, L., & Nelson, C. M. (1988). The regular education initiative: Patent medicine for behavioral disorders. *Exceptional Children, 55,* 21–28.

Bradby, M. K. (1919). *Psycho-analysis and its place in life.* London: Henry Frowde.

Brantlinger, E. (1997). Using ideology: Cases of nonrecognition of the politics of research and practice in special education. *Review of Educational Research, 67,* 425–459.

Bremner, R. H. (Ed.). (1970). *Children and youth in America: A documentary history: Vol. 1. 1600–1865.* Cambridge, MA: Harvard University Press.

Bremner, R. H. (Ed.). (1971). *Children and youth in America: A documentary history: Vol. 2. 1866–1932.* Cambridge, MA: Harvard University Press.

Brentro, L. K., Brokenleg, M., & Van Bockern, S. (1998). *Reclaiming youth at risk: Our hope for the future.* Bloomington, IN: National Educational Service.

Brigham, A. (1845a). Article V. Selected cases. *American Journal of Insanity, 2,* 68–75.

Brigham, A. (1845b). Schools in lunatic asylums. *American Journal of Insanity, 1,* 326–340.

Brigham, A. (1847). The moral treatment of insanity. *American Journal of Insanity, 4,* 1–15.

Brigham, A. (1848). Schools and asylums for the idiotic and imbecile. *American Journal of Insanity, 5,* 19–33.

Brigham, F. J., & Kauffman, J. M. (1998). Creating supportive environments for students with emotional or behavioral disorders. *Effective School Practices, 17*(2), 5–35.

Brown, D. (1995, December 8). Researchers, journalists "oversold" gene therapy: NIH advisers cite nearly uniform failure. *The Washington Post,* pp. A1, A22.

Brown, F. A. (1943). A practical program for early detection of atypical children. *Exceptional Children, 10,* 3–7.

Brussel, J. A. (1969). Introduction (to the facsimile edition of W. Battie's *A treatise on madness,* 1758) (pp. v–vii). New York: Brunner/Mazel.

Bullis, M., & Cheney, D. (1999). Vocational and transition interventions for adolescents and young adults with emotional or behavioral disorders. *Focus on Exceptional Children, 31*(7), 1–24.

Bullock, L. M., & Gable, R. A. (Eds.). (2004). *Quality personnel preparation in emotional/behavioral disorders: Current perspectives and future directions.* Denton: University of North Texas.

Burke, D. (1972). Countertheoretical interventions in emotional disturbance. In W. C. Rhodes & M. L. Tracy (Eds.), *A study of child variance: Vol. 2. Interventions* (pp. 573–657). Ann Arbor: University of Michigan.

Caplan, G. (Ed.). (1961). *Prevention of mental disorders in children: Initial explorations.* New York: Basic Books.

Caplan, R. B. (1969). *Psychiatry and the community in nineteenth century America.* New York: Basic Books.

Carey, G., & Goldman, D. (1997). The genetics of antisocial behavior. In D. M. Stoff, J. Breiling, & J. D. Maser (Eds.), *Handbook of antisocial behavior* (pp. 243–254). New York: Wiley.

Carlberg, C., & Kavale, K. (1980). The efficacy of special versus regular class placement for exceptional children: A meta-analysis. *The Journal of Special Education, 29,* 155–162.

Carlson, E. T., & Dain, N. (1960). The psychotherapy that was moral treatment. *American Journal of Psychiatry, 117,* 519–524.

Carpenter, B., & Bovair, K. (1996). Learning with dignity: Educational opportunities for students with emotional and behavioral difficulties. *Canadian Journal of Special Education, 11*(1), 6–16.

Carstens, C. C. (1932). *Organization for the care of handicapped children: Section 4. The handicapped: Prevention, maintenance, protection.* New York: Century.

Cavan, R. S., & Ferdinand, T. N. (1975). *Juvenile delinquency* (3rd ed.). New York: Lippincott.

Cheney, C., & Morse, W. C. (1972). Psychodynamic intervention in emotional disturbance. In W. C. Rhodes & M. L. Tracy (Eds.), *A study of child variance: Vol. 2. Interventions* (pp. 253–393). Ann Arbor: University of Michigan.

Cheney, D., & Bullis, M. (2004). The school-to-community transition of adolescents with emotional or behavioral disorders. In R. B. Rutherford, M. M. Quinn, & S. R. Mathur (Eds.), *Handbook of research in emotional and behavioral disorders* (pp. 369–384). New York: Guilford Press.

Chesapeake Institute. (1994, September). *National agenda for achieving better results for children and youth with serious emotional disturbance.* Washington, DC: Author.

Clark, H. B., & Clarke, R. T. (1996). Research on the wraparound process and individualized services for children with multiple-system needs. *Journal of Child and Family Studies, 5,* 1–5.

Clarke, R. T., Schaefer, M., Burchard, J. D., & Welkowitz, J. W. (1992). Wrapping community–based mental health services around children with a severe behavioral disorder: An evaluation of Project Wraparound. *Journal of Child and Family Studies, 1,* 241–261.

Cline, D. H. (1990). A legal analysis of policy initiatives to exclude handicapped/disruptive students from special education. *Behavioral Disorders, 15,* 159–173.

Cocco, M. (2004, May 12). At FDA, science subdued by conservative ideology. *Charlottesville Daily Progress,* p. A6.

Cohen, R. (2004, April 27). The cultural divides of war. *The Washington Post,* p. A21.

Cole, T. (2005). Emotional and behavioural difficulties: An historical perspective. In P. Clough, P. Garner, J. T. Pardeck, & F. K. O. Yuen (Eds.), *Handbook of emotional and behavioral difficulties in education* (pp. 26–37). London: Sage.

Collins, F., Green, E. D., Guttmacher, A. E., & Guyer, E. S. (2003). A vision for the future of genomics research. *Nature, 422,* 835–847.

Colvin, G. (1992). *Managing acting-out behavior.* Video and workbooks. Eugene, OR: Behavior Associates.

Colvin, G., Sugai, G., & Patching, B. (1993). Precorrection: An instructional approach for managing predictable problem behaviors. *Intervention in School and Clinic, 28,* 143–150.

Conquest, R. (2000). *Reflections on a ravaged century.* New York: Norton.

Conroy, M. A., Hendrickson, J. M., & Hester, P. P. (2004). Early identification and prevention of emotional and behavioral disorders. In R. B. Rutherford, M. M. Quinn, & S. R. Mathur (Eds.), *Handbook of research in emotional and behavioral disorders* (pp. 199–215). New York: Guilford Press.

Coppock, B. A., & Wood, F. H. (Eds.). (1980). *Mental health, emotional disturbance and Afro-American children and youth: Theories, strategies, services and training.* Minneapolis: University of Minnesota, Department of Psychoeducational Studies.

Crissy, M. S. (1975). Mental retardation: Past, present, and future. *American Psychologist, 30,* 800–808.

Crockett, J. B., & Kauffman, J. M. (1999). *The least restrictive environment: Its origins and interpretations in special education.* Mahwah, NJ: Erlbaum.

Cruickshank, W. M. (Ed.). (1955). *Psychology of exceptional children and youth.* Englewood Cliffs, NJ: Prentice Hall.

Cruickshank, W. M. (1967). The development of education for exceptional children. In W. M. Cruickshank & G. O. Johnson (Eds.), *Education of exceptional children and youth.* Englewood Cliffs, NJ: Prentice Hall.

Cruickshank, W. M. (1974). Foreword. In J. M. Kauffman & C. D. Lewis (Eds.), *Teaching children with behavior disorders: Personal perspectives* (pp. v–xi). Columbus, OH: Merrill.

Cruickshank, W. M. (1976). William M. Cruickshank. In J. M. Kauffman & D. P. Hallahan (Eds.), *Teaching children with learning disabilities: Personal reflections* (pp. 94–127). Columbus, OH: Merrill.

Cruickshank, W. M., Bentzen, F., Ratzeburg, F., & Tannhauser, M. A. (1961). *A teaching method for brain-injured and hyperactive children.* Syracuse, NY: Syracuse University Press.

Cruickshank, W. M., & Johnson, G. O. (Eds.). (1958). *Education of exceptional children and youth.* Englewood Cliffs, NJ: Prentice Hall.

Cruickshank, W. M., Paul, J. L., & Junkala, J. B. (1969). *Misfits in the public schools.* Syracuse, NY: Syracuse University Press.

Cullinan, D. (2002). *Students with emotional and behavior disorders: An introduction for teachers and other helping professionals.* Upper Saddle River, NJ: Merrill/Prentice Hall.

Cullinan, D., & Epstein, M. H. (1979). Administrative definitions of behavior disorders: Status and directions. In F. H. Wood & K. C. Lakin (Eds.), *Disturbing, disordered, or disturbed? Perspectives on the definition of problem behavior in educational settings* (pp. 17–28). Minneapolis: University of Minnesota, Department of Psychoeducational Studies, Advanced Training Institute.

Cullinan, D., Epstein, M. H., & Kauffman, J. M. (1982). The behavioral model and children's behavior disorders: Foundations and evaluation. In R. L. McDowell, G. W. Adamson, & F. H. Wood (Eds.), *Teaching emotionally disturbed children* (pp. 15–46). Boston: Little, Brown.

Cullinan, D., Epstein, M. H., & Lloyd, J. W. (1991). Evaluation of conceptual models of behavior disorders. *Behavioral Disorders, 16,* 148–157.

Daly, P. M. (1985). The educateur: An atypical childcare worker. *Behavioral*

Disorders, 11, 35–41.

Danforth, S. (2001). A pragmatic evaluation of three models of disability in special education. *Journal of Developmental and Physical Disabilities, 13*, 343–359.

Danforth, S., & Rhodes, W. C. (1997). Deconstructing disability: A philosophy for education. *Remedial and Special Education, 18*, 357–366.

Davenport, C. (2004, January 26). Bottom line for mentally ill: Md. deficit limiting options for care. *The Washington Post*, pp. B1, B6.

Davids, L. (1975). Therapeutic approaches to children in residential treatment: Changes from the mid-1950s to the mid-1970s. *American Psychologist, 30*, 809–814.

Dembinski, R. J., Schultz, E. W., & Walton, W. T. (1982). Curriculum intervention with the emotionally disturbed student: A psychoeducational perspective. In R. L. McDowell, G. W. Adamson, & F. H. Wood (Eds.), *Teaching emotionally disturbed children* (pp. 206–234). Boston: Little, Brown.

DeMyer, M. K., Barton, S., Alpern, G. D., Kimberlin, C., Allen, J., & Steele, R. (1974). The measured intelligence of autistic children. *Journal of Autism and Childhood Schizophrenia, 4*, 42–60.

Denham, S., Blair, K., Schmidt, M., & DeMulder, E. (2002). Compromised emotional competence: Seeds of violence sown early? *American Journal of Orthopsychiatry, 72*, 70–82.

Dennison, G. (1969). *The lives of children*. New York: Random House.

Des Jarlais, D. C. (1972). Mental illness as social deviance. In W. C. Rhodes & M. L. Tracy (Eds.), *A study of child variance: Vol. 1. Theories* (pp. 259–322). Ann Arbor: University of Michigan.

Despert, J. L. (1965). *The emotionally disturbed child—Then and now*. New York: Brunner.

Despert, J. L. (1968). *Schizophrenia in children*. New York: Brunner.

Deutsch, A. (1948). *The shame of the states*. New York: Harcourt, Brace, & World.

Devany, J., Rincover, A., & Lovaas, O. I. (1981). Teaching speech to nonverbal children. In J. M. Kauffman & D. P. Hallahan (Eds.), *Handbook of special education* (pp. 512–529). Upper Saddle River, NJ: Prentice Hall.

Dobbs, M. (2004, April 22). "No child" law leaves schools' old ways behind. *The Washington Post*, pp. A1, A12–A13.

Dokecki, P. R., Strain, B. A., Bernal, J. J., Brown, C. S., & Robinson,

M. E. (1975). Low-income and minority groups. In N. Hobbs (Ed.), *Issues in the classification of children* (Vol. 1, pp. 312–348). San Francisco: Jossey-Bass.

Doll, E. A. (1962). A historical survey of research and management of mental retardation in the United States. In E. P. Trapp & P. Himelstein (Eds.), *Readings on the exceptional child: Research and theory* (pp. 21–68). New York: Appleton-Century-Crofts.

Doll, E. A. (1967). Trends and problems in the education of the mentally retarded: 1900–1940. *American Journal of Mental Deficiency, 72,* 175–183.

Donovan, M. S., & Cross, C. T., National Research Council. (Eds.). (2002). *Minority students in special and gifted education.* Washington, DC: National Academy Press.

Dorney, W. P. (1967). Growth and development of education in a detention setting. In P. H. Berkowitz & E. P. Rothman (Eds.), *Public education for disturbed children in New York City* (pp. 124–142). Springfield, IL: Thomas.

Dumont, M. P. (1995). Our lady of the state hospital. *Readings: A Journal of Reviews and Commentary in Mental Health, 10*(4), 8–11.

Duncan, B. B., Forness, S. R., & Hartsough, C. (1995). Students identified as seriously emotionally disturbed in day treatment: Cognitive, psychiatric, and special education characteristics. *Behavioral Disorders, 20,* 238–252.

Dunn, L. M. (Ed.). (1963). *Exceptional children in the schools.* New York: Holt, Rinehart, & Winston.

Dupre, A. P. (1996). Should students have constitutional rights? Keeping order in the public schools. *George Washington Law Review, 65*(1), 49–105.

Dupre, A. P. (1997). Disability and the public schools: The case against "inclusion." *Washington Law Review, 72,* 775–858.

Dupre, A. P. (2000). A study in double standards, discipline, and the disabled student. *Washington Law Review, 75,* 1–96.

Dwyer, K. P., & Bernstein, R. (1998). Mental health in the schools: "Linking islands of hope in a sea of despair." *School Psychology Review, 27,* 277–286.

Eber, L., & Keenan, S. (2004). Collaboration with other agencies: Wraparound and systems of care for children and youth with EBD. In R. B. Rutherford, M. M. Quinn, & S. R. Mathur (Eds.), *Handbook of research in emotional and behavioral disorders* (pp. 502–518). New York: Guilford Press.

Eddy, J. M., Reid, J. B., & Curry, V. (2002). The etiology of youth antisocial behavior, delinquency, and violence and a public health approach to prevention. In M. R. Shinn, H. M. Walker, & G. Stoner (Eds.), *Interventions for academic and behavior problems II: Preventive and remedial approaches* (pp. 27–52). Bethesda, MD: National Association of School Psychologists.

Edelman, P. (2001). *Searching for America's heart: RFK and the renewal of hope*. Boston: Houghton Mifflin.

Edgar, E. B. (1987). Secondary programs in special education: Are many of them justifiable? *Exceptional Children, 53*, 555–561.

Edgar, E., & Siegel, S. (1995). Postsecondary scenarios for troubled and troubling youth. In J. M. Kauffman, J. W. Lloyd, D. P. Hallahan, & T. A. Astuto (Eds.), *Issues in educational placement: Students with emotional and behavioral disorders* (pp. 251–283). Hillsdale, NJ: Erlbaum.

Eggleston, C. (1987). Correctional special education: Our rich history. In C. M. Nelson, R. B. Rutherford, & B. I. Wolford (Eds.), *Special education in the criminal justice system* (pp. 19–23). Upper Saddle River, NJ: Merrill/Prentice Hall.

Eissler, K. R. (1949). *Searchlights on delinquency*. New York: International Universities Press.

Elkins, D. (1956). How the classroom teacher can help the emotionally disturbed child. In M. E. Frampton & E. D. Gall (Eds.), *Special education for the exceptional: Vol. 3. Mental and emotional deviates and special problems* (pp. 338–345). Boston: Porter Sargent.

Ellis, L. (1974). Treatment of deviance by the educational system: Case study. In W. C. Rhodes & S. Head (Eds.), *A study of child variance: Vol. 3. Service delivery systems* (pp. 145–165). Ann Arbor: University of Michigan.

Epstein, M. H., Kutash, K., & Duchnowski, A. (Eds.). (1998). *Outcomes for children and youth with emotional and behavioral disorders and their families: Programs and evaluation of best practices*. Austin, TX: PRO-ED.

Esquirol, E. (1845). *Mental maladies: A treatise on insanity* (E. K. Hunt, Trans.). Philadelphia: Lea & Blanchard.

Esquirol, E. (1849). Incendiary monomania—Pyromania. *American Journal of Insanity, 5*, 237–245.

Fagen, S. A. (1979). Psychoeducational management and self-control. In

D. Cullinan & M. H. Epstein (Eds.), *Special education for adolescents: Issues and perspectives* (pp. 235–271). Upper Saddle River, NJ: Merrill/Prentice Hall.

Fagen, S. A., Long, N. J., & Stevens, D. J. (1975). *Teaching children self-control.* Upper Saddle River, NJ: Merrill/Prentice Hall.

Fallis, D. S. (2004a, May 23). A dangerous place. Assisted living in Virginia. As care declines, cost can be injury, death. *The Washington Post,* pp. A1, A15–A17.

Fallis, D. S. (2004b, May 26). A dangerous place. Failure to regulate. Weak laws let deficient facilities stay open. *The Washington Post,* pp. A1, A12–A13.

Fallis, D. S. (2004c, May 25). A dangerous place. Lost in life and death. Assisted living facility's chaos bred wide neglect. *The Washington Post,* pp. A1, A6.

Fallis, D. S. (2004d, May 24). A dangerous place. A volatile mix of residents. In Vag's assisted living homes, violent preyed on the vulnerable. *The Washington Post,* pp. A1, A6–A7.

Faris, R. E. L. (1944). Ecological factors in human behavior. In J. McV. Hunt (Ed.), *Personality and the behavior disorders: A handbook based on experimental and clinical research* (Vol. 2, pp. 736–757). New York: Ronald Press.

Farson, M. R. (1940). Education of the handicapped child for social competency. *Exceptional Children, 6,* 138–144, 150.

Fay, T. S. (1935). *The scientist looks at the emotionally unstable child: Part 1. Behavior problems in children: The importance of training and conditioning.* Langhorne, PA: Child Research Clinic of the Woods Schools.

Feagans, L. (1972). Ecological theory as a model for constructing a theory of emotional disturbance. In W. C. Rhodes & M. L. Tracy (Eds.), *A study of child variance: Vol. 1. Theories* (pp. 323–389). Ann Arbor: University of Michigan.

Fenichel, C. (1966). Psychoeducational approaches for seriously disturbed children in the classroom. In P. Knoblock (Ed.), *Intervention approaches in educating emotionally disturbed children* (pp. 5–18). Syracuse, NY: Syracuse University Press.

Fenichel, C. (1974). Carl Fenichel. In J. M. Kauffman & C. D. Lewis (Eds.), *Teaching children with behavior disorders: Personal perspectives* (pp. 50–75). Upper Saddle River, NJ: Merrill/Prentice Hall.

Fenichel, C., Freedman, A. M., & Klapper, Z. (1960). A day school for schizophrenic children. *American Journal of Orthopsychiatry, 30,* 130–143.

Feynman, R. P. (1999). *The pleasure of finding things out.* Cambridge, MA: Helix.

Fine, A. H. (1991). Behavior disorders in childhood: The psychodynamic interpretation. *Journal of Developmental and Physical Disabilities, 3,* 245–266.

Flannery, D. J., & Huff, C. R. (Eds.). (1999). *Youth violence: Prevention, intervention, and social policy.* Washington, DC: American Psychiatric Press.

Flannery, R. B. (1999). *Preventing youth violence: A guide for parents, teachers, and counselors.* New York: Continuum.

Forehand, R., & McKinney, B. (1993). Historical overview of child discipline in the United States: Implications for mental health clinicians and researchers. *Journal of Child and Family Studies, 2,* 221–228.

Forness, S. R. (1988). Planning for the needs of children with serious emotional disturbance: The national special education and mental health coalition. *Behavioral Disorders, 13,* 127–133.

Forness, S. R., & Kavale, K. A. (2001). Ignoring the odds: Hazards of not adding the new medical model to special education decisions. *Behavioral Disorders, 26,* 269–281.

Forness, S. R., & Knitzer, J. (1992). A new proposed definition and terminology to replace "serious emotional disturbance" in Individuals with Disabilities Education Act. *School Psychology Review, 21,* 12–20.

Forness, S. R., & MacMillan, D. L. (1970). The origins of behavior modification with exceptional children. *Exceptional Children, 37,* 93–99.

Fox, J. J., & Gable, R. A. (2004). Functional behavioral assessment. In R. B. Rutherford, M. M. Quinn, & S. R. Mathur (Eds.), *Handbook of research in emotional and behavioral disorders* (pp. 143–162). New York: Guilford Press.

Frampton, M. E., & Gall, E. D. (Eds.). (1955a). *Special education for the exceptional: Vol. 1. Introduction and problems.* Boston: Porter Sargent.

Frampton, M. E., & Gall, E. D. (Eds.). (1955b). *Special education for the exceptional: Vol. 2. The physically handicapped and special health problems.* Boston: Porter Sargent.

Frampton, M. E., & Gall, E. D. (Eds.). (1956). *Special education for the exceptional: Vol. 3. Mental and emotional deviates and special problems.* Boston: Porter Sargent.

Fraser, M. (1974). The treatment of deviance by the mental health system:

History. In W. C. Rhodes & S. Head (Eds.), *A study of child variance: Vol. 3. Service delivery systems* (pp. 241–270). Ann Arbor: University of Michigan.

Freud, A. (1946). *The ego and the mechanisms of defense*. New York: International Universities Press.

Freud, A. (1954). *Psychoanalysis for teachers and parents* (Barbara Low, Trans.). New York: Emerson.

Freud, A. (1965). The relation between psychoanalysis and pedagogy. In N. J. Long, W. C. Morse, & R. G. Newman (Eds.), *Conflict in the classroom* (pp. 159–163). Belmont, CA: Wadsworth.

Fuchs, D., & Fuchs, L. S. (1994). Inclusive schools movement and the radicalization of special education reform. *Exceptional Children, 60,* 294–309.

Fuchs, D., & Fuchs, L. S. (1995). Special education can work. In J. M. Kauffman, J. W. Lloyd, D. P. Hallahan, & T. A. Astuto (Eds.), *Issues in educational placement: Students with emotional and behavioral disorders* (pp. 363–377). Mahwah, NJ: Erlbaum.

Furlong, M. J., & Morrison, G. M. (1994). Introduction to the mini-series: School violence and safety in perspective. *School Psychology Review, 23,* 139–150.

Furlong, M. J., Morrison, G. M., & Jimerson, S. (2004). Externalizing behaviors of aggression and violence and the school context. In R. B. Rutherford, M. M. Quinn, & S. R. Mathur (Eds.), *Handbook of research in emotional and behavioral disorders* (pp. 243–261). New York: Guilford Press.

Gadow, K. D. (1979). *Children on medication: A primer for school personnel.* Reston, VA: Council for Exceptional Children.

Gallagher, D. J. (1998). The scientific knowledge base of special education: Do we know what we think we know? *Exceptional Children, 64,* 493–502.

Gallagher, D. J. (Ed.). (2004). *Challenging orthodoxy in special education: Dissenting voices.* Denver, CO: Love.

Garrison, K. C., & Force, D. G. (1959). *The psychology of exceptional children* (3rd ed.). New York: Ronald Press.

Gartner, A., & Lipsky, D. K. (1989). *The yoke of special education: How to break it.* Rochester, NY: National Center on Education and the Economy.

Gay, G. (1998, Winter). Coming of age ethnically: Teaching young adolescents of color. *Prevention Researcher,* 7–9.

166

Gelman, J. A., Pullen, P. A., & Kauffman, J. M. (2005). The meaning of highly qualified and a clear roadmap to accomplishment. *Exceptionality, 12*, 195–207.

Gerber, M. M. (1996). Reforming special education: Beyond "inclusion." In C. Christensen & F. Rizvi (Eds.), *Disability and the dilemmas of education and justice* (pp. 156–174). Philadelphia: Open University Press.

Gesell, A. (1921). *Exceptional children and public school policy*. New Haven, CT: Yale University Press.

Gibbs, J. T., & Huang, L. N. (Eds.). (1997). *Children of color: Psychological interventions with culturally diverse youth*. San Francisco: Jossey-Bass.

Gliona, M. F., Gonzales, A. K., & Jacobson, E. S. (2005). Dedicated, not segregated: Suggested changes in thinking about instructional environments and in the language of special education. In J. M. Kauffman & D. P. Hallahan (Eds.), *The illusion of full inclusion: A comprehensive critique of a current special education bandwagon* (2nd ed., pp. 135–146). Austin, TX: PRO-ED.

Goldapple, K., Segal, Z., Garson, C., Lau, M., Bieling, P., Kennedy, S., & Mayberg, H. (2004). Modulation of cortical-limbic pathways in major depression: Treatment-specific effects of cognitive behavior therapy. *Archives of General Psychiatry, 61*, 34–40.

Gollaher, D. (1995). *Voice for the mad: The life of Dorothea Dix*. New York: Free Press.

Goodall, K. (1972). Shapers at work. *Psychology Today, 6*(6), 53–63, 132–138.

Goodlad, J. I., & Lovitt, T. C. (Eds.). (1993). *Integrating general and special education*. Upper Saddle River, NJ: Merrill/Prentice Hall.

Gould, S. J. (1996). *The mismeasure of man* (rev. ed.). New York: Norton.

Gould, S. J. (1997a). The positive power of skepticism. Foreword in M. Shermer, *Why people believe weird things: Pseudoscience, superstition, and other confusions of our time*. New York: W. H. Freeman.

Gould, S. J. (1997b). *Questioning the millennium. A rationalist's guide to a precisely arbitrary countdown*. New York: Harmony.

Graubard, P. S. (1976). The use of indigenous grouping as the reinforcing agent in teaching disturbed delinquents to learn. In N. J. Long, W. C. Morse, & R. G. Newman (Eds.), *Conflict in the classroom* (3rd ed., pp. 342–346). Belmont, CA: Wadsworth.

Graubard, P. S., Rosenberg, H., & Miller, M. (1971). Ecological approaches to social deviancy. In E. Ramp & B. L. Hopkins (Eds.), *A new direction for education: Behavior analysis 1971* (pp. 80–101). Lawrence: University of Kansas, Department of Human Development.

Gresham, F. M., & MacMillan, D. L. (1997a). Autistic recovery? An analysis and critique of the empirical evidence on the Early Intervention Project. *Behavioral Disorders, 22,* 185–201.

Gresham, F. M., & MacMillan, D. L. (1997b). Denial and defensiveness in the place of fact and reason: Rejoinder to Smith and Lovaas. *Behavioral Disorders, 22,* 219–230.

Grob, G. N. (1973). *Mental institutions in America: Social policy to 1875.* New York: Free Press.

Grosenick, J. K., & Huntze, S. L. (1979). *National needs analysis in behavior disorders: A model for a comprehensive needs analysis in behavior disorders.* Columbia: University of Missouri, Department of Special Education.

Grosenick, J. K., & Huntze, S. L. (1983). *More questions than answers: Review and analysis of programs for behaviorally disordered children and youth.* Columbia: University of Missouri, Department of Special Education.

Grossman, H. (1972). *Nine rotten lousy kids.* New York: Holt, Rinehart & Winston.

Groszmann, M. P. E. (1917). *The exceptional child.* New York: Charles Scribner's Sons.

Haines, T. H. (1925). State laws relating to special classes in schools for mentally handicapped children in the public schools. *Mental Hygiene, 9,* 545–551.

Hallahan, D. P., & Cruickshank, W. M. (1973). *Psychoeducational foundations of learning disabilities.* Upper Saddle River, NJ: Prentice Hall.

Hallahan, D. P., & Kauffman, J. M. (1976). *Introduction to learning disabilities: A psycho–behavioral approach.* Englewood Cliffs, NJ: Prentice Hall.

Hallahan, D. P., & Kauffman, J. M. (2006). *Exceptional learners: Introduction to special education* (10th ed.). Boston: Allyn & Bacon.

Hallahan, D. P., Kauffman, J. M., & Lloyd, J. W. (1999). *Introduction to learning disabilities* (2nd ed.). Boston: Allyn & Bacon.

Hallahan, D. P., Lloyd, J. W., Kauffman, J. M., Weiss, M., & Martinez, E. (2005). *Learning disabilities: Foundations, characteristics, and effective teaching* (3rd ed.). Boston: Allyn & Bacon.

Hallenbeck, B. A., & Kauffman, J. M. (1994). The United States. In K. Mazurek & M. A. Winzer (Eds.), *Comparative studies in special education* (pp. 403–419). Washington, DC: Gallaudet University Press.

Hammond, W. A. (1891). *A treatise on insanity and its medical relations*. New York: Appleton.

Hare, E. H. (1962). Masturbatory insanity: The history of an idea. *Journal of Mental Science, 108*, 1–25.

Haring, N. G. (1968). *Attending and responding*. San Rafael, CA: Dimensions.

Haring, N. G. (1974a). Norris G. Haring. In J. M. Kauffman & C. D. Lewis (Eds.), *Teaching children with behavior disorders: Personal perspectives* (pp. 76–112). Upper Saddle River, NJ: Merrill/Prentice Hall.

Haring, N. G. (1974b). Social and emotional behavior disorders. In N. G. Haring (Ed.), *Behavior of exceptional children* (pp. 253–293). Upper Saddle River, NJ: Merrill/Prentice Hall.

Haring, N. G., & Phillips, E. L. (1962). *Educating emotionally disturbed children*. New York: McGraw-Hill.

Haring, N. G., & Phillips, E. L. (1972). *Analysis and modification of classroom behavior*. Upper Saddle River, NJ: Prentice Hall.

Haring, N. G., & Whelan, R. J. (1965). Experimental methods in education and management. In N. J. Long, W. C. Morse, & R. G. Newman (Eds.), *Conflict in the classroom* (pp. 389–405). Belmont, CA: Wadsworth.

Harms, E. (1967). *Origins of modern psychiatry*. Springfield, IL: Thomas.

Hay, L. (1953). A new school channel for helping the troubled child. *American Journal of Orthopsychiatry, 23*, 678–683.

Hayman, M. (1939). The interrelations between mental defect and mental disorder. *Journal of Mental Science, 85*, 1183–1193.

Healy, W. (1915). *The individual delinquent*. Boston: Little, Brown.

Healy, W. (1917). *Mental conflicts and misconduct*. Boston: Little, Brown.

Healy, W. (1931). *Reconstructing behavior in youth: A study of problem children in foster homes*. New York: Knopf.

Healy, W., & Bronner, A. F. (1969). *Delinquents and criminals: Their making and unmaking*. New York: Batterson-Smith. (Original work published in 1926)

Hecht, J. M. (2003). *Doubt: A history*. San Francisco: Harper.

Heck, A. O. (1940). *The education of exceptional children: Its challenge to teachers, parents, and laymen*. New York: McGraw-Hill.

Hefferman, H. (1935). Meeting the needs of exceptional children in rural schools. *Exceptional Children, 2*, 49–50.

Hendershott, A. B. (2002). *The politics of deviance*. San Francisco: Encounter Books.

Henry, N. B. (Ed.). (1950). The education of exceptional children. *Forty-ninth yearbook of the National Society for the Study of Education, Part 2.* Chicago: University of Chicago Press.

Hester, P. P., & Kaiser, A. P. (1998). Early intervention for the prevention of conduct disorder: Research issues in early identification, implementation, and interpretation of treatment outcomes. *Behavioral Disorders, 24,* 57–65.

Heuchert, C. M., & Long, N. J. (1980). A brief history of life-space interviewing. *Pointer, 25*(2), 5–8.

Heward, W. L. (2003). Ten faulty notions about teaching and learning that hinder the effectiveness of special education. *The Journal of Special Education, 36,* 186–205.

Heward, W. L., & Silvestri, S. M. (2005). The neutralization of special education. In J. W. Jacobson, J. A. Mulick, & R. M. Foxx (Eds.), *Fads: Dubious and improbable treatments for developmental disabilities* (pp. 193–214). Mahwah, NJ: Erlbaum.

Hewett, F. M. (1964a). A hierarchy of educational tasks for children with learning disorders. *Exceptional Children, 31,* 207–214.

Hewett, F. M. (1964b). Teaching reading to an autistic boy through operant conditioning. *Reading Teacher, 18,* 613–618.

Hewett, F. M. (1965). Teaching speech to an autistic boy through operant conditioning. *American Journal of Orthopsychiatry, 35,* 927–936.

Hewett, F. M. (1966). A hierarchy of competencies for teachers of emotionally handicapped children. *Exceptional Children, 33,* 7–11.

Hewett, F. M. (1967). Educational engineering with emotionally disturbed children. *Exceptional Children, 33,* 459–471.

Hewett, F. M. (1968). *The emotionally disturbed child in the classroom.* Boston: Allyn & Bacon.

Hewett, F. M. (1970a). A behavioral approach to the education of the emotionally disturbed child: Building the bridge from the other side. In P. A. Gallagher & L. L. Edwards (Eds.), *Educating the emotionally disturbed: Theory to practice* (pp. 18–35). Lawrence: University of Kansas.

Hewett, F. M. (1970b, November). The Madison Plan really swings. *Today's Education, 59,* 15–17.

Hewett, F. M. (1971). Introduction to the behavior modification approach to special education: A shaping procedure. In N. J. Long, W. C. Morse, & R. G. Newman (Eds.), *Conflict in the classroom* (2nd ed., pp. 360–365). Belmont, CA: Wadsworth.

Hewett, F. M. (1974). Frank M. Hewett. In J. M. Kauffman & C. D. Lewis (Eds.), *Teaching children with behavior disorders: Personal perspectives* (pp. 114–140). Upper Saddle River, NJ: Merrill/Prentice Hall.

Hewett, F. M., & Forness, S. R. (1974). *Education of exceptional learners.* Boston: Allyn & Bacon.

Hirsch, E. D., Jr. (1996). *The schools we need and why we don't have them.* New York: Anchor.

Hirschberg, J. C. (1953). The role of education in the treatment of emotionally disturbed children through planned ego development. *American Journal of Orthopsychiatry, 23,* 684–690.

Hirschberg, J. C. (1956). The management by the general practitioner of emotional problems of children. In M. E. Frampton & E. D. Gall (Eds.), *Special education for the exceptional: Vol. 3. Mental and emotional deviates and special problems* (pp. 312–321). Boston: Porter Sargent.

Hobbs, N. (1965). How the Re-ED plan developed. In N. J. Long, W. C. Morse, & R. G. Newman (Eds.), *Conflict in the classroom* (pp. 286–294). Belmont, CA: Wadsworth.

Hobbs, N. (1966). Helping the disturbed child: Psychological and ecological strategies. *American Psychologist, 21,* 1105–1115.

Hobbs, N. (1974). Nicholas Hobbs. In J. M. Kauffman & C. D. Lewis (Eds.), *Teaching children with behavior disorders: Personal perspectives* (pp. 142–167). Upper Saddle River, NJ: Merrill/Prentice Hall.

Hobbs, N. (1975a). *The futures of children.* San Francisco: Jossey-Bass.

Hobbs, N. (Ed.). (1975b). *Issues in the classification of children* (Vols. 1 and 2). San Francisco: Jossey-Bass.

Hoffman, E. (1974a). The treatment of deviance by the educational system: History. In W. C. Rhodes & S. Head (Eds.), *A study of child variance: Vol. 3. Service delivery systems* (pp. 41–80). Ann Arbor: University of Michigan.

Hoffman, E. (1974b). The treatment of deviance by the educational system: Structure. In W. C. Rhodes & S. Head (Eds.), *A study of child variance: Vol. 3. Service delivery systems* (pp. 81–144). Ann Arbor: University of Michigan.

Hoffman, E. (1975). The American public school and the deviant child: The origins of their involvement. *The Journal of Special Education, 9,* 415–423.

Hollingworth, L. S. (1923). *Special talents and defects: Their significance for education.* New York: Macmillan.

Hollister, W. G., & Goldston, S. E. (1962). *Considerations for planning classes for the emotionally disturbed.* Washington, DC: Council for Exceptional Children.

Homme, L. E. (1969). *How to use contingency contracting in the classroom.* Champaign, IL: Research Press.

Homme, L. (1970). Using behavioral technology to alter children's behavior. In P. A. Gallagher & L. L. Edwards (Eds.), *Educating the emotionally disturbed: Theory to practice* (pp. 57–67). Lawrence: University of Kansas.

Horn, J. L. (1924). *The education of exceptional children: A consideration of public school problems and policies in the field of differentiated education.* New York: Century.

Hosp, J. L., & Reschly, D. J. (2004). Disproportionate representation of minority students in special education: Academic, demographic, and economic predictors. *Exceptional Children, 70,* 185–199.

Howe, S. G. (1851). On training and educating idiots: The second annual report to the legislature of Massachusetts. *American Journal of Insanity, 8,* 97–118.

Howe, S. G. (1852). Third and final report of the Experimental School for Teaching and Training Idiotic Children; also, the first report of the trustees of the Massachusetts School for Idiotic and Feebleminded Youth. *American Journal of Insanity, 9,* 20–36.

Huefner, D. S. (2000). *Getting comfortable with special education law: A framework for working with children with disabilities.* Norwood, MA: Christopher-Gordon.

Hunt, J. McV. (Ed.). (1944a). *Personality and the behavior disorders: A handbook based on experimental and clinical research* (Vol. 1). New York: Ronald Press.

Hunt, J. McV. (Ed.). (1944b). *Personality and the behavior disorders: A handbook based on experimental and clinical research* (Vol. 2). New York: Ronald Press.

Hunter, R., & Macalpine, I. (Eds.). (1963). *Three hundred years of psychiatry, 1535–1860: A history in selected English texts.* London: Oxford University Press.

Hunter, R., & Macalpine, I. (1974). *Psychiatry for the poor. 1851 Colney Hatch Asylum–Friends Hospital. 1973: A medical and social history.* Kent, England: Dawsons of Pall Mall.

Ialongo, N. S., Vaden-Kiernan, N., & Kellam, S. (1998). Early peer rejection and aggression: Longitudinal relations with adolescent behavior. *Journal of Developmental and Physical Disabilities, 10*, 199–213.

Ingram, C. P., & Schumacher, H. C. (1950). The prevention of handicaps in children. In N. B. Henry (Ed.), *The education of exceptional children.* Forty–ninth Yearbook of the National Society for the Study of Education (Part 2, pp. 302–319). Chicago: University of Chicago Press.

Itard, J. M. G. (1962). *The wild boy of Aveyron.* New York: Appleton-Century-Crofts/Prentice Hall.

James, M., & Long, N. (1992). Looking beyond behavior and seeing my needs: A red flag interview. *Journal of Emotional and Behavioral Problems, 1*(2), 35–38.

Jarvis, E. (1852). On the supposed increase of insanity. *American Journal of Insanity, 8*, 333–364.

Johns, B. H. (2003). NCLB and IDEA: Never the twain should meet. *Learning Disabilities: A Multidisciplinary Journal, 12*(3), 89–91.

Johnson, J. L. (1969). Special education and the inner city: A challenge for the future or another means of cooling the mark out? *The Journal of Special Education, 3*, 241–251.

Johnson, J. L. (1971). Croton-on-campus: Experiment in the use of the behavioral sciences to educate black ghetto children. In N. J. Long, W. C. Morse, & R. G. Newman (Eds.), *Conflict in the classroom* (2nd ed., pp. 372–382). Belmont, CA: Wadsworth.

Jones, V., Dohrn, E., & Dunn, C. (2004). *Creating effective programs for students with emotional and behavioral disorders.* Boston: Allyn & Bacon.

Kameya, L. I. (1972a). Behavioral interventions in emotional disturbance. In W. C. Rhodes & M. L. Tracy (Eds.), *A study of child variance: Vol. 2. Interventions* (pp. 159–252). Ann Arbor: University of Michigan.

Kameya, L. I. (1972b). Biophysical interventions in emotional disturbance. In W. C. Rhodes & M. L. Tracy (Eds.), *A study of child variance: Vol. 2. Interventions* (pp. 75–158). Ann Arbor: University of Michigan.

Kamps, D. M., & Tankersley, M. (1996). Prevention of behavioral and conduct disorders: Trends and research issues. *Behavioral Disorders, 22*, 41–48.

Kanner, L. (1943). Autistic disturbances of affective contact. *Nervous Child, 2*, 217–250.

Kanner, L. (1944). Behavior disorders in childhood. In J. McV. Hunt (Ed.),

Personality and the behavior disorders: A handbook based on experimental and clinical research (Vol. 2, pp. 761–793). New York: Ronald Press.

Kanner, L. (1957). *Child psychiatry.* Springfield, IL: Thomas.

Kanner, L. (1960). Child psychiatry: Retrospect and prospect. *American Journal of Psychiatry, 117,* 15–22.

Kanner, L. (1962). Emotionally disturbed children: A historical review. *Child Development, 33,* 97–102.

Kanner, L. (1964). *History of the care and treatment of the mentally retarded.* Springfield, IL: Thomas.

Kanner, L. (1973a). The birth of early infantile autism. *Journal of Autism and Childhood Schizophrenia, 3,* 93–95.

Kanner, L. (1973b). *Childhood psychosis: Initial studies and new insights.* Washington, DC: Winston.

Kanner, L. (1973c). Historical perspective on developmental deviations. *Journal of Autism and Childhood Schizophrenia, 3,* 187–198.

Kantor, J. (1974). The treatment of deviance by the mental health system: A case study. In W. C. Rhodes & S. Head (Eds.), *A study of child variance: Vol. 3. Service delivery systems* (pp. 317–328). Ann Arbor: University of Michigan.

Kauffman, J. M. (1974a). Conclusion: Issues. In J. M. Kauffman & C. D. Lewis (Eds.), *Teaching children with behavior disorders: Personal perspectives* (pp. 275–284). Columbus, OH: Merrill.

Kauffman, J. M. (1974b). Series editors' foreword. In J. M. Kauffman & C. D. Lewis (Eds.), *Teaching children with behavior disorders: Personal perspectives* (pp. iii–iv). Columbus, OH: Merrill.

Kauffman, J. M. (1974c). Severely emotionally disturbed. In N. G. Haring (Ed.), *Behavior of exceptional children* (pp. 377–410). Columbus, OH: Merrill.

Kauffman, J. M. (1976). Nineteenth-century views of children's behavior disorders: Historical contributions and continuing issues. *The Journal of Special Education, 10,* 335–349.

Kauffman, J. M. (1977). *Characteristics of children's behavior disorders.* Columbus, OH: Merrill.

Kauffman, J. M. (1979). An historical perspective on disordered behavior and an alternative conceptualization of exceptionality. In F. H. Wood & K. C. Lakin (Eds.), *Disturbing, disordered, or disturbed? Perspectives on the definition of problem behavior in educational settings* (pp. 49–70). Minneapolis: University of Minnesota, Department of Psychoeducational Studies, Advanced Training Institute.

Kauffman, J. M. (1981). Historical trends and contemporary issues in special education in the United States. In J. M. Kauffman & D. P. Hallahan (Eds.), *Handbook of special education* (pp. 3–23). Upper Saddle River, NJ: Prentice Hall.

Kauffman, J. M. (1984). Saving children in the age of Big Brother: Moral and ethical issues in the identification of deviance. *Behavioral Disorders, 10,* 60–70.

Kauffman, J. M. (1989). The regular education initiative as Reagan–Bush education policy: A trickle-down theory of education of the hard-to-teach. *The Journal of Special Education, 23,* 256–278.

Kauffman, J. M. (1991). Restructuring in sociopolitical context: Reservations about the effects of current reform proposals on students with disabilities. In J. W. Lloyd, A. C. Repp, & N. N. Singh (Eds.), *The regular education initiative: Alternative perspectives on concepts, issues, and methods* (pp. 57–66). DeKalb, IL: Sycamore.

Kauffman, J. M. (1993). How we might achieve the radical reform of special education. *Exceptional Children, 60,* 6–16.

Kauffman, J. M. (1994, March 16). Taming aggression in the young: A call to action. *Education Week, 13*(25), 43.

Kauffman, J. M. (1995). Why we must celebrate a diversity of restrictive environments. *Learning Disabilities Research and Practice, 10,* 225–232.

Kauffman, J. M. (1996). Think about these things: Gentleness, truth, justice, excellence. *Education and Treatment of Children, 19,* 218–232.

Kauffman, J. M. (1997). Conclusion: A little of everything, a lot of nothing is an agenda for failure. *Journal of Emotional and Behavioral Disorders, 5,* 76–81.

Kauffman, J. M. (1999a). Comments on social development research in emotional and behavioral disorders. *Journal of Emotional and Behavioral Disorders, 7,* 189–191.

Kauffman, J. M. (1999b). Educating students with emotional or behavioral disorders: What's over the horizon? In L. M. Bullock & R. A. Gable (Eds.), *Educating students with emotional and behavioral disorders: Historical perspective and future directions* (pp. 38–59). Reston, VA: Council for Children with Behavioral Disorders.

Kauffman, J. M. (1999c). How we prevent the prevention of emotional and behavioral disorders. *Exceptional Children, 65,* 448–468.

175

Kauffman, J. M. (1999d). The role of science in behavioral disorders. *Behavioral Disorders, 24*, 265–272.

Kauffman, J. M. (1999e). Today's special education and its messages for tomorrow. *The Journal of Special Education, 32*, 244–254.

Kauffman, J. M. (1999f). What we make of difference and the difference we make. Foreword in V. L. Schwean & D. H. Saklofske (Eds.), *Handbook of psychosocial characteristics of exceptional children* (pp. ix–xii). New York: Plenum.

Kauffman, J. M. (1999–2000). The special education story: Obituary, accident report, conversion experience, reincarnation, or none of the above? *Exceptionality, 8*(1), 61–71.

Kauffman, J. M. (2002). *Education deform: Bright people sometimes say stupid things about education.* Lanham, MD: Scarecrow Education.

Kauffman, J. M. (2003a). Appearances, stigma, and prevention. *Remedial and Special Education, 24*, 195–198.

Kauffman, J. M. (2003b). Reflections on the field. *Behavioral Disorders, 28*, 205–208.

Kauffman, J. M. (2004a). Foreword. In H. M. Walker, E. Ramsey, & F. M. Gresham (Eds.), *Antisocial behavior in school: Strategies and best practices* (2nd ed., pp. xix–xxi). Belmont, CA: Wadsworth.

Kauffman, J. M. (2004b). The President's Commission and the devaluation of special education. *Education and Treatment of Children, 27*, 307–324.

Kauffman, J. M. (2005a). *Characteristics of emotional and behavioral disorders of children and youth* (8th ed.). Upper Saddle River, NJ: Merrill/Prentice Hall.

Kauffman, J. M. (2005b). How we prevent the prevention of emotional and behavioral difficulties in education. In P. Clough, P. Garner, J. T. Pardeck, & F. K. O. Yuen (Eds.), *Handbook of emotional and behavioral difficulties in education* (pp. 429–440). London: Sage.

Kauffman, J. M. (2005c). Waving to Ray Charles: Missing the meaning of disability. *Phi Delta Kappan, 86*, 520–521, 524.

Kauffman, J. M., Bantz, J., & McCullough, J. (2002). Separate and better: A special public school class for students with emotional and behavioral disorders. *Exceptionality, 10*, 149–170.

Kauffman, J. M., Brigham, F. J., & Mock, D. R. (2004). Historical and contemporary perspectives in the field of behavioral disorders. In R. B. Rutherford, M. M. Quinn, & S. R. Mathur (Eds.)., *Handbook of research in emotional and behavioral disorders* (pp. 15–31). New York: Guilford Press.

Kauffman, J. M., & Burbach, H. J. (1997). On creating a climate of classroom civility. *Phi Delta Kappan, 79*, 320–325.

Kauffman, J. M., & Hallahan, D. P. (1993). Toward a comprehensive service delivery system. In J. I. Goodlad & T. C. Lovitt (Eds.), *Integrating general and special education* (pp. 73–102). Upper Saddle River, NJ: Merrill/Prentice Hall.

Kauffman, J. M., & Hallahan, D. P. (Eds.). (1995). *The illusion of full inclusion: A comprehensive critique of a current special education bandwagon.* Austin, TX: PRO-ED.

Kauffman, J. M., & Hallahan, D. P. (Eds.). (2005a). *The illusion of full inclusion: A comprehensive critique of a current special education bandwagon* (2nd ed.). Austin, TX: PRO-ED

Kauffman, J. M., & Hallahan, D. P. (2005b). *Special education: What it is and why we need it.* Boston: Allyn & Bacon.

Kauffman, J. M., & Krouse, J. (1981). The cult of educability: Searching for the substance of things hoped for, the evidence of things not seen. *Analysis and Intervention in Developmental Disabilities, 1*, 53–60.

Kauffman, J. M., & Lewis, C. D. (Eds.). (1974). *Teaching children with behavior disorders: Personal perspectives.* Columbus, OH: Merrill.

Kauffman, J. M., Lloyd, J. W., Baker, J., & Riedel, T. M. (1995). Inclusion of all students with emotional or behavioral disorders? Let's think again. *Phi Delta Kappan, 76*, 542–546.

Kauffman, J. M., Mostert, M. P., Trent, S. C., & Pullen, P. L. (2006). *Managing classroom behavior: A reflective case-based approach* (4th ed.). Boston: Allyn & Bacon.

Kauffman, J. M., & Smucker, K. (1995). The legacies of placement: A brief history of placement options and issues with commentary on their evolution. In J. M. Kauffman, J. W. Lloyd, D. P. Hallahan, & T. A. Astuto (Eds.), *Issues in educational placement: Students with emotional and behavioral disorders* (pp. 21–44). Hillsdale, NJ: Erlbaum.

Kauffman, J. M., & Wiley, A. L. (2004). How the President's Commission on Excellence in Special Education (PCESE) devalues special education. *Learning Disabilities: A Multidisciplinary Journal, 13*(1), 3–6.

Kavale, K. A., & Forness, S. R. (2000). History, rhetoric and reality: Analysis of the inclusion debate. *Remedial and Special Education, 21*, 279–296.

Kazdin, A. E. (1978). *History of behavior modification: Experimental foundations of contemporary research.* Baltimore: University Park Press.

Kazdin, A. E. (1994). Interventions for aggressive and antisocial children. In L. D. Eron, J. H. Gentry, & P. Schlegel (Eds.), *Reason to hope: A psychosocial perspective on violence and youth* (pp. 341–382). Washington, DC: American Psychological Association.

Kazdin, A. E. (1995). *Conduct disorders in childhood and adolescence* (2nd ed.). Thousand Oaks, CA: Sage.

Kazdin, A. E. (1998). Conduct disorder. In R. J. Morris & T. R. Kratochwill (Eds.), *The practice of child therapy* (3rd ed., pp. 199–230). Boston: Allyn & Bacon.

Kazdin, A. E. (2001). *Behavior modification in applied settings* (6th ed.). Belmont, CA: Wadsworth.

Kelly, F. J. (1931). *Special education: The handicapped and gifted, Committee on Special Classes: Section 3. Education and training.* New York: Century.

Keogh, B. K. (2003). *Temperament in the classroom: Understanding individual differences.* Baltimore: Brookes.

Kerr, M. M., & Nelson, C. M. (2002). *Strategies for addressing behavior problems in the classroom* (4th ed.). Upper Saddle River, NJ: Prentice Hall.

Kerr, M. M., Nelson, C. M., & Lambert, D. L. (1987). *Helping adolescents with learning and behavior problems.* Upper Saddle River, NJ: Merrill/Prentice Hall.

Kerr, M. M., & Zigmond, N. (1986). What do high school teachers want? A study of expectations and standards. *Education and Treatment of Children, 9,* 239–249.

Key, E. (1909). *The century of the child.* New York: Putnam.

Killing off housing for the poor. (2004, May 10). *The New York Times,* p. A24.

Kingery, P. M., & Walker, H. M. (2002). What we know about school safety. In M. R. Shinn, H. M. Walker, & G. Stoner (Eds.), *Interventions for academic and behavior problems II: Preventive and remedial approaches* (pp. 71–88). Bethesda, MD: National Association of School Psychologists.

Kirk, S. A. (1962). *Educating exceptional children.* Boston: Houghton Mifflin.

Kirk, S. A. (1976). Samuel A. Kirk. In J. M. Kauffman & D. P. Hallahan (Eds.), *Teaching children with learning disabilities: Personal perspectives* (pp. 238–269). Columbus, OH: Merrill.

Kirk, S. A. (1984). Introspection and prophecy. In B. Blatt & R. Morris (Eds.), *Perspectives in special education: Personal orientations* (pp. 25–55). Glenview, IL: Scott, Foresman.

Kirk, S. A., & Lord, F. E. (Eds.). (1974). *Exceptional children: Educational resources and perspectives*. Boston: Houghton Mifflin.

Knitzer, J. (1982). *Unclaimed children: The failure of public responsibility to children and adolescents in need of mental health services*. Washington, DC: Children's Defense Fund.

Knitzer, J., & Aber, J. L. (1995). Young children in poverty: Facing the facts. *American Journal of Orthopsychiatry, 65*, 174–176.

Knitzer, J., Steinberg, Z., & Fleisch, F. (1990). *At the schoolhouse door: An examination of programs and policies for children with behavioral and emotional problems*. New York: Bank Street College of Education.

Knoblock, P. (Ed.). (1965). *Educational programming for emotionally disturbed children: The decade ahead*. Syracuse, NY: Syracuse University Press.

Knoblock, P. (Ed.). (1966). *Intervention approaches in educating emotionally disturbed children*. Syracuse, NY: Syracuse University Press.

Knoblock, P. (1970). A new humanism for special education: The concept of the open classroom for emotionally disturbed children. In P. A. Gallagher & L. L. Edwards (Eds.), *Educating the emotionally disturbed: Theory to practice* (pp. 68–85). Lawrence: University of Kansas.

Knoblock, P. (1973). Open education for emotionally disturbed children. *Exceptional Children, 39*, 358–365.

Knoblock, P. (1979). Educational alternatives for adolescents labeled emotionally disturbed. In D. Cullinan & M. H. Epstein (Eds.), *Special education for adolescents: Issues and perspectives* (pp. 273–304). Upper Saddle River, NJ: Merrill/Prentice Hall.

Knoblock, P. (1983). *Teaching emotionally disturbed children*. Boston: Houghton Mifflin.

Knoblock, P., & Goldstein, A. (1971). *The lonely teacher*. Boston: Allyn & Bacon.

Knoblock, P., & Johnson, J. L. (Eds.). (1967). *The teaching-learning process in educating emotionally disturbed children*. Syracuse, NY: Syracuse University Press.

Kohl, H. (1970). *The open classroom*. New York: Vintage.

Kohn, A. (1993). *Punished by rewards*. Boston: Houghton Mifflin.

Konopasek, D. E. (1996). *Medication fact sheets: A medication reference guide for the non-medical professional*. Anchorage, AK: Arctic Tern.

Konopasek, D., & Forness, S. R. (2004). Psychopharmacology in the treatment of emotional and behavioral disorders. In R. B. Rutherford, M. M.

Quinn, & S. R. Mathur (Eds.), *Handbook of research in emotional and behavioral disorders* (pp. 352–368). New York: Guilford Press.

Kornberg, L. (1955). *A class for disturbed children: A case study and its meaning for education.* New York: Teachers College Press.

Kozol, J. (1972). *Free schools.* Boston: Houghton Mifflin.

Krasner, L., & Ullmann, L. P. (Eds.). (1965). *Research in behavior modification: New developments and implications.* New York: Holt, Rinehart & Winston.

Kreuter, M. (1967). The prison school. In P. H. Berkowitz & E. P. Rothman (Eds.), *Public education for disturbed children in New York City* (pp. 143–161). Springfield, IL: Thomas.

Krugman, M. (1953). Symposium: The education of emotionally disturbed children. *American Journal of Orthopsychiatry, 23,* 667–731.

Lamb, H. R., & Weinberger, L. E. (Eds.). (2001). *Deinstitutionalization: Promise and problems.* San Francisco: Jossey-Bass.

Landrum, T. J., & Kauffman, J. M. (in press). Behavioral approaches to classroom management. In C. M. Evertson & C. S. Weinstein (Eds.), *Handbook of classroom management: Research, practice, and contemporary issues.* Mahwah, NJ: Erlbaum.

Lane, H. (1976). *The wild boy of Aveyron.* Cambridge, MA: Harvard University Press.

Lane, K. L. (2004). Academic instruction and tutoring interventions for students with emotional/behavioral disorders: 1990 to the present. In R. B. Rutherford, M. M. Quinn, & S. R. Mathur (Eds.), *Handbook of research in emotional and behavioral disorders* (pp. 462–486). New York: Guilford Press.

Lee, B. (1971). Curriculum design: The re–education approach. In N. J. Long, W. C. Morse, & R. G. Newman (Eds.), *Conflict in the classroom* (2nd ed., pp. 383–394). Belmont, CA: Wadsworth.

Leone, P. E., Rutherford, R. B., & Nelson, C. M. (1991). *Special education in juvenile corrections.* Reston, VA: Council for Exceptional Children.

Lerman, D. C., & Vorndran, C. M. (2002). On the status of knowledge for using punishment: Implications for treating behavior disorders. *Journal of Applied Behavior Analysis, 35,* 431–464.

Lewis, C. D. (1974). Introduction: Landmarks. In J. M. Kauffman & C. D. Lewis (Eds.), *Teaching children with behavior disorders: Personal perspectives* (pp. 2–23). Columbus, OH: Merrill.

Lewis, T. J., Lewis-Palmer, T., Newcomer, L., & Stichter, J. (2004). Applied behavior analysis and the education and treatment of students with emotional and behavioral disorders. In R. B. Rutherford, M. M. Quinn, & S. R. Mathur (Eds.), *Handbook of research in emotional and behavioral disorders* (pp. 523–545). New York: Guilford Press.

Lewis, W. W. (1982). Ecological factors in successful residential treatment. *Behavioral Disorders, 7*, 149–156.

Liaupsin, C. J., Jolivette, K., & Scott, R. M. (2004). Schoolwide systems of behavior support: Maximizing student success in schools. In R. B. Rutherford, M. M. Quinn, & S. R. Mathur (Eds.), *Handbook of research in emotional and behavioral disorders* (pp. 487–501). New York: Guilford Press.

Lieberman, L. (1985). Special and regular education: A merger made in heaven? *Exceptional Children, 51*, 513–517.

Lipsky, D. K., & Gartner, A. (1996). Inclusion, school restructuring, and the remaking of American society. *Harvard Educational Review, 66*, 762–796.

Liss, E. (1935). *The scientist looks at the emotionally unstable child: Part 2. Play techniques in child analysis* (pp. 15–22). Langhorne, PA: Child Research Clinic of the Woods Schools.

Lloyd, J. W., Singh, N. N., & Repp, A. C. (Eds.). (1991). *The Regular Education Initiative: Alternative perspectives on concepts, issues, and models*. Sycamore, IL: Sycamore.

Locke, E. A. (2002). The dead end of postmodernism. *American Psychologist, 57*, 458.

Loeber, R., Farrington, D. P., Stouthamer-Loeber, M., & Van Kammen, W. B. (1998a). *Antisocial behavior and mental health problems: Explanatory factors in childhood and adolescence*. Mahwah, NJ: Erlbaum.

Loeber, R., Farrington, D. P., Stouthamer-Loeber, M., & Van Kammen, W. B. (1998b). Multiple risk factors for multi-problem boys: Co-occurrence of delinquency, substance use, attention deficit, conduct problems, physical aggression, covert behavior, depressed mood, and shy/withdrawn behavior. In R. Jessor (Ed.), *New perspectives on adolescent risk behavior* (pp. 90–149). New York: Cambridge University Press.

Loeber, R., Green, S. M., Lahey, B. B., Christ, M. A. G., & Frick, P. J. (1992). Developmental sequences in the age of onset of disruptive child behaviors. *Journal of Child and Family Studies, 1*, 21–41.

Long, N. J. (1974). Nicholas J. Long. In J. M. Kauffman & C. D. Lewis (Eds.), *Teaching children with behavior disorders: Personal perspectives* (pp. 168–196). Upper Saddle River, NJ: Merrill/Prentice Hall.

Long, N. J., Fecser, F. A., & Brendtro, L. K. (1998). Life space crisis intervention: New skills for reclaiming students showing patterns of self-defeating behavior. *Healing, 3*(2), 2–22.

Long, N. J., Morse, W. C., & Newman, R. G. (Eds.). (1965). *Conflict in the classroom*. Belmont, CA: Wadsworth.

Long, N. J., & Newman, R. G. (1965). Managing surface behavior of children in school. In N. J. Long, W. C. Morse, & R. G. Newman (Eds.), *Conflict in the classroom* (pp. 352–362). Belmont, CA: Wadsworth.

Lovaas, O. I. (1966). A program for the establishment of speech in psychotic children. In J. K. Wing (Ed.), *Early childhood autism: Clinical, educational and social aspects*. New York: Pergamon.

Lovaas, O. I. (1967). A behavior therapy approach to the treatment of childhood schizophrenia. In J. P. Hill (Ed.), *Minnesota symposia on child psychology* (Vol. 1, pp. 108–157). Minneapolis: University of Minnesota Press.

Lovaas, O. I. (1987). Behavioral treatment and normal educational and intellectual functioning in young autistic children. *Journal of Consulting and Clinical Psychology, 55*, 3–9.

Lovaas, O. I., & Koegel, R. L. (1973). Behavior therapy with autistic children. In C. Thoresen (Ed.), *Behavior modification in education*. Chicago: University of Chicago Press.

Lovaas, O. I., Koegel, R. L., Simmons, J. Q., & Long, J. S. (1973). Some generalization and follow-up measures on autistic children in behavior therapy. *Journal of Applied Behavior Analysis, 6*, 131–166.

Lovaas, O. I., Young, D. B., & Newsom, C. D. (1978). Childhood psychosis: Behavioral treatment. In B. B. Wolman (Ed.), *Handbook of treatment of mental disorders in childhood and adolescence* (pp. 385–420). Upper Saddle River, NJ: Prentice Hall.

Mackie, R. P., Kvaraceus, W. C., & Williams, H. M. (1957). *Teachers of children who are socially and emotionally maladjusted*. Washington, DC: U.S. Department of Health, Education and Welfare, Office of Education.

MacMillan, D. L., Gresham, F. M., & Forness, S. R. (1996). Full inclusion: An empirical perspective. *Behavioral Disorders, 21*, 145–159.

MacMillan, D. L., & Hendrick, I. G. (1993). Evolution and legacies. In J. I. Goodlad & T. C. Lovitt (Eds.), *Integrating general and special education* (pp. 23–48). Columbus, OH: Merrill/Macmillan.

MacMillan, M. B. (1960). Extra-scientific influences in the history of childhood psychopathology. *American Journal of Psychiatry, 116,* 1091–1096.

Mahler, M. S. (1952). On child psychosis and schizophrenia. *Psychoanalytic Study of the Child, 7,* 286–305.

Mahoney, M. J. (1974). *Cognition and behavior modification.* Cambridge, MA: Ballinger.

Malone, J. C. (2003). Advances in behaviorism: It's not what it used to be. *Journal of Behavioral Education, 12,* 85–89.

Mann, L. (1979). *On the trail of process: A historical perspective on cognitive processes and their training.* New York: Grune & Stratton.

Marquez, G. G. (2003). *Living to tell the tale* (E. Grossman, Trans.). New York: Knopf.

Martella, R. C., Nelson, J. R., & Marchand-Martella, N. E. (2003). *Managing disruptive behaviors in the schools: A schoolwide, classroom, and individualized learning approach.* Boston: Allyn & Bacon.

Martens, E. H. (1941). Education for a strong America. *Exceptional Children, 8,* 36–41.

Martens, E. H., & Russ, H. (1932). Adjustment of behavior problems of school children: A description and evaluation of the clinical program in Berkeley, Calif. Washington, DC: U.S. Government Printing Office.

Martin, E. W. (1972). Individualism and behaviorism as future trends in educating handicapped children. *Exceptional Children, 38,* 517–525.

Martin, L. C. (1940). Shall we segregate our handicapped? *Exceptional Children, 6,* 223–225, 237.

Mateer, F. (1924). *The unstable child: An interpretation of psychopathy as a source of unbalanced behavior in abnormal and troublesome children.* New York: Appleton.

Maudsley, H. (1880). *The pathology of the mind.* New York: Appleton.

Mayo, T. (1839). *Elements of pathology of the human mind.* Philadelphia: Waldie.

McCandless, B. R. (1956). The emotionally disturbed. In M. E. Frampton & E. D. Gall (Eds.), *Special education for the exceptional: Vol. 3. Mental and emotional deviates and special problems* (pp. 274–307). Boston: Porter Sargent.

McDowell, R. L., Adamson, G. W., & Wood, F. H. (Eds.). (1982). *Teaching emotionally disturbed children.* Boston: Little, Brown.

McGee, K. A., & Kauffman, J. M. (1989). Educating teachers with emotional disabilities: A balance of private and public interests. *Teacher Education and Special Education, 12*(3), 110–116.

McMahon, R. J., & Wells, K. C. (1998). Conduct problems. In E. J. Mash & R. A. Barkley (Eds.), *Treatment of childhood disorders* (2nd ed., pp. 111–207). New York: Guilford Press.

McManus, M. E., & Kauffman, J. M. (1991). Working conditions of teachers of students with behavioral disorders: A national survey. *Behavioral Disorders, 16*, 247–259.

Meichenbaum, D. (1977). Cognitive-behavior modification: An integrative approach. New York: Plenum.

Menninger, K. (1963). *The vital balance*. New York: Viking.

Menolascino, F. J. (1972). Primitive, atypical, and abnormal-psychotic behavior in institutionalized mentally retarded children. *Journal of Autism and Childhood Schizophrenia, 3*(1), 49–64.

Menolascino, F. J. (1990). The nature and types of mental illness in the mentally retarded. In M. Lewis & S. M. Miller (Eds.), *Handbook of developmental psychopathology* (pp. 397–408). New York: Plenum.

Merrell, K. W., & Walker, H. M. (2004). Deconstructing a definition: Social maladjustment versus emotional disturbance and moving the EBD field forward. *Psychology in the Schools, 41*, 899–910.

Mesinger, J. F. (1985). A commentary on "A rationale for the merger of special and regular education." *Exceptional Children, 51*, 510–513.

Miller, S. R., Ewing, N. J., & Phelps, L. A. (1980). Career and vocational education for the handicapped: A historical perspective. In L. Mann & D. A. Sabatino (Eds.), *The fourth review of special education* (pp. 341–366). New York: Grune & Stratton.

Mitchell, R. (2004, April 27). Dumbing down our schools. *The Washington Post*, p. A21.

Mock, D. R., Jakubecy, J. J., & Kauffman, J. M. (2003). Special education, history of. In J. W. Guthrie (Ed.), *Encyclopedia of education* (2nd ed., pp. 2278–2284). New York: Macmillan Reference.

Mock, D., & Kauffman, J. M. (2002). Preparing teachers for full inclusion: Is it possible? *Teacher Educator, 37*, 202–215.

Mock, D. R., & Kauffman, J. M. (2005). The delusion of full inclusion. In J. W. Jacobson, R. M. Foxx, & J. A. Mulick (Eds.), *Controversial therapies for developmental disabilities: Fad, fashion, and science in professional practice* (pp. 113–128). Mahwah, NJ: Erlbaum.

Moore, B. (1974a). Counter cultural alternatives to modern institutions. In

W. C. Rhodes & S. Head (Eds.), *A study of child variance: Vol. 3. Service delivery systems* (pp. 41–80). Ann Arbor: University of Michigan.

Moore, B. (1974b). The roots of counter institutions. In W. C. Rhodes & S. Head (Eds.), *A study of child variance: Vol. 3. Service delivery systems* (pp. 595–635). Ann Arbor: University of Michigan.

Morgan, J. J. B. (1937). *The psychology of the unadjusted school child.* New York: Macmillan.

Morse, W. C. (1953). The development of a mental hygiene milieu in a camp program for disturbed boys. *American Journal of Orthopsychiatry, 23*, 826–833.

Morse, W. C. (1958). The education of socially maladjusted and emotionally disturbed children. In W. M. Cruickshank & G. O. Johnson (Eds.), *Education of exceptional children and youth* (pp. 557–608). Englewood Cliffs, NJ: Prentice Hall.

Morse, W. C. (1965a). The crisis teacher. In N. J. Long, W. C. Morse, & R. G. Newman (Eds.), *Conflict in the classroom* (pp. 251–254). Belmont, CA: Wadsworth.

Morse, W. C. (1965b). Intervention techniques for the classroom teacher. In P. Knoblock (Ed.), *Educational programming for emotionally disturbed children: The decade ahead* (pp. 29–41). Syracuse, NY: Syracuse University Press.

Morse, W. C. (1971a). The crisis or helping teacher. In N. J. Long, W. C. Morse, & R. G. Newman (Eds.), *Conflict in the classroom* (2nd ed., pp. 294–296). Belmont, CA: Wadsworth.

Morse, W. C. (1971b). Crisis intervention in school mental health and special classes for the disturbed. In N. J. Long, W. C. Morse, & R. G. Newman (Eds.), *Conflict in the classroom* (2nd ed., pp. 459–464). Belmont, CA: Wadsworth.

Morse, W. C. (1974). William C. Morse. In J. M. Kauffman & C. D. Lewis (Eds.), *Teaching children with behavior disorders: Personal perspectives* (pp. 198–216). Upper Saddle River, NJ: Merrill/Prentice Hall.

Morse, W. C. (1985). *The education and treatment of socioemotionally impaired children and youth.* Syracuse, NY: Syracuse University Press.

Morse, W. C. (1994). Comments from a biased point of view. *The Journal of Special Education, 27*, 531–542.

Morse, W. C., Ardizzone, J., MacDonald, C., & Pasick, P. (1980). *Affective education for special children and youth.* Reston, VA: Council for Exceptional Children.

Morse, W. C., Cutler, R. L., & Fink, A. H. (1964). *Public school classes for the emotionally handicapped: A research analysis.* Washington, DC: Council for Exceptional Children.

Morse, W. C., & Wineman, D. (1965). Group interviewing in a camp for disturbed boys. In N. J. Long, W. C. Morse, & R. G. Newman (Eds.), *Conflict in the classroom* (pp. 374–380). Belmont, CA: Wadsworth.

Mostert, M. P., Kauffman, J. M., & Kavale, K. A. (2003). Truth and consequences. *Behavioral Disorders, 28,* 333–347.

Motto, J. J., & Wilkins, G. S. (1968). Educational achievement of institutionalized emotionally disturbed children. *Journal of Educational Research, 61,* 218–221.

Murphy, D. M. (Ed.). (1986a). Handicapped juvenile offenders [Special issue]. *Remedial and Special Education, 7*(3).

Murphy, D. M. (1986b). The prevalence of handicapping conditions among juvenile delinquents. *Remedial and Special Education, 7*(3), 7–17.

National Research Council. (2001). *Educating children with autism.* Washington, DC: National Academy Press.

National Research Council. (2002). *Minority students in special and gifted education.* Committee on Minority Representation in Special Education. In M. S. Donovan & C. T. Cross (Eds.), Division of Behavior and Social Sciences Education. Washington, DC: National Academy Press.

Neff, A. (1974). The treatment of deviance by the legal-correctional system: A case study. In W. C. Rhodes & S. Head (Eds.), *A study of child variance: Vol. 3. Service delivery systems* (pp. 217–240). Ann Arbor: University of Michigan.

Neier, A. (2001, October 9). Warring against modernity. *The Washington Post,* p. A29.

Neill, A. S. (1927). *The problem child.* New York: Robert M. McBride.

Neill, A. S. (1960). *Summerhill.* New York: Hart.

Nelson, C. M. (Ed.). (1978). *Field-based teacher training: Applications in special education.* Minneapolis: University of Minnesota, Department of Psychoeducational Studies.

Nelson, C. M., Leone, P. E., & Rutherford, R. B. (2004). Youth delinquency: Prevention and intervention. In R. B. Rutherford, M. M. Quinn, & S. R. Mathur (Eds.), *Handbook of research in emotional and behavioral disorders* (pp. 282–301). New York: Guilford Press.

Nelson, C. M., & Pearson, C. A. (1991). *Integrating services for children and youth with emotional and behavioral disorders.* Reston, VA: Council for Exceptional Children.

Nelson, C. M., Rutherford, R. B., & Wolford, B. I. (Eds.). (1987). *Special education in the criminal justice system.* Upper Saddle River, NJ: Merrill/ Prentice Hall.

Nemetz-Carlson, A. (1974). A case study of alternative institutions in Noah. In W. C. Rhodes & S. Head (Eds.), *A study of child variance: Vol. 3. Service delivery systems* (pp. 637–667). Ann Arbor: University of Michigan.

Odiorne, D. M. (1934). *Emotional instability: A case study.* Langhorne, PA: Child Research Clinic of the Woods Schools.

Ollendick, T. H., & Hersen, M. (1983). A historical overview of child psychopathology. In T. H. Ollendick & M. Hersen (Eds.), *Handbook of child psychopathology* (pp. 3–11). New York: Plenum Press.

Osher, D., Cartledge, G., Oswald, D., Sutherland, K. S., Artiles, A. J., & Coutinho, M. (2004). Cultural and linguistic competency and disproportionate representation. In R. B. Rutherford, M. M. Quinn, & S. R. Mathur (Eds.), *Handbook of research in emotional and behavioral disorders* (pp. 54–77). New York: Guilford Press.

Pate, J. E. (1963). Emotionally disturbed and socially maladjusted children. In L. M. Dunn (Ed.), *Exceptional children in the schools* (pp. 239–283). New York: Holt, Rinehart & Winston.

Patterson, G. R. (1965a). An application of operant conditioning techniques to the control of a hyperactive child. In L. P. Ullmann & L. Krasner (Eds.), *Case studies in behavior modification.* New York: Holt, Rinehart & Winston.

Patterson, G. R. (1965b). A learning theory approach to the treatment of the school phobic child. In L. P. Ullmann & L. Krasner (Eds.), *Research in behavior modification: New developments and implications.* New York: Holt, Rinehart & Winston.

Patterson, G. R. (1973). Reprogramming the families of aggressive boys. In C. Thoresen (Ed.), *Behavior modification in education.* Chicago: University of Chicago Press.

Patterson, G. R. (1975). The aggressive child: Victim or architect of a coercive system? In L. A. Hammerlynck, L. C. Handy, & E. J. Mash (Eds.), *Behavior modification and families* (pp. 267–316). New York: Brunner/ Mazel.

Patterson, G. R. (1980). Mothers: The unacknowledged victims. *Monographs of the Society for Research in Child Development, 45*(5, Serial No. 186).

Patterson, G. R. (1982). *Coercive family process.* Eugene, OR: Castalia.

Patterson, G. R. (1986). Performance models for antisocial boys. *American Psychologist, 41,* 432–444.

Patterson, G. R., & Forgatch, M. (1987). *Parents and adolescents living together.* Eugene, OR: Castalia.

Patterson, G. R., Reid, J. B., & Dishion, T. J. (1992). *Antisocial boys.* Eugene, OR: Castalia.

Patterson, G. R., Reid, J. B., Jones, R. R., & Conger, R. E. (1975). *A social learning approach to family intervention: Vol. 1. Families with aggressive children.* Eugene, OR: Castalia.

Patton, S. (Producer), Mondale, S. (Director), & Monmaney, T. (Writer). (1988). *Asylum.* [Videotape]. Washington, DC: Stone Lantern Films.

Peacock Hill Working Group. (1991). Problems and promises in special education and related services for children and youth with emotional or behavioral disorders. *Behavioral Disorders, 16,* 299–313.

Pekarsky, D. (1974a). The treatment of deviance by the religious institutions: History. In W. C. Rhodes & S. Head (Eds.), *A study of child variance: Vol. 3. Service delivery systems* (pp. 441–498). Ann Arbor: University of Michigan.

Pekarsky, D. (1974b). The treatment of deviance by the religious institutions: Structure. In W. C. Rhodes & S. Head (Eds.), *A study of child variance: Vol. 3. Service delivery systems* (pp. 499–558). Ann Arbor: University of Michigan.

Peterson, R., & Ishii-Jordan, S. (Eds.). (1994). *Multicultural issues in the education of students with behavioral disorders.* Cambridge, MA: Brookline.

Phillips, E. L. (1962). Contributions to a learning-theory account of childhood autism. In E. P. Trapp & P. Himelstein (Eds.), *Readings on the exceptional child: Research and theory* (pp. 602–609). New York: Appleton-Century-Crofts.

Phillips, E. L. (1967). Problems in educating emotionally disturbed children. In N. G. Haring & E. L. Phillips (Eds.), *Methods in special education* (pp. 137–158). New York: McGraw-Hill.

Phillips, E. L., & Haring, N. G. (1959). Results from special techniques for teaching emotionally disturbed children. *Exceptional Children, 26,* 64–67.

Phillips, L., Draguns, J. G., & Bartlett, D. P. (1975). Classification of behavior disorders. In N. Hobbs (Ed.), *Issues in the classification of children* (Vol. 1, pp. 26–55). San Francisco: Jossey-Bass.

Pinker, S. (2002). *The blank slate: The modern denial of human nature*. New York: Viking.

Pollak, R. (1997). *The creation of Dr. B: A biography of Bruno Bettelheim*. New York: Simon & Schuster.

Postel, H. H. (1937). The special school versus the special class. *Exceptional Children, 4*, 12–13, 18–19.

Potter, H. W. (1933). Schizophrenia in children. *American Journal of Psychiatry, 89*, 1253–1270.

Potter, H. W. (1935). *The scientist looks at the emotionally unstable child: Part 2. Family situations in relation to the emotionally unstable child* (pp. 5–13). Langhorne, PA: Child Research Clinic of the Woods Schools.

Proceedings of the First Annual Meeting of the International Council for the Education of Exceptional Children. (n.d.). Arlington, VA: Council for Exceptional Children.

Prugh, D. G., Engel, M., & Morse, W. C. (1975). Emotional disturbance in children. In N. Hobbs (Ed.), *Issues in the classification of children* (Vol. 1, pp. 261–299). San Francisco: Jossey-Bass.

Quay, H. C. (1975). Classification in the treatment of delinquency and antisocial behavior. In N. Hobbs (Ed.), *Issues in the classification of children* (Vol. 1, pp. 377–392). San Francisco: Jossey-Bass.

Quay, H. C. (1977). Measuring dimensions of deviant behavior: The Behavior Problem Checklist. *Journal of Abnormal Child Psychology, 5*, 277–289.

Quinn, K. P., Epstein, M. H., & Cumblad, C. L. (1995). Developing comprehensive, individualized, community-based services for children and youth with emotional and behavior disorders: Direct service providers' perspectives. *Journal of Child and Family Studies, 4*, 19–42.

Rank, B. (1949). Adaptation of the psychoanalytic techniques for the treatment of young children with atypical development. *American Journal of Orthopsychiatry, 19*, 130–139.

Rautman, A. L. (1944). Special class placement. *Exceptional Children, 10*, 99–102.

Ravlin, M. (1974). The treatment of deviance by the social welfare system: A case study. In W. C. Rhodes & S. Head (Eds.), *A study of child variance: Vol. 3. Service delivery systems* (pp. 415–439). Ann Arbor: University of Michigan.

Ray, I. (1846). Observations of the principal hospitals for the insane, in Great Britain, France, and Germany. *American Journal of Insanity, 2,* 289–390.

Ray, I. (1852, May 18). On the best methods of saving our hospitals for the insane from the odium and scandal to which such institutions are liable, and maintaining their place in the popular estimation: Including the consideration of the question, How far is the community to be allowed access to such hospitals? Paper presented at a meeting of the Association of Medical Superintendents of American Institutions for the Insane, New York, NY. (Reprinted in *American Journal of Insanity, 9,* 36–65.)

Raymer, R. (1992, April 13). Annals of science: A silent childhood. *The New Yorker,* pp. 41–81, 43–77.

Redl, F. (1959a). The concept of the life space interview. *American Journal of Orthopsychiatry, 29,* 1–18.

Redl, F. (1959b). The concept of a therapeutic milieu. *American Journal of Orthopsychiatry, 29,* 721–734.

Redl, F. (1966). Designing a therapeutic classroom environment for disturbed children: The milieu approach. In P. Knoblock (Ed.), *Intervention approaches in educating emotionally disturbed children* (pp. 79–98). Syracuse, NY: Syracuse University Press.

Redl, F., & Wattenberg, W. W. (1951). *Mental hygiene in teaching.* New York: Harcourt, Brace, & World.

Redl, F., & Wineman, D. (1951). *Children who hate.* New York: Free Press.

Redl, F., & Wineman, D. (1952). *Controls from within.* New York: Free Press.

Rees, T. P. (1957). Back to moral treatment and community care. *Journal of Mental Science, 103,* 303–313.

Reich, R. B. (2004). *Reason: Why liberals will win the battle for America.* New York: Knopf.

Reisman, J. M. (1976). *A history of clinical psychology* (enlarged ed.). New York: Irvington.

Rezmierski, V. E., Knoblock, P., & Bloom, R. B. (1982). The psychoeducational model: Theory and historical perspective. In R. L. McDowell, G. W. Adamson, & F. H. Wood (Eds.), *Teaching emotionally disturbed children* (pp. 47–69). Boston: Little, Brown.

Rezmierski, V., & Kotre, J. (1972). A limited literature review of theory of the psychodynamic model. In W. C. Rhodes & M. L. Tracy (Eds.), *A study of child variance: Vol. 1. Theories* (pp. 181–258). Ann Arbor: University of Michigan.

Rhodes, W. C. (1963). Curriculum and disordered behavior. *Exceptional Children, 30,* 61–66.

Rhodes, W. C. (1965). Institutionalized displacement and the disturbing child. In P. Knoblock (Ed.), *Educational programming for emotionally disturbed children: The decade ahead* (pp. 42–57). Syracuse, NY: Syracuse University Press.

Rhodes, W. C. (1967). The disturbing child: A problem of ecological management. *Exceptional Children, 33,* 449–455.

Rhodes, W. C. (1970). A community participation analysis of emotional disturbance. *Exceptional Children, 37,* 309–314.

Rhodes, W. C. (1972a). Introductory overview. In W. C. Rhodes & M. L. Tracy (Eds.), *A study of child variance: Vol. 1. Theories* (pp. 9–36). Ann Arbor: University of Michigan.

Rhodes, W. C. (1972b). Overview of intervention. In W. C. Rhodes & M. L. Tracy (Eds.), *A study of child variance: Vol. 2. Interventions* (pp. 19–73). Ann Arbor: University of Michigan.

Rhodes, W. C. (1972c). An overview: Toward a synthesis of models of disturbance. In W. C. Rhodes & M. L. Tracy (Eds.), *A study of child variance: Vol. 1. Theories* (pp. 541–602). Ann Arbor: University of Michigan.

Rhodes, W. C. (1975). *A study of child variance: Vol. 4. The future.* Ann Arbor: University of Michigan.

Rhodes, W. C. (1987). Ecology and the new physics. *Behavioral Disorders, 13,* 58–61.

Rhodes, W. C. (1992). Navigating the paradigm change. *Journal of Emotional and Behavioral Problems, 1*(2), 28–34.

Rhodes, W. C., & Doone, E. M. (1992). One boy's transformation. *Journal of Emotional and Behavioral Problems, 1*(2), 10–15.

Rhodes, W. C., & Head, S. (Eds.). (1974). *A study of child variance: Vol. 3. Service delivery systems.* Ann Arbor: University of Michigan.

Rhodes, W. C., & Paul, J. L. (1978). *Emotionally disturbed and deviant children: New views and approaches.* Upper Saddle River, NJ: Prentice Hall.

Rhodes, W. C., & Sagor, M. (1974). Overview. In W. C. Rhodes & S. Head (Eds.), *A study of child variance: Vol. 3. Service delivery systems* (pp. 11–39). Ann Arbor: University of Michigan.

Rhodes, W. C., & Tracy, M. L. (Eds.). (1972a). *A study of child variance: Vol. 1. Theories.* Ann Arbor: University of Michigan.

Rhodes, W. C., & Tracy, M. L. (Eds.). (1972b). *A study of child variance: Vol. 2. Interventions.* Ann Arbor: University of Michigan.

Rich, H. L., Beck, M. A., & Coleman, T. W. (1982). Behavior management: The psychoeducational model. In R. L. McDowell, G. W. Adamson, & F. H. Wood (Eds.), *Teaching emotionally disturbed children* (pp. 131–166). Boston: Little, Brown.

Richards, E. L. (1932). *Behaviour aspects of child conduct.* New York: Macmillan.

Rie, H. E. (1971). Historical perspective of concepts of child psychopathology. In H. E. Rie (Ed.), *Perspectives in child psychopathology.* Chicago: Aldine Atherton.

Robins, L. N. (1966). *Deviant children grown up.* Baltimore: Williams & Wilkins.

Robins, L. N. (1974). Antisocial behavior disturbances of childhood: Prevalence, prognosis, and prospects. In E. J. Anthony & C. Koupernik (Eds.), *The child in his family: Children at psychiatric risk* (pp. 447–460). New York: Wiley.

Robins, L. N. (1979). Follow-up studies. In H. C. Quay & J. S. Werry (Eds.), *Psychopathological disorders of childhood* (2nd ed., pp. 483–513). New York: Wiley.

Robins, L. N. (1986). The consequences of conduct disorder in girls. In D. Olweus, J. Block, & M. Radke-Yarrow (Eds.), *Development of antisocial and prosocial behavior: Research, theories, and issues* (pp. 385–414). New York: Academic Press.

Robinson, F. J., & Vitale, L. J. (1954). Children with circumscribed interest patterns. *American Journal of Orthopsychiatry, 24,* 755–766.

Rogers, C. (1983). *Freedom to learn for the 80s.* Upper Saddle River, NJ: Merrill/Prentice Hall.

Rosenberg, H. E., & Graubard, P. S. (1975). Peer use of behavior modification. *Focus on Exceptional Children, 7*(6), 1–10.

Rosenblum, S. (1962). Practices and problems in the use of tranquilizers with exceptional children. In E. P. Trapp & P. Himelstein (Eds.), *Readings on the exceptional child: Research and theory* (pp. 639–657). New York: Appleton-Century-Crofts.

Rothman, D. (1971). *The discovery of the asylum: Social order and disorder in the new republic.* Boston: Little, Brown.

Rothman, E. P. (1970). *The angel inside went sour.* New York: McKay.

Rothman, E. P. (1974). Esther P. Rothman. In J. M. Kauffman & C. D. Lewis (Eds.), *Teaching children with behavior disorders: Personal perspectives* (pp. 218–239). Upper Saddle River, NJ: Merrill/Prentice Hall.

Rothman, E. P., & Berkowitz, P. H. (1967a). The clinical school—A paradigm. In P. H. Berkowitz & E. P. Rothman (Eds.), *Public education for disturbed children in New York City* (pp. 355–369). Springfield, IL: Thomas.

Rothman, E. P., & Berkowitz, P. H. (1967b). The concept of clinical teaching. In P. H. Berkowitz & E. P. Rothman (Eds.), *Public education for disturbed children in New York City* (pp. 327–343). Springfield, IL: Thomas.

Rothman, E. P., & Berkowitz, P. H. (1967c). Some aspects of reading disability. In P. H. Berkowitz & E. P. Rothman (Eds.), *Public education for disturbed children in New York City* (pp. 344–354). Springfield, IL: Thomas.

Rubenstein, E. A. (1948). Childhood mental disease in America. *American Journal of Orthopsychiatry, 18*, 314–321.

Ruscio, J. (2002). *Clear thinking with psychology: Separating sense from nonsense.* Pacific Grove, CA: Wadsworth.

Russ, D. F. (1972). A review of learning and behavior theory as it relates to emotional disturbance in children. In W. C. Rhodes & M. L. Tracy (Eds.), *A study of child variance: Vol. 1. Theories* (pp. 95–179). Ann Arbor: University of Michigan.

Rutherford, R. B., Nelson, C. M., & Forness, S. R. (Eds.). (1987). *Severe behavior disorders of children and youth.* Boston: College-Hill.

Rutherford, R. B., Nelson, C. M., & Forness, S. R. (Eds.). (1988). *Severe behavior disorders of children and youth.* Boston: College-Hill.

Rutherford, R. B., Nelson, C. M., & Wolford, B. I. (1985). Special education in the most restrictive environment: Correctional/special education. *The Journal of Special Education, 19*, 59–71.

Rutherford, R. B., Nelson, C. M., & Wolford, B. I. (1986). Special education programming in juvenile corrections. *Remedial and Special Education, 7*(3), 27–33.

Rutherford, R. B., Quinn, M. M., & Mathur, S. R. (Eds.). (2004). *Handbook of research in emotional and behavioral disorders.* New York: Guilford Press.

Sagor, M. (1972). Biological bases of childhood behavior disorders. In W. C. Rhodes & M. L. Tracy (Eds.), *A study of child variance: Vol. 1. Theories* (pp. 37–94). Ann Arbor: University of Michigan.

Sagor, M. (1974). The treatment of deviance by the mental health system: Structure. In W. C. Rhodes & S. Head (Eds.), *A study of child variance: Vol. 3. Service delivery systems* (pp. 271–316). Ann Arbor: University of Michigan.

Sailor, W., & Paul, J. L. (2004). Framing positive behavior support in the ongoing discourse concerning the politics of knowledge. *Journal of Positive Behavior Interventions, 6,* 37–49.

Sarason, S. B., & Doris, J. (1979). *Educational handicap, public policy, and social history: A broadened perspective on mental retardation.* New York: Macmillan.

Sasso, G. M. (2001). The retreat from inquiry and knowledge in special education. *The Journal of Special Education, 34,* 178–193.

Savage, G. H. (1891). *Insanity and allied neuroses: Practical and clinical.* London: Cassell.

Sayles, M. B., & Nudd, H. W. (1929). *The problem child in school: Narratives from case records of visiting teachers.* New York: Commonwealth Fund.

Schultz, E. W., Heuchert, C. M., & Stampf, S. W. (1973). *Pain and joy in school.* Champaign, IL: Research Press.

Scull, A. T. (1975). From madness to mental illness: Medical men as moral entrepreneurs. *Archives of European Sociology, 16,* 218–251.

Seguin, E. O. (1866). *Idiocy and its treatment by the physiological method.* New York: W. Wood.

Shapiro, J. P., Loeb, P., Bowermaster, D., Wright, A., Headden, S., & Toch, T. (1993, December). Separate and unequal. *U.S. News and World Report, 115*(23), 46–60.

Shattuck, R. (1994). *The forbidden experiment: The story of the Wild Boy of Aveyron.* New York: Kodansha International.

Simpson, R. L. (2004). Inclusion of students with behavior disorders in general education settings: Research and measurement issues. *Behavioral Disorders, 30,* 19–31.

Singer, J. D. (1988). Should special education merge with regular education? *Educational Policy, 2,* 409–424.

Singh, N. N. (1996). Cultural diversity in the 21st century: Beyond E Pluribus Unum. *Journal of Child and Family Studies, 5,* 121–136.

Skinner, B. F. (1953). *Science and human behavior.* New York: Free Press.

Skrtic, T. M., & Sailor, W. (1996). School-linked services integration: Crisis and opportunity in the transition to postmodern society. *Remedial and Special Education, 17,* 271–283.

Smith, J. D. (Ed.). (1998). The history of special education: Essays honoring the bicentennial of the work of Jean Itard [Special issue]. *Remedial and Special Education, 19*(4).

Smith, J. O. (1962). Criminality and mental retardation. *Training School Bulletin, 59,* 74–80.

Smith, P. (1999). Drawing new maps: A radical cartography of developmental disabilities. *Review of Educational Research, 69,* 117–144.

Smith, P. (2001). Inquiry cantos: Poetics of developmental disability. *Mental Retardation, 39,* 379–390.

Smith, R. G., & Churchill, R. M. (2002). Identification of environmental determinants of behavior disorders through functional analysis of precursor behaviors. *Journal of Applied Behavior Analysis, 35,* 125–136.

Smith, T., & Lovaas, O. I. (1997). The UCLA Young Autism Project: A reply to Gresham and MacMillan. *Behavioral Disorders, 22,* 202–218.

Spaulding, W. B., & Kavaraceus. W. C. (1944). Sex discrimination in special class placement. *Exceptional Children, 11,* 42–44.

Stage, S. A., & Quiroz, D. R. (1997). A meta-analysis of interventions to decrease disruptive classroom behavior in public education settings. *School Psychology Review, 26,* 333–368.

Stainback, W., & Stainback, S. (1984). A rationale for the merger of special and regular education. *Exceptional Children, 51,* 102–111.

Stainback, W., & Stainback, S. (1991). A rationale for integration and restructuring: A synopsis. In J. W. Lloyd, N. N. Singh, & A. C. Repp (Eds.), *The Regular Education Initiative: Alternative perspectives on concepts, issues, and models* (pp. 226–239). Sycamore, IL: Sycamore.

Stevenson, G. S. (1944). The prevention of personality disorders. In J. McV. Hunt (Ed.), *Personality and the behavior disorders: A handbook based on experimental and clinical research* (Vol. 2, pp. 1164–1191). New York: Ronald Press.

Strain, P. S., & Timm, M. A. (2001). Remediation and prevention of aggression: An evaluation of the Regional Intervention Program over a quarter century. *Behavioral Disorders, 26,* 297–313.

Strand, P. S., Barnes-Holmes, Y., & Barnes-Holmes, D. (2003). Educating the whole child: Implications of behaviorism as a science of meaning. *Journal of Behavioral Education, 12,* 105–117.

Strauss, A. A., & Kephart, N. C. (1955). *Psychopathology and education of the brain-injured child: Vol. 2. Progress in theory and clinic.* New York: Grune & Stratton.

Strauss, A. A., & Lehtinen, L. E. (1947). *Psychopathology and education of the brain-injured child*. New York: Grune & Stratton.

Stribling, F. T. (1842). Physician and superintendent's report. In *Annual Reports to the Court of Directors of the Western Lunatic Asylum to the Legislature of Virginia* (pp. 1–70). Richmond, VA: Shepherd & Conlin.

Stullken, E. H. (1950). Special schools and classes for the socially maladjusted. In N. B. Henry (Ed.), *The education of exceptional children. Forty-ninth yearbook of the National Society for the Study of Education* (Part 2, pp. 281–301). Chicago: University of Chicago Press.

Suerken, H., & Bloch, D. A. (1956). Juvenile delinquency. In M. E. Frampton & E. D. Gall (Eds.), *Special education for the exceptional: Vol. 3. Mental and emotional deviates and special problems* (pp. 361–426). Boston: Porter Sargent.

Sutton, N. (1997). *Bettelheim: A Life and a Legacy*. New York: Basic Books.

Swap, S. (1974). Disturbing classroom behaviors: A developmental and ecological view. *Exceptional Children, 41*, 163–172.

Swap, S. (1978). The ecological model of emotional disturbance in children: A status report and proposed synthesis. *Behavioral Disorders, 3*, 186–196.

Swap, S., Prieto, A. G., & Harth, R. (1982). Ecological perspectives on the emotionally disturbed child. In R. L. McDowell, G. W. Adamson, & F. H. Wood (Eds.), *Teaching emotionally disturbed children* (pp. 70–98). Boston: Little, Brown.

Tenny, J. W. (1944). Adjustment of special class pupils to regular classes. *Exceptional Children, 10*, 139–145.

Thomas, A., Chess, S., & Birch, H. G. (1968). *Temperament and behavior disorders in children*. New York: New York University Press.

Tobin, T. J., & Sugai, G. M. (1999). Using sixth-grade school records to predict school violence, chronic discipline problems, and high school outcomes. *Journal of Emotional and Behavioral Disorders, 7*, 40–53.

Tracy, M. L., Reimer, E., & Bron, A. (1972). Counter theory. In W. C. Rhodes & M. L. Tracy (Eds.), *A study of child variance: Vol. 1. Theories* (pp. 391–540). Ann Arbor: University of Michigan.

Trieschman, A. E., Whittaker, J. K., & Brendtro, L. K. (1969). *The other 23 hours*. Chicago: Aldine.

Trippe, M. J. (1966). Educational dimensions of emotional disturbance—Past and forecast. In P. Knoblock (Ed.), *Intervention approaches in educating emotionally disturbed children* (pp. 19–33). Syracuse, NY: Syracuse University Press.

Trippe, M. J. (1970, April). *Love of life, love of truth, love of others.* Presidential address, annual meeting of the Council for Children with Behavioral Disorders, Gary, IN.

Ullmann, L. P., & Krasner, L. (Eds.). (1965). *Case studies in behavior modification.* New York: Holt, Rinehart & Winston.

Ullmann, L. P., & Krasner, L. (1969). *A psychological approach to abnormal behavior.* Upper Saddle River, NJ: Prentice Hall.

Ulrich, R., Stachnik, T., & Mabry, J. (Eds.). (1966). *Control of human behavior.* Glenview, IL: Scott, Foresman.

Ulrich, R., Stachnik, T., & Mabry, J. (Eds.). (1970). *Control of human behavior: From cure to prevention.* Glenview, IL: Scott, Foresman.

Unger, C. (1974a). The treatment of deviance by the social welfare system: History. In W. C. Rhodes & S. Head (Eds.), *A study of child variance: Vol. 3. Service delivery systems* (pp. 329–369). Ann Arbor: University of Michigan.

Unger, C. (1974b). The treatment of deviance by the social welfare system: Structure. In W. C. Rhodes & S. Head (Eds.), *A study of child variance: Vol. 3. Service delivery systems* (pp. 371–413). Ann Arbor: University of Michigan.

U.S. Department of Education. (1994). *Sixteenth annual report to Congress on implementation of the Individuals with Disabilities Education Act.* Washington, DC: Author.

U.S. Department of Education. (1995). *Seventeenth annual report to Congress on implementation of the Individuals with Disabilities Act.* Washington, DC: Author.

U.S. Department of Health and Human Services. (2001). *Report of the Surgeon General's conference on children's mental health: A national action agenda.* Washington, DC: Author.

Van Hasselt, V. B., & Hersen, M. (Eds.). (1991a). *Journal of Developmental and Physical Disabilities* [Special issue], 3(3).

Van Hasselt, V. B., & Hersen, M. (Eds.). (1991b). *Journal of Developmental and Physical Disabilities* [Special issue], 3(4).

Votel, S. M. (1985). Special education in France for the emotionally/behaviorally disordered as it relates to that of the United States. In S. Braaten, R. B. Rutherford, & W. Evans (Eds.), *Programming for adolescents with behavioral disorders* (Vol. 2, pp. 127–135). Reston, VA: Council for Children with Behavioral Disorders.

Wagner, M. (1972). Environmental interventions in emotional disturbance.

In W. C. Rhodes & M. L. Tracy (Eds.), *A study of child variance: Vol. 2. Interventions* (pp. 395–571). Ann Arbor: University of Michigan.

Wagner, M. (1991). *Dropouts with disabilities: What do we know? What can we do?* Menlo Park, CA: SRI International.

Walk, A. (1964). The pre-history of child psychiatry. *British Journal of Psychiatry, 110*, 754–767.

Walker, H. M. (1995). *The acting-out child: Coping with classroom disruption* (2nd ed.). Longmont, CO: Sopris West.

Walker, H. M. (2003, February 20). *Comments on accepting the Outstanding Leadership Award from the Midwest Symposium for Leadership in Behavior Disorders*, Kansas City, KS. Unpublished remarks.

Walker, H. M., & Buckley, N. K. (1973, May). Teacher attention to appropriate and inappropriate classroom behavior. *Focus on Exceptional Children*, pp. 5–12.

Walker, H. M., & Bullis, M. (1991). Behavior disorders and the social context of regular class integration: A conceptual dilemma? In J. W. Lloyd, N. N. Singh, & A. C. Repp (Eds.), *The Regular Education Initiative: Alternative perspectives on concepts, issues, and models* (pp. 75–93). Sycamore, IL: Sycamore.

Walker, H. M., Colvin, G., & Ramsey, E. (1995). *Antisocial behavior in school: Strategies and best practices*. Pacific Grove, CA: Brooks/Cole.

Walker, H. M., Forness, S. R., Kauffman, J. M., Epstein, M. H., Gresham, F. M., Nelson, C. M., & Strain, P. S. (1998). Macro-social validation: Referencing outcomes in behavioral disorders to societal issues and problems. *Behavioral Disorders, 24*, 7–18.

Walker, H. M., Hops, H., & Fiegenbaum, E. (1976). Deviant classroom behavior as a function of combinations of social and token reinforcement and cost contingency. *Behavior Therapy, 7*, 76–88.

Walker, H. M., Hops, H. G., & Greenwood, C. R. (1981). RECESS: Research and development of a behavior management package for remediating social aggression in the school. In P. S. Strain (Ed.), *The utilization of classroom peers as behavior change agents* (pp. 261–303). New York: Plenum.

Walker, H. M., Kavanagh, K., Stiller, B., Golly, A., Severson, H., & Feil, E. G. (1998). First Step to Success: An early intervention approach for preventing school antisocial behavior. *Journal of Emotional and Behavioral Disorders, 6*, 66–80.

Walker, H. M., McConnell, S., Holmes, D., Todis, B., Walker, J., & Golden, N. (1983). *The Walker social skills curriculum: The ACCEPTS program.* Austin, TX: PRO-ED.

Walker, H. M., Ramsey, E., & Gresham, F. M. (2004). *Antisocial behavior in school: Strategies and best practices* (2nd ed.). Pacific Grove, CA: Brooks/ Cole.

Walker, H. M., Reavis, H. K., Rhode, G., & Jenson, W. R. (1985). A conceptual model for delivery of behavioral services to behavior disordered children in educational settings. In P. H. Bornstein & A. E. Kazdin (Eds.), *Handbook of clinical behavior therapy with children* (pp. 700–741). Homewood, IL: Dorsey.

Walker, H. M., & Severson, H. H. (1990). *Systematic Screening for Behavior Disorders (SSBD): A multiple gating procedure.* Longmont, CO: Sopris West.

Walker, H. M., Severson, H. H., & Feil, E. G. (1994). *The Early Screening Project: A proven child-find process.* Longmont, CO: Sopris West.

Walker, H. M., & Shinn, M. R. (2002). Structuring school-based interventions to achieve integrated primary, secondary and tertiary prevention goals for safe and effective schools. In M. R. Shinn, H. M. Walker, & G. Stoner (Eds.), *Interventions for academic and behavior problems II: Preventive and remedial approaches* (pp. 1–26). Bethesda, MD: National Association of School Psychologists.

Walker, H. M., & Sprague, J. R. (1999). The path to school failure, delinquency, and violence: Causal factors and some potential solutions. *Interventions in School and Clinic, 35,* 67–73.

Wallin, J. E. W. (1924). *The education of handicapped children.* Boston: Houghton Mifflin.

Weiner, J. (1999). *Time, love, memory: A great biologist and his quest for the origins of behavior.* New York: Knopf.

Weinstein, L. (1969). Project Re-ED schools for emotionally disturbed children: Effectiveness as viewed by referring agencies, parents, and teachers. *Exceptional Children, 35,* 703–711.

Whelan, R. J. (1963). Educating emotionally disturbed children: Reflections upon educational methods and therapeutic processes. *Forum for Residential Therapy, 1,* 9–14.

Whelan, R. J. (1966). The relevance of behavior modification procedures for teachers and emotionally disturbed children. In P. Knoblock (Ed.),

Intervention approaches in educating emotionally disturbed children (pp. 35–78). Syracuse, NY: Syracuse University Press.

Whelan, R. J. (1974). Richard J. Whelan. In J. M. Kauffman & C. D. Lewis (Eds.), *Teaching children with behavior disorders: Personal perspectives* (pp. 240–270). Upper Saddle River, NJ: Merrill/Prentice Hall.

Whelan, R. J. (Ed.). (1998). *Emotional and behavioral disorders: A 25–year focus.* Denver, CO: Love.

Whelan, R. J. (1999). Historical perspective. In L. M. Bullock & R. A. Gable (Eds.), *Educating students with emotional and behavioral disorders: Historical perspective and future directions* (pp. 3–36). Reston, VA: Council for Children with Behavioral Disorders.

Whelan, R. J., & Gallagher, P. A. (1972). Effective teaching of children with behavior disorders. In N. G. Haring & A. H. Hayden (Eds.), *The improvement of instruction* (pp. 183–218). Seattle: Special Child Publications.

Whelan, R. J., & Haring, N. G. (1966). Modification and maintenance of behavior through systematic application of consequences. *Exceptional Children, 32,* 281–289.

White House Conference on Child Health and Protection called by President Hoover, 1930. (1931). *Addresses and abstracts of committee reports.* New York: Century.

Wickman, E. K. (1929). *Children's behavior and teachers' attitudes.* New York: Commonwealth Fund, Division of Publications.

Will, M. (1986). Educating children with learning problems: A shared responsibility. *Exceptional Children, 52,* 411–416.

Wilson, E. O. (1998). *Consilience: The unity of knowledge.* New York: Vintage.

Winzer, M. A. (1993). *The history of special education: From isolation to integration.* Washington, DC: Gallaudet University Press.

Winzer, M. A. (2005). International comparisons in EBD: Critical issues. In P. Clough, P. Garner, J. T. Pardeck, & F. K. O. Yuen (Eds.), *Handbook of emotional and behavioral difficulties in education* (pp. 18–25). London: Sage.

Wise, P. M. (1889). General index, 1844–1889. *American Journal of Insanity.*

Witt, J. C., VanDerHeyden, A. M., & Gilbertson, D. (2004). Instruction and classroom management: Prevention and intervention research. In R. B. Rutherford, M. M. Quinn, & S. R. Mathur (Eds.), *Handbook of research in emotional and behavioral disorders* (pp. 426–445). New York: Guilford Press.

Wood, F. H. (Ed.). (1977a). *Preparing teachers to foster personal growth in emotionally disturbed students*. Minneapolis: University of Minnesota, Department of Psychoeducational Studies.

Wood, F. H. (Ed.). (1977b). *Preparing teachers for severely emotionally disturbed children with autistic characteristics*. Minneapolis: University of Minnesota, Department of Psychoeducational Studies.

Wood, F. H. (Ed.). (1977c). *The socialization process*. Minneapolis: University of Minnesota, Department of Psychoeducational Studies.

Wood, F. H. (Ed.). (1978). *Preparing teachers to develop and maintain therapeutic educational environments*. Minneapolis: University of Minnesota, Department of Psychoeducational Studies.

Wood, F. H. (Ed.). (1980). *Preparation of teachers for seriously emotionally disturbed and behaviorally disordered youth: Issues and trends*. Minneapolis: University of Minnesota, Department of Psychoeducational Studies.

Wood, F. H. (1987). Special education law and correctional education. In C. M. Nelson, R. B. Rutherford, & B. I. Wolford (Eds.), *Special education in the criminal justice system* (pp. 85–99). Upper Saddle River, NJ: Merrill/Prentice Hall.

Wood, F. H. (Ed.). (1990). When we talk with children: The life space interview. *Behavioral Disorders* [Special section], *15*, 110–126.

Wood, F. H. (1999). CCBD: A record of accomplishment. *Behavioral Disorders, 24*, 273–283.

Wood, F. H. (2004). Foreword. In R. B. Rutherford, M. M. Quinn, & S. R. Mathur (Eds.), *Handbook of research in emotional and behavioral disorders* (pp. xi–xii). New York: Guilford Press.

Wood, F. H., & Lakin, K. C. (Eds.). (1982a). *Disturbing, disordered or disturbed? Perspectives on the definition of problem behavior in educational settings*. Reston, VA: Council for Exceptional Children.

Wood, F. H., & Lakin, K. C. (Eds.). (1982b). *Punishment and aversive stimulation in special education: Legal, theoretical and practical issues in their use with emotionally disturbed children and youth*. Reston, VA: Council for Exceptional Children.

Wood, F. H., Smith, C. R., & Grimes, J. (Eds.). (1985). *The Iowa assessment model in behavioral disorders: A training manual*. Des Moines: Iowa Department of Public Instruction.

Wood, F. H., Zabel, R. H., & Uhlemann, D. C. (1977). *Problem behavior in the schools: A bibliography*. Minneapolis: University of Minnesota, Department of Psychoeducational Studies.

Wood, M. M., & Long, N. J. (1991). *Life space intervention: Talking with children and youth in crisis*. Austin, TX: PRO-ED.

Wright, W. G. (1967). The Bellevue Psychiatric Hospital School. In P. H. Berkowitz & E. P. Rothman (Eds.), *Public education for disturbed children in New York City* (pp. 78–123). Springfield, IL: Thomas.

Yell, M. L. (1998). *The law and special education*. Upper Saddle River, NJ: Prentice Hall.

Yell, M. L., Rogers, D., & Rogers, E. L. (1998). The legal history of special education: What a long, strange trip it's been! *Remedial and Special Education, 19*, 219–228.

Yell, M. L., & Shriner, J. G. (1997). The IDEA amendments of 1997: Implications for special and general education teachers, administrators, and teacher trainers. *Focus on Exceptional Children, 30*(1), 1–19.

Zanglis, I., Furlong, M. J., & Casas, J. M. (2000). Case study of a community mental health collaborative: Impact on identification of youths with emotional or behavioral disorders. *Behavioral Disorders, 25*, 359–371.

Zigmond, N. (2003). Where should students with disabilities receive special education services? Is one place better than another? *The Journal of Special Education, 37*, 193–199.

Zimmerman, J., & Zimmerman, E. (1962). The alteration of behavior in a special class situation. *Journal of the Experimental Analysis of Behavior, 5*, 59–60.

Author Index

Subject Index

About the Authors

JAMES M. KAUFFMAN is the professor emeritus of education at the University of Virginia, where he has been chair of the Department of Special Education, associate dean for research, the Charles S. Robb Professor of Education, and the William Clay Parrish Jr. Professor of Education. He joined the University of Virginia faculty in 1970 and retired from full-time teaching in 2003. A former teacher in both general elementary and special education, Kauffman received his EdD degree in special education from the University of Kansas in 1969. He is currently director of doctoral study in special education at the University of Virginia and teaches a doctoral seminar in special education.

Kauffman is a past president of the Council for Children with Behavioral Disorders (a division of the Council for Exceptional Children) and has been coeditor (with Rick Brigham) of the division's journal, *Behavioral Disorders*. He is the recipient of the 1991 Award for Outstanding Service in Behavior Disorders from the Midwest Symposium for Leadership in Behavior Disorders, the 1994 Research Award of the Council for Exceptional Children, a Special Kuhn Barnett Award from the Virginia Federation of the Council for Exceptional Children in 1995, the Outstanding Faculty Award from the Curry School of Education Foundation in 1997, and the Outstanding Leadership Award from the Council for Children with Behavioral Disorders, 2002.

Kauffman's primary research interests are emotional and behavioral disorders, learning disabilities, and the history of special education. He has published over 100 articles in refereed journals and authored or coauthored more than a dozen books.

TIMOTHY J. LANDRUM is an associate professor on the general faculty in the Curry School of Education at the University of Virginia. He taught students with emotional and behavioral disorders in both public school and residential settings before earning his doctorate in special education from the University of Virginia in 1990. He has been a member of the Executive Board of the Division for Research since 1993 and is currently chair of the Publications Committee for that division. He also serves as a member of the Publications Committee of the Council for Children with Behavioral Disorders. He is author or coauthor of more than 40 journal articles and book chapters. His research and writing focuses on emotional and behavioral disorders, classroom and behavior management, and the translation of research into practice. He received the Carl Fenichel Memorial Lectureship Award from the Council for Children with Behavioral Disorders in 1990.